D1528135

THE PULSE
OF DEMOCRACY

The Public-Opinion Poll

and How It Works

by

George Gallup

and

Saul Forbes Rae

GREENWOOD PRESS, PUBLISHERS
NEW YORK   1968

★

Foreword

★

WHAT is the common man thinking? The life history of democracy can be traced as an unceasing search for an answer to this vital question. The following pages provide a modern answer on the basis, not of guesswork, but of facts. They tell the story of a new instrument—the public-opinion poll—and describe how it works to provide a continuous chart of the opinions of the man in the street. Through a network of trained interviewers, in thousands of week-to-week conversations, the front-page issues of the day are placed squarely before him, with the query: "What's your opinion?" His reply, along with the replies of thousands of others like and unlike himself—a cross section of the vast American public—then forms a composite public opinion which is published for all to see. The application of sampling has made it possible to predict the divisions and trends of public sentiment with a high degree of accuracy.

In this book we shall describe how polls have developed from the straw-vote stage to the continuous cross-section surveys of the present day. We shall show the competition of the old and new techniques in the test of the 1936 presidential election; we shall take the reader behind the scenes and point out the actual problems that face those who administer the polls. Because we feel that such surveys fill a real need in the existing structure of democracy, we propose

*to show how the polls covered specific and major conflicts
of public opinion during the past few years. Finally, we
hope to discuss the various questions and criticisms that the
polls have stimulated. Will the modern polls go the way
of* The Literary Digest? *How is the representative cross
section built up? Can this instrument measure the intensity
of opinion? Does its application to elections and issues create a band-wagon vote? What about the implications of
these polls for the machinery of democracy? Will they lead
to a new form of direct democracy? Are polls a "positive
menace tending to destroy the effectiveness of the real ballot"? or do they represent "an advance in human relationships and a forward step in self-government"? Above all, do
their results show that public opinion is stupid and unreliable as a guide in politics, or is there a basis in fact for
the faith which all believers in democracy have toward
their system of government?*

*The object of this book, then, is to describe and defend
this new instrument, because we firmly believe that it per-
forms a necessary and useful task in a democratic society
based on an electorate of some sixty million eligible voters.
We believe that by bringing all the arguments together
and presenting the case for the polls as we see it, the methods and implications of public-opinion measurement can
be more clearly understood.*

*It is not the object of this book to present a final and
definitive statement of the uses and value of public-opinion
polls. Just out of their swaddling clothes, with their future
development subject to shifts and adjustments, public-opinion polls will require new evaluations in the years ahead.
What we can present at this stage is essentially an interim
report describing work in progress. The polls are charting*

unmapped territory. These are pages from a notebook of exploration.

Secondly, this book does not present a comprehensive theory of public opinion and its processes. The action of public opinion is continuous, and the factual observation of its processes is still an infant science. It is not too hopeful to suggest, however, that the continuous collection of facts about public opinion will provide the theorists of the future with a solid groundwork on which to base a realistic theory of public opinion as it actually works in everyday life. As public-opinion research proceeds on many fronts and as more facts become available, both the advocates and the critics of democracy will have a body of evidence as a common point of departure in the debate.

Most of the factual findings represented in this study have been based upon the work of the American Institute of Public Opinion, but it need hardly be emphasized that other organizations—notably the Fortune *Survey—are also doing pioneer work in this new field.*

Many persons have helped directly and indirectly in the preparation of this book. The authors would like to express their warm thanks to those who have worked at close hand with the various polling problems, and who have contributed their time and experience to the material of these pages, especially to Edward G. Benson, Lawrence E. Benson, Paul Perry, and Donald F. Saunders of the Institute's research and statistical staff, and to William A. Lydgate and John K. Tibby of the editorial staff. The authors are indebted also to the army of interviewers whose labors over the past few years have provided the raw material for this study. For friendly advice and acute criticism, thanks are due to Hadley Cantril of Princeton University and Claude

Robinson of the Opinion Research Corporation, and for a careful reading of the manuscript to Harwood Childs of Princeton University and Lloyd Free, editor of the Public Opinion Quarterly. *Indirectly we must include also the many students of public opinion, political observers, newspaper editors, and members of the general public who have criticized the polls, generally in the helpful spirit of intelligent skepticism. Without this constant barrage of advice, attack, and study, the polls would never have attained their present stage of development.*

Finally, to the editors and publishers of American newspapers who have made this new venture in reporting public opinion possible, a special word of tribute is due. The newspapers and those who make them have stood by the Institute's researches since the earliest experimental days, and have played their part loyally in backing continuous and independent surveys of what people think. In publishing the results of surveys even when these results have violently disagreed with the opinions expressed in their editorial columns, these newspapers act as the twentieth-century weathercocks for a vast democracy.

GEORGE GALLUP
SAUL FORBES RAE

American Institute of Public Opinion
Princeton, N. J.
May 5, 1940

Table of Contents

★

PART I

★   ★

THE METHOD

★   ★

CHAPTER ONE

★

A Powerful, Bold, and Unmeasurable Party?

ON STATE STREET in downtown Boston early in May, 1940, a stockbroker stops to answer the questions of a young man with a sheaf of ballots and a lead pencil:

"Whom would you like to see elected President in November?" the young man asks.

"Well, my first choice would be for Wendell Willkie," says the stockbroker, "but I don't know whether or not the politicians would take to him. In any case, put *me* down for Willkie."

"What do you think is the most important problem before the American people today?"

"As I see it—this country must try to avoid getting mixed up in this war in Europe. I'm strongly against our looking for trouble overseas."

The scene shifts to a backwoods road in Arkansas. The man who asks the questions wears a cap; the man who answers them wears the faded overalls of a back-country farmer. But the questions are the same. Both the stockbroker and the farmer agree that keeping the United States out of war is the crucial problem facing Americans today. The Arkansas farmer wants a third term for President Roosevelt. Both men are chance cogs in an endlessly functioning machine that samples public opinion. Both were selected on

3

the initiative of the field investigator, but only after careful and detailed directions had come from the office of the American Institute of Public Opinion in Princeton. Multiplied hundreds of times, these interviews provide continuous descriptions of what Americans are thinking about unemployment, relief, agriculture, the President's popularity, the third-term issue, labor problems, the Wagner Act, child labor, about the war in Europe, reciprocal trade treaties, conscription, rearmament, birth control, disease prevention, capital punishment, prohibition, the Dies Committee, and the prospects of rival candidates, parties, and pressure groups.

In thousands of week-to-week conversations with the men and women voters of America, such issues are presented to the public by the shock troops of public-opinion research. These interviewers know what it is to drive through a Maine snowstorm to make a farm interview; to trudge across Kansas wheat fields on a blistering day to interview a thresher on the job; to travel through the red-clay mud of Georgia in a drenching rainstorm. Their assignments may take them into a third-floor tenement in New York City's East Side, or require them to argue their way past a uniformed doorman guarding a smart Park Avenue apartment. They talk to the prominent industrialist who runs a huge factory employing thousands of employees, just as they talk to the old lady who silently mops his office when everyone else has gone home. As vital issues emerge from the fast-flowing stream of modern life, the public-opinion polls conducted by such organizations as the American Institute and the *Fortune* Survey enable the American people to speak for themselves. Nor is this new phenomenon exclusively confined to the United States. Similar Institutes of Public Opinion have been organized in Great Britain and in

France, directly affiliated with the American Institute. From 1938 to the present day, continuing throughout the course of the war, the *News Chronicle* of London has regularly published the results of frequent sampling surveys made by the British Institute. The findings of the French Institute were reported in the French newspaper, *Paris-Soir*, until the present European conflict began.

When the shadow of war fell across Europe in late August, 1939, an instrument was in readiness to test America's attitudes and reactions. Even before the outbreak of hostilities, selected interviewers in every state had received ballots especially designed to test public opinion objectively. In 1917, it was necessary to rely on impression and speculation to assess the reactions of public opinion. In 1939, a more reliable method was ready to be placed in operation. As German troops advanced into western Poland, interviewers went out to talk to the man in the street, and listened closely to what he had to say to such questions as:

> Do you think the United States will go into this war?
> Should the United States allow its citizens to travel on ships of countries which are now at war?
> Do you think the United States should declare war on Germany at once and send our Army and Navy abroad to help England, France, and Poland?

Replies were swiftly returned to the Institute, which tabulated the final results and distributed them to its subscribing newspapers throughout the country.

Such a test taken at a moment when the attention of every citizen was riveted on events abroad is typical of hundreds. For in our own day, the study of public opinion has developed from a glorified kind of fortunetelling into a practical way of learning what the nation thinks. The surveys of the last five years chart the main alignments and

changes in public opinion. Their basic principle is simply
this: by sounding the opinions of a relatively small number
of persons, proportionate to each major population group
in every section of the country, the opinions of the whole
population can be determined with a high degree of accuracy.

Is this sampling instrument merely a passing fad or
does it fill a genuine need in American public life? Many
signs suggest that opinion sampling has come to stay.
Not only have the polls demonstrated by their accuracy
that public opinion *can* be measured; there is a growing
conviction that public opinion *must* be measured. What the
mass of the people thinks puts governments in and out of
office, starts and stops wars, sets the tone of morality, makes
and breaks heroes. We know that democrats think public
opinion is important because continuous efforts have been
made throughout the history of popular government to improve and clarify its expression. We know, too, that autocrats think public opinion is important because they devote
vast sums and careful attention to curbing and controlling it.

Throughout the history of politics this central problem
has remained: shall the common people be free to express
their basic needs and purposes, or shall they be dominated
by a small ruling clique? Shall the goal be the free expression
of public opinion, or shall efforts be made to ensure its
repression? In the democratic community, the attitudes of
the mass of the people determine policy. "With public
opinion on its side," said Abraham Lincoln in the course of
his famous contest with Douglas, "everything succeeds.
With public opinion against it, nothing succeeds." But public opinion is also important in the totalitarian state. Contemporary dictators must inevitably rule through the minds

of their people—otherwise they would quickly dispense with their elaborate propaganda machines. "Our ordinary conception of public opinion," Adolf Hitler has written in *Mein Kampf,* "depends only in very small measure on our personal experience or knowledge, but mainly, on the other hand, on what we are told; and this is presented to us in the form of so-called 'enlightenment,' persistent and emphatic." Whether his ultimate goal is to encourage the clear and honest expression of public opinion, or merely to create an "enlightened" majority, no ruler can stay in power without having some measure of the mind of the mass of the people.

What channels are open in a dictatorship? How can public opinion be known? Immediately after Herr Hitler had made his spectacular entry into Vienna on the occasion of the *Anschluss* with Austria, the National Socialist party held a lightning plebiscite and presently informed the world that 99.7 per cent of the electorate had voted in favor of the Führer's action. Election returns from Soviet Russia tell us from time to time that Joseph Stalin has been re-elected by the Moscow Soviet with 99.4 per cent or 99.6 per cent of the total vote.

But when elections merely confirm the *status quo,* when the opportunity to oppose the official candidate or regime must be weighed against the rigors of the concentration camp, such expressions of "public opinion" merit considerable skepticism. The artificial creation of an apparent majority, whether in a vote which allows no freedom of choice, or in the organized enthusiasm of a popular rally supervised by the secret police, provides a poor index of public opinion. Not only does the outside world remain unconvinced that the people have really spoken; the dictator himself can never be certain whether he is hearing the people's voice or the echo of his own. For if there is opinion which is static, controlled, stamped with the seal of official approval, there is another kind of opinion as well. To find it one must go into the concentration camps, and visit the distant wastes of Siberia. It is not voiced at party rallies, but behind locked doors. It is expressed in whispers and jokes, grumbling and curses, when uniforms are hung in closets and men gather together to talk furtively in small groups. One can hear this opinion in fugitive radio messages; one can read it between the lines of letters which from time to time drift past the rigid censorship. It is intangible, but it is always present.

The kind of public opinion implied in the democratic ideal is tangible and dynamic. It springs from many sources deep in the day-to-day experience of individuals who constitute the political public, and who formulate these opinions as working guides for their political representatives. This public opinion listens to many propagandas, most of them contradictory. It tries in the clash and conflict of argument and debate to separate the true from the false. It needs criticism for its very existence, and through criticism it is constantly being modified and molded. It acts and learns by action. Its truths are relative and contingent upon the results which its action achieves. Its chief faith is a faith in experiment. It believes in the value of every individual's contribution to political life, and in the right of ordinary human beings to have a voice in deciding their fate. Public opinion, in this sense, is the pulse of democracy.

Between these two points of view there can be no compromise. For the past decade, the democratic faith in public opinion has been challenged by totalitarian critics. Signor Mussolini insists that Fascism has "thrown on the dump heap" the "lifeless theories" of democracy; Comrade Stalin decries the democratic way as a sham and a delusion, and in the name of liberty has strengthened his dictatorship over the Russian people. Herr Hitler scoffs at the "foolish masses," the "granite stupidity of mankind"; he regards the common people as "mere ballot cattle."

This name-calling has been echoed in contemporary America by the would-be imitators of this triumvirate. Even in our own midst we can hear the pseudo autocrats argue that dictatorship is a better way of life than democracy, because dictatorship rests on the will and action of a single, all-powerful individual. Unhampered by "critics" and "obstructionists," responsible only to his own iron will, the Leader, it is maintained, can take immediate and decisive action in domestic as well as in foreign affairs. "Democracy is cumbersome and slow-moving," we have been told. "The twentieth century belongs to the swift. You must either copy the tactics of the Strong Men, or go to the wall."

This attack on democracy, with the crisis which has swiftly developed in world affairs, has inevitably led to self-questioning. It strikes both at the basis and the methods of popular government. From this challenge spring two fundamental questions to which an answer must be given. *Is democracy really inferior to dictatorship? Can democracy develop new techniques to meet the impact of this strange new decade?* Such questions are not academic. They have long been matters of profound concern to many thinking persons in this country and in all countries where faith in free institutions still runs high.

Remarkably few people in the United States really believe that dictatorship is superior to democracy as a way of life. In spite of the prophets of calamity, propaganda condemning the methods and purposes of popular government

has received an extremely cool reception. The challenge of
dictatorship, whether of foreign or domestic origin, has
made only minor dents on the surface of America's political
consciousness. Even the Dies Committee on un-American
activities failed to discover that the lure of totalitarianism
had seduced Americans in the mass from their fundamental
democratic allegiance. The following excerpt from the
15,000-word report that the Committee laid before Congress on January 4, 1940, makes the point clear:

> One of the greatest facts of all that should be recorded in
> the report of this Committee is that, on the basis of evidence
> presented to the Committee, not over 1,000,000 people in the
> United States can be said to have been seriously affected by
> these essentially foreign or un-American activities. That leaves
> about 131,000,000 Americans who in spite of Nazis, Fascists,
> Communists, self-styled saviors of America and all the rest,
> and in spite of the suffering and distress of ten years of unem-
> ployment and depression, are still as sound and loyal to
> American institutions and the democratic way of life as they
> ever were.

All the signs point to a growing immunity to the virulent
attack which insists that democracy is doomed, that this
country must follow the totalitarian pattern, that ordinary
citizens must resign in favor of the dictator and the bureau-
crat. For the vast majority of the American people feel in
their bones that the case for dictatorship is riddled with
weaknesses. They believe that the "unity" about which we
hear so much is synthetic rather than real; that it disguises,
but fails to solve, fundamental conflicts within the state
itself. They are aware that the great flaw in the dictator's
armor lies in his inability to know the real mind of his
people, and that when he tries to get a true measure of
public opinion, he is like a blind man groping in a dark
room for a light that isn't there. They know that, having

cut the communication lines on which political stability ultimately rests, the self-chosen are driven to rely on propaganda and brute force to ensure outward conformity.

What of the second question: "Can democracy develop new techniques and be made more efficient?"

To the charge that some of the machinery of democratic government is archaic and unfitted for the speed-up of the twentieth century, Americans have lent a more sympathetic ear. Always an inventive people, they have not confined their ingenuity to building automobiles and radios, bridges and skyscrapers. They have also applied it, although far more gradually, to their political system, and to their methods of living together. They have learned by experience to preserve an open mind to inventions which might make democracy work more effectively. They have met new needs by creating new techniques.

To the solution of the problem of making democracy work more effectively, single or simple answers will be wholly inadequate. Democracy can function efficiently only when the economic system is doing its best to provide for the needs of all its citizens. It can work well only when education and literacy are widespread, and when the people have reliable facts and information on which to base their opinions. It demands the exposure of pressure groups and powerful interests (and the Dies Committee has by no means covered them all) who speak in the name of democracy while abusing its freedom to destroy its structure. Above all, democracy recognizes the essential dignity of the individual citizen as such; it assumes that our economic, political, and cultural institutions must be geared to the fundamental right of every person to give free expression to the worth that is in him.

What has been obvious these past few years is that the right to vote, to choose between this party or that, is by itself not true democracy. Democracy is more than a legal right which the citizen exercises on a certain day of the year when he enters a tiny polling booth to mark an anonymous "X" on a ballot form. It is a process of constant thought and action on the part of the citizen. It is self-educational. It calls for participation, information, the capacity to make up one's own mind. "The people," it has been truly said, "must understand and participate in the basic ideals of democracy if these ideals are to be defended against attack. They must learn that it is not shibboleth but a vital truth that the state is their own, that they are free citizens with rights and responsibilities." [1]

In an enormous community of more than 130,000,000 persons, this goal has not always been easy to attain. We are not living in an age like that of the Founding Fathers of the American Republic, when "participation in the basic ideals of democracy" was limited exclusively to the "wise, the rich, and the good." Public opinion is not today, as it was then, the opinion of a small and exclusive minority of educated persons enjoying a monopoly of economic and political power. Nor can we restore the practice of direct democracy which operated in the early town-hall meetings of New England, or revive the political intimacy of the rural corner store with its cracker barrel.

For good or evil, public opinion today plays its role on a stage as vast as the American scene itself. The impetus of a growing industrialism, the revolutions in transport and communication, the emergence of factories, towns, and great cities destroyed for all time the rural localism of early

---

[1] Lederer, E., "Public Opinion," in *Political and Economic Democracy*, ed. Ascoli, M., and Lehmann, F., New York, 1937, p. 291.

America. A new kind of public opinion appeared. It was no longer the opinion of a small, exclusive class; it embraced all classes and sections of the community.

The enormous expansion of social and political life broke down the old face-to-face relationships of the small governing class. The rise of what the late Graham Wallas once called the Great Society occurred only because political parties, nation-wide associations, newspapers, the telephone, the motion picture, and radio came upon the scene. Ideas and information had to be disseminated to an ever-growing public. To reach the outlying districts of the country, to bring the immigrant and the newly franchised groups closer to their government, the newspaper and the school fought a continuous battle.

Inevitably, these new agencies of communication gave those who controlled them the power to influence as well as to express public opinion. More and more voices claimed they spoke for the people. Powerful newspapers called themselves the true *vox populi*. Glib party leaders declared that their policies were inscribed in the hearts of the American workingman. Motion-picture and radio executives asserted their belief that at last "the public was getting what it wanted." As the old equality of participation gradually disappeared, the voice of the common man grew faint in the din and clatter of other voices speaking in his name. Basically that is why Walter Lippmann in his search for "public opinion" found only a "phantom public." It is the background of his gloomy picture of the disenchanted man living in a world "which he cannot see, does not understand, and is unable to direct."

The problem of building machinery for directly approaching the mass of the people and hearing what they have to say demands solution. Between infrequent elections, legislators must depend on all sorts of indirect and impressionistic ways of learning the popular will, and finding out how the mass of the people are reacting to the events and propaganda of the day. Unless the ordinary citizen can find channels of self-expression, the common man may become the forgotten man. When such a situation develops, when public opinion cannot get itself expressed, democracy lays itself open to its hostile critics. For public opinion can be a satisfactory guide only if we can hear it and, what is equally important, if it can hear itself.

The following pages tell the story of a new instrument which may help to bridge the gap between the people and those who are responsible for making decisions in their name. The public-opinion polls provide a swift and efficient method by which legislators, educators, experts, and editors, as well as ordinary citizens throughout the length and breadth of the country, can have a more reliable measure of the pulse of democracy. The study of public opinion is still in the experimental stage. But the blueprints for a new technique of investigation have been drawn up and real working models are already in operation. The public-opinion polls represent but one attempt to give an answer to these vital questions. When many more efforts have been made, all of us who believe in democracy will be in a better position to give sound reasons—based upon evidence—for the faith that is in us. One thing is certain: we cannot avoid the problem of trying to get a better measure of public opinion, for our failure to solve it would be a step in the direction which finally identifies the wishes of the people with the hysterical speeches of a "minister of enlightenment."

"Public Opinion," wrote Montaigne, "is a powerful, bold, and unmeasurable party." It is precisely *because* it is powerful and bold that we must try to devise better instruments for measuring it. In a democratic society the views of the majority must be regarded as the ultimate tribunal for social and political issues. Moreover, a large-scale democracy like our own has a special incentive to improve its knowledge of public opinion because of the fundamental need to combine maintenance of popular government with more decisive and efficient legislative action. It is far too late in the day to take refuge in blanket condemnations or in eulogies of the common man. It is not sufficient to do as some mystical democrats have done and urge that public opinion is some kind of supernatural force which will automatically operate to make democracy create the best of all possible worlds. The voice of the people is not the voice of God—at all times and under all conditions. Public opinion is not a deity, neither is it infallible. It is not something above and superior to the opinions of ordinary men and women organized in a political community. It is as good, or as bad, as the human beings whose ideas and aspirations make up the total stream of opinion. It is not the product of an omniscient group mind, but rather a dynamic process resulting from the communication and interaction of individuals in an ever-moving society. Having chosen a way of life which consults the mass of the people in the formulation of policy, we must listen to what the people themselves have to say, for public opinion can only be of service to democracy if it can be heard.

★

★

CHAPTER TWO

The Voices of the People

"THE obvious weakness of government by opinion," wrote James Bryce, "is the difficulty of ascertaining it."

Few political observers have matched Bryce's remarkable insight into the forces behind popular government. Like most of the generalizations which abound in the pages of his *American Commonwealth*, written in 1888, and in later sketches of modern democracies at work, this truth is as valid today as it was at the turn of the century.

Bryce based his analysis of democracy on a conception of public opinion. He did not regard public opinion as a superentity, but as the "aggregate of the views men hold regarding matters that affect or interest the community." And because he saw nothing mystical about public opinion, he advanced definitions which illuminate the problems of democracy in the present day.

"Thus understood," he wrote, "public opinion is a congeries of all sorts of discrepant notions, beliefs, fancies, prejudices, aspirations. It is confused, incoherent, amorphous, varying from day to day and week to week. But in the midst of this diversity and confusion every question as it arises into importance is subjected to a process of consolidation and clarification until there emerge and take shape certain views or sets of interconnected views, each held and advocated in common by bodies of citizens. It is to the power exerted by any such views or set of views, when held by an apparent majority of citizens, that we refer when we talk of Public Opinion as approving or disapproving a certain doctrine or proposal, and thereby becoming a guiding or ruling power."

This public opinion he felt to be the moving force behind the institutions of government, and the "real ruler of America." Yet he was quick to sense the basic problems arising from popular rule: he knew that the multitude of voices claiming to speak for the people might prevent the people themselves from being heard. He therefore proceeded to survey the available methods of estimating the trends of public opinion, by posing the question:

"How does this vague, fluctuating, complex thing we call public opinion—omnipotent yet indeterminate—a sovereign to whose voice everyone listens, yet whose words, because he speaks with as many tongues as the waves of a boisterous sea, it is so hard to catch—how does public opinion express itself in America? By what organs is it declared and how, since these organs often contradict one another, can it be discovered which of them speak most truly for the mass?"

In giving his answer, Bryce emphasized that the first, and by all odds the most valuable, index to public opinion was the popular vote at local, state, and national elections. After the campaigning, the shouting, and the torchlight parades— when the last ballot had been cast and the final announcement of defeat and victory had been declared to the populace—the will of the people was said to have been expressed. It was assumed that national presidential elections reflected the main divisions of public sentiment, and the elected candidate was widely regarded as the symbol of the desires and aspirations of the majority. State and local elections, he suggested, might also indicate the public will, because in these, too, the people could directly express their views by marking ballots for rival candidates. Of all the available methods, in Bryce's view, the vote at elections was the best, because it was the most direct.

But even elections did not provide completely infallible indices of public opinion. Bryce knew that periodic voting might fail to elicit real divisions of opinion on public questions because of the tendency to confuse issues and men. "At elections," he wrote, "it is for a candidate that votes are given, and as his personality or his local influence may count for more than his principles, the choice of one man against another is an imperfect way of expressing the mind of a constituency." He understood, too, that many social and economic conflicts arose and should be settled at intervals not allowed for in the electoral clauses of the American Constitution: "The action of opinion is continuous, that of voting occasional, and in the intervals between the elections of legislative bodies changes may take place materially affecting the views of the voters."

The problem of interpreting the vote at elections is equally pressing in our own day. The confusion between candidates, on the one hand, and fundamental issues, on the other, is still with us. How can we tell whether the people are voting for the man or his platform? How do we know whether the people favor all the views put forward by the candidate or merely some of them? The successful candidate is frequently tempted to regard his election as a blanket endorsement of his entire program, although, in point of fact, this may not express the real intention of the mass of his supporters.

In recent American experience, for example, President Roosevelt's critics maintained that he should have made his Supreme Court reorganization plan a campaign issue in the

1936 election. They argued that if President Roosevelt had done this he could then have correctly assumed that his re-election constituted a mandate to proceed with the proposed Court changes. Yet even if the President had made the Supreme Court an issue in his 1936 campaign, his huge popular vote would not necessarily have indicated majority support on that particular issue. Indeed, the later resistance of large sections of the voting public to the proposal indicated that this sweeping majority was not always voting for specific issues. The voters were merely re-electing President Roosevelt because they preferred him as their presidential candidate in 1936 to Mr. Landon.

Even in years when an election is fought on a single issue, party lines and allegiances make clear interpretation of the result difficult, if not impossible. In 1928, for example, a dry Southern Democrat could not vote for his party's candidate, Alfred E. Smith, without fearing that his ballot might be interpreted as a vote to repeal the Eighteenth Amendment. And, in like manner, the wet Republican could not vote for Herbert Hoover without having his vote misinterpreted in the other direction. If, however, the prohibition question had been divorced from personalities and submitted to a vote of the people, it is probable that the public might have voted strongly for repeal in 1928. Indeed, *The Literary Digest* prohibition poll in 1930 indicated majorities for repeal in 43 of the 48 states.

It is difficult in elections, then, to separate issues from men, not only because elected representatives employ the mandate theory to justify their actions, but also because party lines demand generalized conformity and allegiance and require the average voter to support issues which he might at times prefer to reject. Moreover, at all elections rival candidates are chiefly concerned in getting votes, and the heat of party battle does not always provide the best atmosphere for a clear discussion of issues. "In elections," as Bryce clearly saw, "the spirit of party or class, and the combative ardour which such a spirit inspires, cloud the mind of many voters, making them think of party triumph rather than of either a candidate's merits or his principles. A large percentage of the votes may be given with little reference to the main issues involved." It is true, too, that some elections have failed completely to represent the will of the people. Democratic safeguards have not eliminated the occasional demagogue who claims to represent the popular will which he himself has created by using techniques ranging from simple deception to the more robust forms of vote getting.

There is still another reason why successful candidates occasionally may fail adequately to represent public opinion. In theory, the legislator is supposed to focus the interests of all the voters in his district. Under a rigorous two-party system, there is a tendency for him to yield only to the demands of his own party, and to ignore criticism from groups originally in opposition to him. Party discipline and the need to "play ball" with his leaders may bring pressure to bear on the Congressman who keenly desires re-election. Thus, his political behavior may at times be molded not by what his district thinks but rather by what the party leaders demand.

Moreover, a bird's-eye view of Congress sometimes reveals that it is not truly representative of the main divisions of party sentiment in the country as a whole. The 1936 election gave the Democrats an almost five-to-one preponderance in the Senate although the electorate had voted Democratic by a ratio of only three to two. Advocates of a scheme of proportional representation have frequently emphasized the great disparities which may exist under a system which calls for one representative from each district rather than representation based upon the broad divisions of public opinion in the state or in the country itself.

For all these reasons, elections can never be the sole channel for the expression of public opinion, although they remain, at particular times, probably the best single measure of public opinion obtainable. But there is still a need, even in the best of representative systems, for keeping the legislator in constant touch with public opinion. For whether he chooses to follow public opinion or not, even if his conscience and experience tell him that the opinions of the majority are sometimes wise and at other times foolish, the representative must try to learn what people in his own community, and in the nation itself, are thinking. It is the legislator's duty to educate and instruct the people, just as it is the people's privilege to urge their views upon those whom they have elected. If the legislator thinks the people are right, he must try to get a measure of public opinion. If he thinks they are wrong, he must know what the errors are and where they lie, in order to correct them. For there is a growing belief that representative government works best when the representative combines the roles of leader and follower.

One problem instantly confronts the legislator. It is the old difficulty of judging between the bewildering variety of voices, all of which claim to represent the will of the people. Shall he judge public opinion by the daily newspapers? Shall he estimate opinion by the number or nature of the telegrams from eager constituents? Shall he check the attendance at protest meetings held throughout the country? Does public opinion express itself through the National Association of Manufacturers or the American Federation of Labor? Through the Anti-Saloon League or through its "wet" opponents? Through the delegations which harass his political life at Washington or through the resolutions which emanate from individual meetings held throughout the country? Admitting that the legislator is sincerely trying to sound the depths of the public mind, which instrument shall he use?

James Bryce considered the press an indispensable guide to public opinion. In his time, as in our own, newspapers were part of the daily diet of politicians, government officers, students, and other observers of the movements of opinion. He sensed how close a free press lay to the very basis of democratic government. Long before Bryce wrote, newspapers had been acclaimed as "tribunes of the people," as the vital link between the aspirations of the public and the operation of the government. "If it were left to me," wrote Thomas Jefferson, "to decide whether we should have a government without newspapers, or newspapers without a government, I should not hesitate a moment to prefer the latter." Since Jefferson's time every spokesman of liberal democracy has continued to insist on the importance of the press in reporting the facts on which political decision must rest.

Bryce was quick to see that the newspapers played not a single, but a threefold role. They were at once, as he said, "narrators," "advocates," and "weathercocks." They told what was happening, in their news columns. Their editorials made them propagandists for their own adopted causes. And in their third capacity, they "indicated by their attitude what those who conduct them and are interested in their circulation take to be the prevailing opinion of their readers." Because of the overlapping of these various functions, Bryce felt that newspapers, while indispensable as guides, were not by themselves a sure signpost to public opinion.

These general truths still hold good today. The student of public opinion, the legislator, and the citizen must use the newspaper as a "primary source" in charting the trends of popular thought. In the modern community, the newspaper habit is practically universal, and huge circulations testify to the fact that the newspaper is in all literalness the Bible of democracy. But, obviously, the press does not bear a constant relationship to the intellectual life of all the individuals in a democracy. For some groups the newspaper is almost the sole source of information, while for others it merely provides first impressions. Some individuals swear by their daily paper, while others swear *at* it. But the fact remains that the newspaper provides most people with the groundwork of their knowledge of what other people are thinking, saying, and doing. The press, then, occupies a key position in the democratic structure. But because newspapers mold, as well as reflect, public opinion, and because their influence is often exerted in quite opposite and contradictory directions, they sometimes make very confusing "weathercocks." The busy legislator who scans the day's editorial columns drawn from a wide geographical area, or even from within the confines of a single city, is instantly struck by the divergent interpretations and conflicting courses which are urged upon him. One editorial insists that the people call for a firm stand in support of the embargo on arms and munitions; another solemnly announces that public opinion demands immediate revision. Which is he to believe? Which represents public opinion, or preponderant opinion? The press is not a single unit. Behind each newspaper there is a dynamic of conflicting views and opinions.

That is the essence of a free press. It is only in a dictatorship that the Leader can expect the press to emit a monotonous blast.

For his own peace of mind, the legislator may work out
certain rule-of-thumb methods of estimating the force of
the view put forward by a given newspaper. He may learn
that circulations are not always a satisfactory index of influence, that sometimes the most influential newspaper may
have a comparatively small readership. He will be aware
of the biases of individual newspaper owners, and the pet
ideas of the leading political writers and columnists. He
will distinguish between different newspapers according to
the various political publics to which their arguments are
addressed. He will try to assess the relative importance and
influence of the mass-circulation newspapers in large urban
centers as compared with the small dailies which furnish
most information and opinion to small country towns.
Above all, he will probably realize that democracy's newspapers speak with many voices, and that each of these voices
represents only a single note in the chorus around him. So
many unknown factors stand between what the newspapers
say and what the public thinks that the legislator is forced
to seek further illumination about public opinion.

What about the expressions of sentiment which crystallize in public meetings, and in the claims of countless political, economic, religious, racial, and welfare associations? In
Bryce's day, such groups and associations were growing into
lusty manhood. "Such associations," he wrote, "have great
importance in the development of public opinion, for they
rouse attention, excite discussion, formulate principles,
submit plans, embolden and stimulate their members, and
produce that impression of a spreading movement which

goes so far towards success with a sympathetic and sensitive people." Yet, as he well knew, this ability to produce the "impression of a spreading movement" had its dangers, for there was such a thing as "an artificially created and factitious opinion." "The art of propaganda has been much studied in our time," Bryce observed, "and it has attained a development which enables its practitioners by skilfully and sedulously applying false or one-sided statements of fact to beguile and mislead those who have not the means or the time to ascertain the facts for themselves."

The propaganda which was an art in Bryce's era has become a science in our own. The twentieth century is the age of the expert who knows how to build a private interest into a public demonstration. In this day of pressure groups, telegram barrages, and other forms of protest, the worried legislator must cope with such techniques and therefore may mistakenly identify all the noise and clamor with public opinion.

"I don't merely rely on newspapers," a Congressman may say. "Delegations, petitions, telegrams are also things which you just can't ignore. One false step here and I would have an avalanche of criticism sent to me by courtesy of Western Union; hundreds of people would besiege my office in Washington; petitions would flow in from dozens of organizations all over the country. There's your real public opinion. That's the thing that makes and breaks governments."

Undeniably, letters, telegrams, petitions, and delegations often provide useful indices of popular opinion. During the Congressional discussions of the Neutrality Act in October, 1939, when American public opinion was agitating "for" and "against" repeal of the embargo clauses of the Act, Congress was flooded with letters and telegrams from anxious constituents and interested groups. Western Union, in an attempt to systematize the flood, even provided a special questionnaire telegram, containing possible choices and points of view, which needed only a check in the appropriate square to register the sender's opinion.

The *Cleveland Plain Dealer,* in its editorial of September 5, 1939, commented on this flood:

> There have been such letter and word telegram avalanches before. One of them helped to keep the United States out of the World Court. Then hundreds of thousands of those who wrote or wired their Congressmen obviously had slight understanding of the merits of the question. Another avalanche came from people when the so-called "death penalty" for holding companies was at issue. At this time, as was proved later, private utility employees copied names out of phone books to forge on "protesting" telegrams.
>
> This does not mean, of course, that many who are now writing to their representatives in Washington are not sincerely and intelligently exercising the right of petition. But when a Congressman is buried by thousands of letters or post cards of practically the same wording, he should not take them too seriously as a manifestation of the preponderant "voice of the people." He might do well to recall the famous legend of the three tailors of Tooley Street who addressed a plea to the King, subscribing themselves, "We, the people of England."

Nobody can question the fundamental right of an individual or a group to petition those entrusted with policy making. But even here there is a latent danger, for one can never be sure that the letter, telegram, or petition avalanche is the product of a genuine protest, or merely the organized effort of a small but powerful pressure group parading as a majority. The claim of the three Tooley Street tailors to represent "the people of England," or the pretensions of some of the groups who bombard American Congressmen in the name of public opinion, must never be accepted uncritically. For even when the petition or delegation is backed by thousands of loyal supporters, it may not truly represent public opinion. Some people look with disdain upon methods of mass pressure and refuse to participate in such action, while countless other obliging souls will sign each and every petition that comes along—in many cases even before they have read its contents. So few checks exist on whether such protests are honest or fraudulent ·that one must be cautious in interpreting these demonstrations as "public" opinion. Indeed, most Congressmen might privately admit doubts on this score.

No country in the world has such numerous and potent private associations, interest groups, and organized lobbies as the United States. Geographic, economic, religious, and welfare associations compete with one another in pushing their pet legislation. Often in such conflicts, narrow self-interest and sectionalism, rather than any generalized conception of the public welfare, dominate the issues and the conflict. It is often difficult to identify these numerous pressure groups or to know when they are in operation. Senator Tydings has mentioned some twenty important organizations representing labor, agriculture, war veterans, pension-plan advocates, chambers of commerce, racial groups, isolationists and internationalists, high-tariff and low-tariff groups, preparedness and disarmament groups, budget balancers and spending advocates, soft-money associations and hard-money associations, transportation groups, and states' righters and centralizationists. The list could be continued indefinitely. Each pressure group focuses upon a special purpose and interprets all political or general issues with reference to its own objectives and interests. Will this piece of legislation hurt the farmer? Let's oppose it! Will this tariff help New England? Let's back it! The groups have a centralizing cause, to which adherents pay their dues and their homage. Loyalty, conformity, and, above all, action—these are the watchwords of the pressure groups. Through press, radio, meetings, and a dozen subtle, un-avowed channels, such groups work night and day to influ-ence the public and to mold the opinion of Congress, even forming their own political parties when the need and occasion arise.

In the growing clamor of voices, each group claims to represent "public opinion." Who has not heard the cham-bers of commerce and the labor unions invoke the same deity in the midst of some industrial strike? Did not Dr. Townsend urge that his old-age-pension movement had the support of an overwhelming majority of voters in the nation? Late in 1934, the Townsend movement gathered momentum in the West, descended on Washington. Town-send Clubs grew up all over the country, claiming converts in district after district like an old-time religious revival. What were Congressmen to do? How was the legislator to know whether or not this movement really represented a dominant current in American opinion, or merely the exuberance of a few apostles of utopia?

These are some of the difficulties which confront observers of public opinion today. But they are also the "weaknesses of public opinion" which Bryce detected when he wrote *The American Commonwealth*, over fifty years ago. Through the years, the central problem of making democracy work has been related to the need to discover the real purposes and opinions of the people. "The more completely popular sovereignty prevails in a country," Bryce declared, "so much the more important is it that the organs of opinion should be adequate to its expression, prompt, full, and unmistakable, in their utterances." Yet in spite of this need, the techniques at our disposal have not always been sufficiently accurate to solve this vital problem.

In modern America, even more than in the democracy of 1888, the problem is pressing indeed. Rapid communication has aided the growth and consolidation of political parties by integrating distant rural areas. Pressure groups representing a wide variety of interests have grown enormously powerful, and this expansion has created a new set of conditions within which public opinion operates.

There is one final point of difference between the America of 1888 and the America of 1940. Fifty-two years ago, Bryce saw a country of boundless opportunity, and commented on its amazing economic and social equality. Income levels, he said, made little or no difference in opinion. "As social distinctions count for less in America, the same tendencies are more generally and uniformly diffused among all classes, and it is not necessary to discount so many special points of difference which may affect the result. As social intercourse is easier, and there is less difference between a person in the higher and in the humbler ranks, a man can better pick up in conversation the sentiment of his poorer neighbors." And again, "In America you cannot appeal from the classes to the masses. What the employer thinks, his workmen think; what the wholesale merchant feels, the retail shopkeeper feels, and the poorer customers feel."

Contemporary students of opinion in the United States know that this condition is disappearing. New alignments of opinion have arisen; the wealthy, the middle class, and the poor do not see all issues eye to eye. The 1936 election and succeeding events revealed a growing chasm between the opinions of those whose incomes come from investments

and those dependent on relief. Uneven economic developments in American society have produced more rigid alignments of opinion, and have even created pockets where
insecurities and frustrations make fertile ground for pressure groups, propagandists, and the rabble-rousers. All the
more necessary, then, for legislators in our own day to be
certain that the view put forward as public opinion is not
merely the view of powerful interests which stand between
the people and their government. In a society which is
becoming increasingly stratified, in which competing interests of section and class are producing a pattern infinitely
more complex and intricate than Americans knew in the
era of "boundless opportunity," the views of all groups must
be taken into account. If government with the consent of
the governed is to be preserved and strengthened, then the
common man, the farmer, the industrial worker, the stenographer, the clerk, and the factory hand must become as
politically articulate as the professional man, the businessman, and the banker.

James Bryce was not a destructive critic. He did not
merely say that the techniques available in his day were
likely to be inaccurate; he also looked forward to a time
when more efficient methods might be devised to aid the
legislator, and provide democracy with a mirror in which
it could see its own likeness. He realized that the popular
vote was the best positive test, but felt that, for obvious
reasons, elections could not be multiplied indefinitely.

The referendum as practiced in the cantons of Switzer-
land impressed him deeply because it allowed the mass of
citizens to participate more actively in government. "The
referendum, or plan of submitting a specific question to the
popular vote," Bryce suggested, "is the logical resource, but

it is troublesome and costly to take the votes of millions of
people over an area so large as that of one of the greater
states; much more, then, is this difficult to apply in federal
matters." Because he felt that the effort and expense
involved would prohibit the use of frequent referendums
in a large-scale democracy, he concluded, with some regret,
that ". . . the machinery for weighing or measuring the
popular will from week to week or month to month is not
likely to be invented."

What then was his final suggestion?

> The best way in which the tendencies which are at work
> in any community may be discovered is by moving freely about
> among all sorts and conditions of men and noting how they
> are affected by the news or arguments brought from day to
> day to their knowledge.
>
> In every neighborhood there are unbiased persons with
> good opportunities for observing, and plenty of skill in "sizing
> up" the attitudes and proclivities of their fellow citizens. Such
> men are invaluable guides.
>
> Talk is the best way of reaching the truth, because in talk,
> one gets directly at the facts, whereas reading gives not so
> much the facts, as what the writer believes, or wished to have
> others believe.

There is a remarkable parallel between Bryce's outline
of the best way of discovering public opinion and the
methods now used by the modern polls of public opinion.
Surveys are conducted in rural and urban areas, among
rich and poor, old and young (*"by moving freely about
among all sorts and conditions of men"*), which ask people
to express their attitudes on the vital issues of the day (". . .
*noting how they are affected by the news or arguments
brought from day to day to their knowledge"*). The modern
polls rely on interviewers (". . . *unbiased persons with
good opportunities for observing"*) who listen to voters

expressing their attitudes in ordinary conversation (*"Talk is the best way of reaching the truth, because in talk, one gets directly at the facts"*).

On just one basic point of technique do the modern polls part company with Bryce's advice. Instead of "sizing up" the attitudes and proclivities of their fellow citizens, the interviewers who travel about America let the people speak for themselves. Thus the polls substitute direct factual reporting for intuition as a guide to public opinion.

Not only have the polls followed Bryce's suggestion that the people should be approached directly; the development of a careful sampling technique has virtually overcome the obstacles of time and expense which caused Bryce to doubt the possibility of continuous nation-wide referendums. By collecting the opinions of a representative sample of voters, they have made possible that week-to-week audit of public opinion, which Bryce himself called the "logical resource."

The sampling referendum, then, is a modern answer to Bryce's problem. But even before he wrote, the rough outlines of a plan for this machinery were beginning to take shape. From the first quarter of the nineteenth century, enterprising individuals were testing out a way of approaching the public directly. Keenly interested in collecting "newsworthy" information, one or two newspaper editors had sent out their reporters to discover what people were thinking. They began by testing sentiment toward candidates for public office. They could not ask all the people about their opinions, but they asked some whom they considered "typical." They could not poll all the individuals in the United States, but they could and did select people from various groups and tried to find out how they were going to vote. They did not sit back in their armchairs and *imagine* the state of public opinion; they anticipated

Bryce's advice and sent out interviewers to collect the opinions of ordinary citizens in towns and villages throughout the country.

Mistakes were inevitable at first. Little was known about the factors which would have to be watched in order to make these "samples" representative of the whole voting population, what the principle of selection was to be, or how the probable limits of accuracy could be determined. The chief interest of the early polls centered upon elections, and on predictions of voting results which would boost circulations and give certain newspapers a reputation for political sagacity. For the most part, they ignored what today has come to be the major interest of sampling studies: the measurement of opinion on issues. Yet these early "straw votes," conducted by harassed journalists and reporters on election eve, and hampered by inaccurate methods, nevertheless gave a clue to improving our knowledge of public opinion. Much credit is due these pioneers who had the courage and the foresight to believe that politics, too, needs its inventions.

CHAPTER THREE

★

A Clue to the Problem

THE presidential election of 1824 provided a free-for-all between the leaders of rival factions within the old Republican party. Who was to succeed to the mantle of James Monroe? After the preliminary stages of the campaign, four candidates remained in the presidential race. From Monroe's cabinet came John Quincy Adams, Secretary of State, and William H. Crawford, Secretary of the Treasury. The new frontier states divided their enthusiasm between Henry Clay of Kentucky and General Andrew Jackson of Tennessee. Twenty-four states participated in the election. Although Jackson led his nearest competitor by 50,000 votes, and had the greatest number of electoral votes, no candidate won a clear majority, and the final choice was left to the House of Representatives. On the first ballot in the House, Adams received the votes of 13 states, with 7 for General Jackson, and 4 for Crawford. A wave of recrimination swept the West. The Jackson men claimed that the people had elected their hero, but that the politicians had deprived him of office. Thus the 1824 election set the stage for the sectional conflicts which emerged with increased vigor in 1828.

It was during this exciting presidential campaign—the second occasion on which the House of Representatives was called upon to break a deadlock—that the earliest counterparts of the modern opinion surveys began. "As we look back at the oldest report of polling which I have seen in print," writes Mr. Emil Hurja, a keen student of the polls, "we come to the conclusion that Americans, in whatever era they live, are generally interested in seeing beyond the rim in politics as in everything else." By way of documentation, Hurja reports two early studies which bear witness to the early nineteenth-century origins of the polling technique of measuring public opinion. The *Harrisburg Pennsylvanian* of July 24, 1824, printed a report of a straw vote taken at Wilmington, Delaware, "without Discrimination of Parties." In this poll, Andrew Jackson received 335 votes; John Quincy Adams, 169; Henry Clay, 19, and William H. Crawford, 9. In Delaware, where the legislature chose the electors, bitter disputes occurred. Again in August of the same year, the *Raleigh Star* undertook to canvass political meetings held in North Carolina "at which the sense of the people was taken." These surveys showed that out of 4256 voters canvassed, Jackson received 3428; Adams, 470, and Crawford, 358. Jackson carried North Carolina in the following November.

Newspapers continued to dominate the picture through the years. In 1883 General Charles H. Taylor, editor of the *Boston Globe,* tried to speed up his reporting of election returns by sending out his reporters to representative precincts to gather early returns. The combined results were then used to indicate what the final count was likely to be.

These pioneer efforts to measure public opinion whetted the interest of other newspaper editors who soon discovered that what people thought, as well as what people did, made good "news." From the turn of the century, newspapers in the larger cities throughout the country extended their reporting to include opinions as well as events. National,

state, and local elections stimulated more and more newspapers to try to find out, and, if possible, to predict, how
the public was going to vote. The early leaders in this field
included the *New York Herald,* the *Cincinnati Enquirer,*
the *Boston Globe,* the *Columbus Dispatch,* the *Chicago
American,* and the *Chicago Record-Herald,* as well as many
others, whose methods and activities have already been well
discussed.[1] Magazines also sensed the value and interest of
polling, and, as early as 1912, the *Farm Journal* began its
series of presidential polls. *The Literary Digest* followed,
and later the *Pathfinder.*

Only occasionally did these early polls deal with issues.
The war of 1914-18 deeply stirred the American public and
focused attention on the vital question of American participation. In 1917, when the public was passionately dis-
cussing the impending declaration of war on Germany,
Ernest Lundeen, then a Congressman of the Fifth Congressional District of Minnesota, conducted a dramatic poll on
the question of whether or not America should enter the
world conflict. Lundeen had debated in the House of Representatives against this country's participation in the war,
arguing that a popular referendum would clearly demonstrate the widespread popularity of his views. He mailed a
ballot card to all the 54,000 registered voters in his district,
containing the declaration:

"I believe that the people should be consulted before
Congress declares war." The question was then asked:
"Shall the United States declare war?" Congressman Lundeen got 8800 replies, of which 8000, or about 90 per cent
of the voters in his district, cast their votes against American
participation in the war.

Such tests of public opinion on issues occurred but seldom

1 Robinson, Claude, *Straw Votes,* 1932, Ch. 6.

and were usually local in scope. But the basic idea of going directly to the people to measure their wishes and intentions had fired the imagination of American newspapermen and publicists. The rapid growth in the polling activities of newspapers and magazines indicated that the urge to "see beyond the rim in politics" was highly contagious.[1]

The methods used in this early period varied enormously from poll to poll. Many of the first newspaper polls resorted to the simple expedient of printing "straw ballots" in the newspaper itself, and asking the reader to cut out and mail the completed form to the sponsoring organization.[2] In this case, the assumption was that the readers of the newspaper concerned would constitute a "typical" sample or cross section of the electorate, an assumption rarely if ever true in fact, since newspapers tend to draw their readers from particular sections of the population. The "ballot-in-the-paper" method tempted pressure groups to buy quantities of the newspaper and vote enthusiastically, thus making their private view look like "public" opinion. Occasionally, early sponsors failed to appreciate the distinction between a public-opinion survey, a popularity contest, and a subscription-raising device. But other sponsors like the *Colum-*

---

1 Robinson tells us that "approximately eighty-five straw polls were held during the Presidential election of 1928. Seventy-five of these undertakings were local in character, being confined to a city, county, or restricted trade area. Four of the enterprises, those of the *Columbus Dispatch, Cincinnati Enquirer, Chicago Tribune,* and *New York Daily News,* extended to the boundaries of the home state or included this state and neighboring commonwealths. Six of the polls were of nation-wide character. These were sponsored by the *Literary Digest,* the *Hearst Newspapers,* the *Farm Journal,* the *Pathfinder,* the *Nation,* and *College Humour.*"

2 The polls conducted by the *Erie Dispatch Herald* (Pennsylvania), the *Omaha World Herald,* and the *Buffalo Evening Times* (New York), some of the newspapers of the Hearst chain, and the *Pathfinder* magazine were examples of this type.

bus Dispatch and the *Cincinnati Enquirer* used careful methods. They hired canvassers, generally reporters and newspapermen, to travel around the area, soliciting votes in offices, at street corners, hotels, theaters, clubs—wherever people would be found. At times, a semipermanent booth was erected in some conspicuous spot, or voting machines were used. Such newspapers frequently achieved a good measure of accuracy through sincere and careful attempts to adhere to a formal procedure. The *Columbus Dispatch,* for example, used trained men, organized them into crews, and assigned each crew to specific sections of the area to be polled. Controls of economic background, nationality, and sex were introduced in order to get a good sample of the voting public. Special checkups were ordered for areas where the voting promised to be close, and rough quotas were worked out for laborers and white-collar workers, for urban and rural districts, for men and women.

But careful polls on the model of the *Columbus Dispatch,* the *Cincinnati Enquirer,* or those made more recently by the *Chicago Times,* and the *Baltimore Sun* were, by and large, the exception. In general, the early polls were hastily organized, and conducted by people with little statistical training. Their sponsors emphasized the theatrical element of vote predicting instead of undertaking the more important task of measuring public reactions to the issues of the day. Because of these difficulties, unreliable predictions almost always followed. Since each sponsor practiced his own method, and since these methods often differed in all their phases, the estimates of public opinion contradicted each other almost as often as they agreed.

In the public mind, one of these early polls stood out as a model. Of all the newspaper and magazine polls, those conducted by *The Literary Digest* received the greatest public attention and acclaim. For years the *Digest* poll stood as a monument of accuracy, and its frequent successes in predicting the outcome of elections drew the plaudits of an admiring public.

The Literary Digest was a magazine with a large nationwide circulation. As far back as 1895, it had begun to collect the names of prospective subscribers, for filing and mailing purposes. This mailing list consisted largely of the names of people in the middle- and upper-income groups who offered the best market for the magazine as well as for the products advertised in its pages. Its social composition included a preponderance of lawyers, doctors, architects, engineers, club members, business people, merchants, and the like. In 1895, the list had 350,000 names; by 1900, it had grown to 685,000. By 1932, the *Digest* mailing list numbered over 20,000,000. As the list grew in size it provided increasing coverage of the major groups, except the groups consisting of people with low incomes.

The year 1916 saw *The Literary Digest* enter the polling field. At that time it asked its readers in all sections of the country to act as reporters and to send news of public opinion as to the chances of President Wilson and Charles Evans Hughes in the coming election. From labor leaders, it also tried to find out how labor would vote, and to this indirect method added a direct postal-card poll of subscribers in Illinois, Indiana, New Jersey, New York, and Ohio.

Before the nominating conventions were held in 1920, 11,000,000 ballots were distributed by mail to residential telephone subscribers, to test sentiment on possible presidential nominees, rather in the manner of an unofficial presidential primary. During the campaign itself, ballots were distributed in California, Illinois, Indiana, New Jersey, New York, and Ohio.

Then came the three national prohibition referendums of 1922, 1930, and 1932. In 1922, 10,108,437 ballot cards were mailed to users of telephones throughout the United States, asking them to choose one of three alternatives:

1. Do you favor the continuance and strict enforcement of the Eighteenth Amendment and Volstead Law? (or)
2. Do you favor a modification of the Volstead Law to permit light wines and beers? (or)
3. Do you favor repeal of the Prohibition Amendment?

Almost 800,000 people in the United States participated by declaring their views. When the final tabulation was made, combining the vote for light wines and beer with that for repeal, the returns showed that "wet" sentiment was then uppermost in 46 states. In 1930, the same questions were asked of 20,000,000 automobile owners and telephone subscribers in the nation, and the enormous number of 5,000,000 votes was received in return. Again, combining the modification and repeal vote, this poll revealed "wet" majorities in 43 of the 48 states.[1] In 1932, approximately the same-sized public was tested.

In February, 1924, 15,000,000 ballots had been mailed to the *Digest*'s "tel-auto public," on attitudes to the Mellon tax-reduction proposal. In 1928, a presidential poll was taken in which 18,000,000 ballots were distributed. It predicted a victory for Herbert Hoover with 63.2 per cent of the total popular vote. Actually the Republican candidate got 58.8 per cent of the total. In the succeeding campaign of

---

1 See Wilcox, W. F., "Public Opinion About Repealing the Eighteenth Amendment," *Journal of the American Statistical Association,* Vol. XXVI (September, 1931), No. 175; Robinson, Claude: *Straw Votes,* Ch. VI, pp. 145-171.

1932, some 20,000,000 ballots were distributed. The *Digest* straws indicated that the Democratic candidate, Franklin D. Roosevelt, would be the next President.

On October 14, 1932, while *The Literary Digest* poll was prophesying a sweeping Roosevelt victory, Democratic Chairman James Farley commented: "Any sane person cannot escape the implication of such gigantic sampling of the popular opinion as is embraced in *The Literary Digest* straw vote. I consider this conclusive evidence as to the desire of the people for a change in the national government. It is a poll fairly and honestly conducted."

Mr. Farley's attitude was more than that of a practical strategist seeking public endorsement of his party's prospect. It was an expression of widespread popular respect for the poll and its accuracy. The brilliance of its past predictions, the huge organization which it had built up to conduct the work, and, above all, the "gigantic sampling," were eulogized on all sides. The poll was widely heralded as "uncanny," "infallible," "amazingly accurate." When it predicted the division of the total popular vote of the two presidential candidates in 1932 within 1.4 per cent, the chorus of praise rang louder than ever.

"The *Digest* poll is still the Bible of millions," declared its editorial of August 22, 1936, just before the polling machinery for the elections of 1936 went into operation. Such a statement was not an idle editorial boast. It was an accurate description of the place which this enormous straw-vote venture occupied in the thinking of the general public, as well as in the minds of many professional political observers. Beginning in August, 1936, the *Digest* prepared with confidence to play the role of the nation's chief prognosticator. Relying on the methods which had apparently proved so accurate in the past, it proceeded to use the "tel-auto" lists, and sent out 10,000,000 ballots in the course of the campaign. Of these, some 2,376,523 ballots were returned—a proportion of about one in four. Occasionally whole towns were canvassed. Ballots were mailed out to every registered voter in certain communities, and to one in every three registered voters in the Chicago area. A fixed and prearranged plan was followed throughout, and returns were totaled and released as they came in.

"Like the outriders of a great army," it was announced, "the first ballots in the great 1936 Presidential campaign march into the open this week to be marshalled, checked and counted. Next week more states will join the parade and there will be thousands of additional votes. Ballots are pouring out by tens of thousands and will continue to flood the country for several weeks. They are pouring back too, in an ever increasing stream. The homing ballots coming from every state, city, and hamlet should write the answer to the question, Roosevelt or Landon? long before Election Day. For in every previous poll, such ballots have enabled the *Digest* to put its finger on the winner."

With this statement made on September 5, the *Digest* introduced its early returns. The preliminary figures, based on the early results in four states, showed Landon with 16,056 votes to Roosevelt's 7645 and Lemke's 754—a lead of more than two to one for the Republican candidate. Throughout the campaign, the weekly releases continued to indicate a Landon victory by a sweeping majority. As ballots poured into headquarters, the *Digest* figures showed that, after three weeks of polling, Landon had 61,190 votes; Roosevelt, 33,423; and Lemke, 4169. When the incoming ballots reached the 250,000 mark, Landon still stood ahead with 153,360 to Roosevelt's 88,815 and Lemke's 10,374.

"As the three round the turn," ran the release of September 19, "it becomes more and more evident that the 1936 Presidential sweepstakes is a wide open sprint." On September 26, the score stood: Landon, 293,972; Roosevelt, 185,495, and Lemke, 19,632. The semifinal report, with 2,158,739 ballots in, gave Landon the lead in 32 states, with 54.8 per cent of the votes, while President Roosevelt was given only 16 states and 40.7 per cent of the total vote. The *Digest's* final report, based on 2,376,523 ballots, pointed to a resounding Landon victory, with Republican margins in 32 states and a total of 370 electoral votes. The poll indicated that Landon would get some 54 per cent of the total vote, or 57 per cent of the major party vote.

In the election which followed the straw vote, when the final ballots had been counted on November 5, President Franklin D. Roosevelt polled 62.5 per cent of the major party vote and was declared elected with the colossal majority of 523 out of a possible 531 electoral votes.

Why did the *Digest* poll fail? Why did this poll, backed by a long record of past successes, conducted by honest administrators, and based on an enormous sample of millions of ballots, completely fail to predict the eventual winner, place some 32 states in the wrong column, and miss the division of the popular vote between candidates by such a huge margin?

★

★

CHAPTER FOUR

The Lessons of 1936

THE glaring discrepancy between the result of *The Literary Digest* poll and the actual vote in the 1936 presidential election moved a few violent partisans to impassioned attack. Charges were hurled about the "honesty" of the sponsors, and insinuations were made that the poll had been "rigged" in some mysterious fashion to suit the needs of the Republican National Committee. Such charges, needless to say, had no basis in fact. The sincerity and honesty of the *Digest*'s sponsors were beyond question and had been established in numerous polls conducted long before 1936. Why, then, did the *Digest* go wrong? The answer lies not in a lack of honesty on the part of the sponsors, but rather in the fact that in this business of polling public opinion, sincerity and honesty, though vitally important, are not in themselves guarantees against errors and inaccuracies. Disaster lay in the *Digest*'s cross section and its sampling methods, not in the morals of its organizers.

In general, there were two kinds of critics. While some individuals ranted and railed at the *Digest* poll *after* the election, others who had studied and observed public opinion had foreseen the disaster long before it actually happened.

Ammunition for this second type of criticism came from two main quarters. The expansion of American industry had led to specialization. This specialization resulted in the emergence of a group of capable market-research analysts who had been applying statistical methods and techniques to the study of consumers' choices and the needs of the national market. Industry needed to know people's opinions about the goods and commodities which they bought or refused to buy. Advertisers wanted to learn about brand preferences, sizes, amounts, buying habits, consumers' interests. To answer these questions, statisticians were called in to develop sampling methods in order to deal with the attitudes of large populations. The research methods which this market analysis had built up furnished yardsticks by which surveys of public opinion could be checked.

Still other critics emerged from academic privacy to point out the basic flaws in the *Digest*'s procedures. The social sciences had become increasingly aware of the uses of statistical methods and their application to the study of attitudes, beliefs, and opinions. Universities and colleges were giving students a theoretical background for the work of these opinion polls.

The leaders in this movement to improve polling techniques included such men as Claude Robinson, W. L. Crum, and Henry C. Link whose experimental studies paved the way for a critical, statistical approach to public-opinion measurement. In the field of practical politics, Emil Hurja was utilizing sampling procedures to indicate the main voting tendencies in different parts of the country. Market research contributed Elmo Roper and Paul Cherrington, who in association with *Fortune* magazine developed the *Fortune* Survey in 1935. Since that time the *Fortune* Survey has remained a regular and important feature of that magazine. Before the election of 1936, Archibald Crossley, also recruited from the field of market research, and with long experience of survey methods, applied sampling techniques in the Crossley poll which appeared as a feature in the Hearst newspapers. After a preliminary period of experiment, beginning in 1933, the American Institute of Public Opinion, with the co-operation and support of a number of American newspapers, began a series of week-by-week national polls which have continued to the present day. The Institute's purpose was to perform the function of fact finding in the realm of opinion in the same general way as the Associated Press, the United Press, and the International News Service functioned in the realm of events. This attempt to improve and objectify the reporting of what people think met with warm response and active encouragement from editors throughout the country.

The growing interest of such individuals and organizations in the theory and practice of public-opinion measurement created, by 1936, a new apparatus of criticism and analysis. From experimental studies of pre-election opinion, the American Institute of Public Opinion had grown aware that political sentiment in 1936 varied strikingly with different income levels. Early in the campaign, statisticians at the Institute made a series of preliminary studies which showed that while Landon was receiving 59 per cent of the ballots drawn from telephone subscribers and 56 per cent of the votes cast by owners of automobiles, he was getting only 18 per cent of the votes drawn from people on relief. This observation suggested an interesting experiment. The Institute took the identical kind of sample which the *Digest* was planning to use, based chiefly on the upper- and middle-income-group voters and ignoring the lower-income-group voters and voters on relief, and, on the basis of the returns from this one-sided sample, predicted that the *Digest* would be wrong in its 1936 prediction, and actually estimated the degree of this probable *Digest* error *within 1 per cent even before the Digest had begun its send-out of ballots.*

Williston Rich has described the incident with considerable vigor:[1]

> . . . Landon was nominated on June 11, 1936. On July 12, Gallup warned his subscribers that the *Digest's* old fashioned methods would point to the wrong man.
>
> Almost as an after-thought he mentioned that its totals would show about 56% for Landon, 44% for Roosevelt.
>
> Inasmuch as the poll was not to begin for six weeks, Wilfred J. Funk, editor of *The Literary Digest,* was outraged. "Never before has anyone foretold what our poll was going to show even before it started!" he snapped. "Our fine statistical friend" should be advised that the *Digest* would carry on "with those old fashioned methods that have produced correct forecasts exactly one hundred per cent of the time."

While the *Digest* was thus "carrying on," still other insistent critics pointed out that its sampling methods would prove inaccurate. In a special series of *New York Post* articles describing the various public-opinion polls before the 1936 election, Claude Robinson repeatedly showed that since the *Digest's* mailing list was drawn from a "tel-auto" public, its sampling method was operating automatically to enfranchise the wealthier classes and disfranchise the poorer groups. Since people who used telephones and owned automobiles tended on the whole to be Republican in their political sympathies, this economic bias produced, as Robinson suggested, a political bias. Comparison of previous *Digest* predictions on a state-by-state basis with the actual division of the party vote indicated that in 128 out

---

1 Rich, Williston "The Human Yardstick," *The Saturday Evening Post,* Jan. 21, 1939. The Institute estimated that the *Digest* returns would show 56 per cent for Landon. The actual *Digest* returns which were finally tabulated showed 57 per cent for Landon.

of 149 *Digest* state reports, the vote of the Republican candidate had been overestimated.

Moreover, political observers in 1936 sensed that class alignments were being drawn with a firmness unknown in American politics since the McKinley-Bryan fight of 1896. The *Digest*'s string of predictive successes from 1916 to 1932 took place in a period when political sentiment favoring each of the major parties was evenly distributed through the different layers of society. The *Digest* poll was accurate in 1932 because sampling any one economic group in American society brought out the same divisions of sentiment as sampling opinion in other economic groups. But in 1936 the bitterness of the struggle between the "haves" and the "have-nots" meant distinct cleavages of political attitude between rich and poor, and pointed to a heavy Democratic vote from the ranks of the "ill-fed, ill-clothed, and ill-housed" lower third of the population—the group to which the *Digest*'s sampling plan failed to give full weight.

Statisticians pointed out the fallacy in piling up cases to the two-million mark when the basis of selecting the sample was itself faulty. They questioned whether it was possible to combine the objectives of accurately measuring public sentiment with the desire to stimulate magazine circulation. They warned that unless extremely careful checks were used, the mail-ballot technique would be bound to contribute still further toward severely weighting the *Digest* sample in favor of the upper-income-group voters, and would therefore magnify the Republican vote, since persons in the upper-income brackets tended to respond to mail canvasses in greater proportion than the less articulate groups in the poorer districts. Added emphasis was given to the cogency of their arguments by the indignation felt by the bulk of wealthier voters toward President Roosevelt's

New Deal measures, moving them to register a powerful vote of protest in the 1936 election. Further, the critics added, the *Digest* sample would be biased in favor of older persons, since it was based on ownership qualifications, and underlined this by warning that the young were, on the whole, going to vote anti-Republican in 1936.

To these warnings of hidden sources of distortion in the sample, still another important cause of error was noted during the campaign. The *Digest*'s practice of totaling the returns week by week introduced still another variable factor in its final estimate inasmuch as it meant a failure to take account of changes in sentiment over time. Since the *Digest* polled steadily throughout several months, and accumulated its returns from week to week, it failed to catch the move of political sentiment toward Roosevelt in the last stages of the campaign.

Criticism of the *Digest* did not merely rest with prophesying the final debacle. In the mounting flood of discussion and argument, one vital point clearly emerged above the din: in an election like the presidential election of 1936, where basic cleavages were becoming apparent between different economic groups within the general voting public, it was realized that no poll based on a faulty sample could hope to survive. Practical demonstration of the *Digest*'s failure to include all the major groups within its cross section was made possible by the advent of new polls whose methods were based on scientific principles. The surprising accuracy of the results obtained by these new polls in 1936, bearing in mind that it was the first real test of scientific sampling in a national election, bears witness to the cogency of the criticisms of the *Digest* poll, and to the underlying soundness of the alternative methods which were put to the test.

Of all the competing straw votes, polls, and sampling studies conducted in 1936, three national polls were outstanding—the Crossley poll, the *Fortune* Survey, and the poll directed by the American Institute of Public Opinion. Before comparing the predictive accuracy of these new efforts with that of the *Digest,* it will be necessary to discuss what is meant by the accuracy of a public-opinion poll.

The Accuracy of the Polls in 1936

Poll accuracy can best be objectively judged by comparing the returns of the poll with those of the election itself. Thus, although a survey of opinion taken in October might provide a fair picture of the main divisions of sentiment at that time, its failure to take account of a basic change in sentiment between October and Election Day early in November must be regarded as a predictive error. The final election result is the mark at which public-opinion polls must shoot, because this is the only objective basis on which the general public can verify the accuracy of competing estimates.

In the election of 1936, Franklin D. Roosevelt was re-elected as President of the United States. He received 60.7 per cent of the total vote awarded to all candidates, or 62.5 per cent of the major party vote; 46 of the 48 states voted for him, and he obtained a total of 523 out of a possible 531 electoral votes. His share of the vote ranged from a high of 98.6 per cent in South Carolina, to a low of 42.8 per cent in Maine.

Once we agree that accuracy is to be tested against election returns, certain questions are bound to emerge. In a presidential election, which "returns" are we to use? The division of the national popular vote? The correct placement of states in the various political columns? Electoral

votes? The state-by-state average error between the predicted and the actual figure? [1]

All the major national polls estimated the division of the
total popular vote between the various candidates. But this
method of judging the accuracy of election polls may at
times be misleading. The President is not elected by the
total popular vote, but by the popular vote cast in each state
separately, the winner of each state obtaining all the electoral votes of that state. For this reason, a more complete
picture of the outcome of a presidential election can be
obtained by a pre-election poll which reports the results for
each state. It can be seen, in certain cases, that a close prediction of the division of the national vote may include errors
made in certain states or regions which are counterbalanced
by errors in the opposite direction made in other areas.

All the major national polls with the exception of the
Fortune Survey, which did not poll in every state, tabulated
their estimates in terms of the division of the total popular
vote between the candidates, the placement of states in the
"Democratic" or "Republican" column, the total electoral
vote of each candidate, and the state-by-state division of the
vote for each candidate. By itself, of course, the correct
placement of states in the prediction of the total electoral
vote can constitute only a rough measure of accuracy since
such methods may fail to indicate how closely the forecast
approximates the distribution of the popular vote within
each state. A pre-election poll might accurately predict the
total electoral vote and yet fall wide of the mark in its
prognosis of the margin of victory in each of the states where

[1] For discussions of the accuracy of the polls in 1936, see: Katz, D., and
Cantril, H., "Public Opinion Polls," *Sociometry*, Vol. 1, 1937; Gosnell,
Harold, "How Accurate Were the Polls?" *Public Opinion Quarterly*, Jan-
uary, 1937.

voting was close. In *The Literary Digest* polls of the 1924 and 1928 presidential elections, for example, the popular vote of the winner was greatly overpredicted, but few states were misrepresented in the electoral college because the real election happened to be one-sided. Thus it is clear that the best criterion is not correct prediction of the electoral-college votes, but rather the ability to forecast the state-by-state division of the vote between candidates. Paradoxically enough, this may even mean that, in some instances, a poll which predicts victory for the wrong man may be judged to be more accurate than one which predicts the winner accurately.

In Crossley's final estimate, as reported in the Hearst newspapers, he indicated that Roosevelt would obtain 55 per cent of the major party vote, and 53.8 per cent of the total popular vote. A total of 27 states were listed as "certain" for Roosevelt, with a total of 250 electoral votes. For Landon, 6 states were reported as "certain" with a total of 73 electoral votes. The remaining 15 states, counting for 208 electoral votes, were regarded as so close as to be difficult to predict. Of these 15 states, 7 were listed as leaning to Roosevelt, with 101 electoral votes, while the remaining 6 states, with 107 electoral votes, were listed as leaning to Landon. In terms of state-by-state error, Crossley's average deviation was 5.8 per cent.

Although the *Fortune* Survey did not publish state-by-state figures in 1936, its popular-vote total was amazingly close to the true division of sentiment. It gave Roosevelt 59.4 per cent, 36.6 per cent opposed, and listed 4 per cent as undecided. This undecided vote, it was assumed, would divide in the same way as the vote of those with opinions. In commenting on its October release, *Fortune* pointed out that some discount of its own estimate was necessary.

Negroes, for example, had voted 84 per cent for Roosevelt in the *Fortune* Survey, yet in the election, it was suggested, such groups would be effectively excluded from voting in many Southern states. This adjustment, *Fortune* pointed out, might take away some 1 per cent from Roosevelt's majority. It was further suggested that the poor groups, strongly pro-Roosevelt, might not vote in as large numbers as the more prosperous who were so strongly pro-Landon. Although *Fortune* did not predict the total national electoral vote for Roosevelt, it reported that the Northeast section, with the greatest weight in the electoral college (143 of the total 531 electoral votes), remained opposed to Roosevelt, with only 43.1 per cent of the voters in favor of Roosevelt and 50.8 per cent against him. Opinion in the states of the Northwest plains, accounting for an additional 70 electoral votes, it was reported, was nearly equal, with a statistical shade opposed to Roosevelt. *Fortune* also inquired as to the Union-party strength amongst the anti-Roosevelt voters, and found that 3.7 per cent favored Lemke, and less than 1 per cent were for Thomas and Browder.

The final prediction made by the American Institute indicated that Roosevelt would receive 53.8 per cent of the total vote for all candidates, or 55.7 per cent of the major party vote. In its estimate of returns by states, the Institute distinguished between "sure" states, where the margin for one candidate was greater than the 3 per cent error to be expected, and the "doubtful" states, which were listed as either "leaning Democratic" or "leaning Republican." Thirty-one states were listed as "sure" for Roosevelt, while only 3 states (Maine, Vermont, and New Hampshire) were listed as "sure" for Landon. In 14 other states where the margin between the candidates was as close as 2 per cent,

9 were stated to be "leaning Democratic," 3 to be "leaning Republican," while Connecticut and Rhode Island were placed on the border line.

The Institute then gave its electoral-vote estimate on the basis of "sure" states, and suggested that Roosevelt would receive a minimum of 315 electoral votes. If the states which were "leaning Democratic" were included, the Institute predicted that, as a maximum, Roosevelt might receive more than the 472 electoral votes he got in 1932.

In terms of state-by-state error the Institute's error was 6.1 per cent as the average for all states. In addition the Institute predicted that Lemke, Union-party candidate for President, would receive 2.2 per cent of the total election vote. He actually received 1.9 per cent. The predicted vote for Norman Thomas, Socialist candidate, was 0.9 per cent, while Thomas actually received 0.4 per cent.

It was apparent that all the modern surveys erred on the side of caution. There was a common realization that many factors might operate to swing close states one way or the other—such factors as the weather on Election Day, the relative efficiency of the rival political machines, and the errors due to size of sample. By any criterion, whether measured by the division of the total vote, by electoral-college estimates, or by state-by-state error, the scientific sampling techniques proved to be far more accurate than the older methods of the *Digest*. As we shall see in the next chapter, there were minor differences of emphasis and method between the three modern national polls in 1936. But between all three and the premises of *The Literary Digest* there was an unbridgeable gulf.

One fundamental lesson became clear in the 1936 election: the heart of the problem of obtaining an accurate measure of public opinion lay in the cross section, and no mere accumulation of ballots could hope to eliminate the error that sprang from a biased sample. Many other lessons were learned by the polls as we shall see. Their first national-election test was by no means a final statement of the accuracy of the results which could be obtained by the sampling method. To understand why the modern polls, using only a small sample, as compared with the "gigantic sampling" of *The Literary Digest,* proved to be more accurate, and to see why this degree of precision has been maintained and improved in successive studies after 1936, we must turn briefly to the theory of sampling on which the method of the modern polls is based.

★

★

CHAPTER FIVE

Building the Miniature Electorate

THERE is nothing startling or magical about sampling. People use sampling in the common-sense "figuring out" of everyday life, just as trained scientists and statistical experts apply it in their researches. The stenographer who hurriedly counts a single line of her typing to see how many words she has typed on the page is taking a rough "sample." The housewife, tasting a spoonful of tomato soup which she is preparing, "samples" the soup. The doctor who extracts a few cubic centimeters of blood from a vein in his patient's arm is taking a "sample" of the blood stream. In each case, a part has been selected from the whole and subjected to analysis or measurement of one kind or another.

Sampling is not only a common phenomenon, it is a procedure made necessary by the very conditions of our complex life. Human beings could not perform a fraction of their usual tasks if they were not able to judge the world about them by abstracting from total experience, by selecting parts to "represent" the whole.

For modern research, the same thing is true. "Sociologists and economists," it has been suggested, "are compelled to employ sampling because like natural scientists, businessmen, government officials, and everyone else, they cannot afford to obtain all the data possible before they can formulate generalizations or make decisions."

The most important requirement of any sample is that it be as representative as possible of the entire group or "universe" from which it is taken. "Universe" simply means the total area or group from which the sample is to be selected. Whether this universe is the housewife's bowl of soup, the stenographer's typed page, or the patient's entire blood stream, a truly representative sample must be compounded of the same elements as are present in the whole.

In some cases it is a comparatively simple matter to select a sample which may be taken as a dependable substitute for the whole. All the housewife has to do, for example, is to stir the tomato soup thoroughly in order to be certain that the various components are well mixed before she tastes it. After the soup has been stirred, she can take a spoonful at random from any part of the bowl and be reasonably sure that it will contain the same mixture of ingredients as the contents of the entire bowl. Because the various ingredients have been thoroughly mixed, the consistency of the bowl of soup is uniform throughout, and successive spoonfuls will generally provide equally good samples.

When the universe is uniform, or *homogeneous* throughout, a sample taken at random will represent the whole within certain measurable limits of accuracy. The laws of probability have been known since the early speculations of the Swiss mathematician, Jakob Bernoulli, in 1713, and used widely in many fields of study. Applied to the problem of scientific sampling, these laws of probability demonstrate that a small number of cases chosen at random from among a very large group of the same kind of cases are almost certain to have the main characteristics of the whole group. The following example may help to clarify the way in which such principles can be used in determining the limits of accuracy in random sampling.

Imagine a wooden box filled with 1000 black and 1000 white marbles, completely mixed together. Now let us suppose a small boy is blindfolded and asked to draw out 100 marbles after they have been thoroughly mixed. His first draw, let us say, shows 51 black and 49 white. When he has finished taking this sample, the marbles are replaced in the box, and the small boy is asked to repeat the experiment, drawing out 100 each time, noting the proportions in each sample, and remixing the marbles after every attempt. Now suppose that we chart five successive samples of 100 drawn in this way:

	Black	White
First Sample	49	51
Second "	44	56
Third "	50	50
Fourth "	52	48
Fifth "	47	53

Thus, it may be seen, in the successive samples, there is a tendency for the proportions drawn in the samples to cluster around the actual proportion of black and white marbles in the box. If every marble is given an equal chance to be drawn, the proportion of white or the proportion of black in the sample tends to be the same as the proportion of each in the total. The samples will tend to show a proportion of 50-50, as in the original. If instead of 5 samples, 500 samples be taken in the same way, it will be seen that the most likely division will be 50-50, the next likely will be 49-51, while only a few samples will be a long way away from this mark. As the number of samples drawn increases, the average result of all the samples will tend to draw closer and closer to the actual 50-50 division. On the basis of other possible divisions, 80-20, 60-40, and the like, it is possible to calculate the size of the sample needed to secure accuracy within certain limits.

This simple experiment indicates that if the items or units are mixed in such a way that the selection of any particular item or unit is due entirely to the operation of chance, the sample thus selected will tend to be representative of the whole universe from which it is chosen. The limits of accuracy fluctuate with the size of the sample.

Although random sampling can be highly accurate in the case of homogeneous populations, and is in many cases the simplest sampling method, there are times when it cannot be used successfully. Sometimes the statistical universe is heterogeneous—that is, it is composed of a number of dissimilar elements which are not evenly distributed throughout the whole. In addition, the universe is sometimes so widely distributed or so inaccessible that it is not feasible to set up a random sampling procedure which will guarantee that each unit has an equally good chance of being included in the sample.

An illustration of such a situation is the problem which confronts the typist who counts the words in one line in order to estimate the number of words she has on a page. A cursory glance will tell her that while some lines may contain only short words like "and" and "but," other lines will consist of words like "anticonstitutional" or "paleontological." In order to obtain a fairly accurate estimate of the total number of words on the page, she must select a line that contains a typical proportion of both short and long words, so that it will be representative of the lines on the entire page. If this is difficult to do by inspection alone, she will probably select several lines, containing both short and long words, as the basis of her estimate. In choosing these lines, she has to exercise an element of selection, and her sample, therefore, is not strictly a random sample.

An even better illustration of this same point may be seen in the problem of sampling public opinion in any community as large and diversified as the United States. The political public is not a homogeneous population, but is divided into groups between which there are significant differences of interest and outlook. In order to sample a population of this sort, the method used is called "stratified" or "controlled" sampling.

In the application of controlled sampling, the voting public, which is the universe of the opinion researcher, is not composed of identical dissociated units, but of human beings who form themselves into distinct groups in certain observable, measurable ways. The voting population, then, is not homogeneous but heterogeneous.

The American public is a mosaic whose complex pattern of individuals is clustered together in a variety of social groups and associations. Individuals do not dwell in a vacuum. Considerations of geography, occupation, age, sex, political affiliation, race, religion, and general cultural background are the basic determinants of their experiences and opinions. The play of such forces divides the public into groups and stimulates common attitudes within the groups themselves. The public is thus made up of men and women living in different geographical sections and earning their daily bread as farmers, mechanics, coal miners, doctors, housewives, businessmen, bankers, merchants, salesgirls, teachers, industrial workers. It is constituted of separate economic classes, age groups, and political parties. Its component individuals represent different racial, religious, and linguistic backgrounds. Human beings are not identical units, for their attitudes and opinions are formed within the circumference of the everyday life experiences and activities which they share with their fellows.

People who live differently think differently; common points of view spring from sharing a common experience. In the political history of the United States, sectional conflicts and sectional similarities have provided a constant keynote. The old differences in attitude between settled and frontier communities have yielded, in modern form, to the conflict between the manufacturing East and the agricultural West and South. The farmer in the Middle West is a different kind of individual from the hardware manufacturer in Connecticut. He has interests and objectives which ally him with others who share his experiences and which separate him from the industrialists, or the factory workers, in other sections of the country.

According to the 1930 census, 21,000,000 Americans live in cities of 500,000 or over, with 14,000,000 of them in New York, Chicago, Philadelphia, and Detroit. About one fourth of all American families live in villages, towns, and cities with less than 25,000 inhabitants, while another fourth live on farms. These different dwelling places mean basic differences of occupation, political background, and attitude toward various issues.

About a third of the country's workers earn their living as skilled and semiskilled workers; about a fifth by working on the land; businessmen and white-collar workers make up another fifth; while about one person in twenty is listed as a member of the professional class.

Different occupations produce different levels of income and involve steep gradations in living standards. The division of the American public into broad economic classes is perhaps the distinguishing feature of modern politics. Viewed from the angle of economic status, the public presents enormous contrasts within itself. The gulf between the wages of the Southern sharecropper and the huge dividends of the multimillionaire, between the experience of the father of four children who is a W.P.A. worker and that of the middle-class suburban bachelor, creates fundamentally opposed views. Differences in economic status tend to stratify the public and mold its opinions along the broad lines of economic class.

If income and economic class are highly significant, still other determinants break up the public into subgroups. Age and sex cannot be ignored. One half the American population is under thirty years of age, while only one tenth is over sixty, and age is often a dividing force in political interests and behavior. The dynamic drive on the part of old people for pension schemes and security, and the enthusiasm of young people for better economic and educational opportunities—such attitudes as these spring from the divergent experiences of youth and old age. Further, many issues reveal political cleavages along the line of sex division within the general public, for, at times, men and women take up distinct views on the main needs and objectives of policy. Race, religion, language—all may operate to induce like-mindedness in areas within the public. Beyond such factors lie interests which spring from education and cultural experiences. Some people bury themselves in the financial page and form a special public for news of mergers and stock prices, just as other people restrict their newspaper reading to the results of the 2:30 at Aqueduct and the standing of their favorite baseball team.

America, then, does not follow a monotonous pattern. Its people are divided and cross-divided. In this sense, there is not one single entity, the American public, but rather several publics which cut across each other. Each of the major groups reveals striking uniformities of attitude and interest. On certain issues, such as labor relations, the businessman in New York has common interests and attitudes with the businessman of Chicago or Detroit. Farmers, as a class, in spite of their rugged individualism, hold similar views on many issues and have at times even united behind a common program of political action. Industrial workers exhibit increasing solidarity. "Reliefers" are possibly the most "solid" group in American politics today. The old and the young are becoming distinct political forces, while in spite of the "melting pot," rival races and creeds continue to act as molds in which common ways of thinking take their shape. On the broadest canvas of all, the interests and activities which stem from such forces express themselves through political parties, and party ties in turn become still another force making for a heterogeneous public. Political loyalties separate Democrat from Republican and minority voters of Left and Right, while within these broad divisions, strong uniformities of attitude may exist. For all these basic reasons, individuals are not atomized, identical units; they are the essential elements of social groups, and they at once reflect and mold the view of the groups of which they are members.

This fundamental fact—that the public consists of people clustered into social groups—is the chief reason why the opinion surveyor makes use of selective sampling to build up his "miniature public." Professor W. L. Crum has stated this point clearly in his discussion of sampling procedures. "The straw-poll problem," he writes, "is, unfortunately, not a simple question of random sampling; for the total population is not a 'homogeneous' body, in that there are within the population several fairly distinct groups which presumably have different voting intentions. Any such group may be fairly homogeneous within itself, and the ordinary method of random sampling can be used in making selections from that group. So far as selection from the entire population is concerned, however, *some attention is needed to ensure that each important group is reached to the proper extent, particularly in case the complete sample is not large."*

Thus, there are two central problems which confront the opinion surveyor who tries to build a representative sample containing groups from the whole population:

I. The character of the cross section, and
II. The size of the cross section.

I. *The Character of the Cross Section*

The prime determinant of accuracy in any sample survey of opinion lies in the character of the cross section—in the way the groups are selected to represent the public as a whole. The failure of most of the early polls may be traced to the lopsided inclusion of different groups in the cross section. Everyone knows that a representative sample of lemon pie, for instance, must include the meringue on top, the lemon in the middle, and the crust on the bottom. *The Literary Digest* sampling procedure in 1936 resembled the action of the small boy who eats the meringue on top and the lemon in the middle, but ignores most of the crust on the bottom. The voters which the *Digest* selected were, for the most part, telephone subscribers and owners of automobiles. But such qualifications excluded large sections of the population. Since, in 1936, voters in the excluded sections tended overwhelmingly to vote for Roosevelt, while Landon's support was recruited largely from the upper- and middle-income groups, the *Digest*'s sample was inevitably biased in favor of Landon.

Public-opinion polls can fall short of accuracy, then, by excluding groups which later participate in the actual election. The inclusion of Southern Negroes in the sample of some polls introduced still another biasing factor in their final returns, since such groups were effectively disfranchised in many Southern states and did not participate in the election. Other factors besides color, such as age, property qualifications, lack of citizenship, inability to read or write, or loss of civil rights, may also operate to disfranchise certain groups.

Thus, it is important to distinguish between two types of cross section used by the modern public-opinion polls: (1) a social cross section which is based on total population figures, limited only by age, and (2) a political cross section which is designed to fit the voting population and is, therefore, based upon estimates of political participation. The social cross section is used primarily in measuring opinion on social subjects. For example, it may be used in studying opinion concerning living standards, distribution of wealth, or similar matters.

The distribution of the social cross section conforms to information about the total population obtained from such sources as the Bureau of the Census, other divisions of the Department of Commerce, and information from the Federal Security Administration. These sources show the distribution of the population as between states, counties, cities, and towns, the distribution between farm dwellers and urban dwellers, country of birth, sex, age, citizenship, and the like. The Bureau of the Census makes available estimates of certain changes in the population in intercensal years. While this information is usually less accurate than the census itself, it obviously helps to allow for trends.

Other governmental agencies provide supplementary information concerning such matters as income and relief status. In 1938, the National Resources Committee made public a study of income based upon work done by the Department of Agriculture and the W.P.A. Information concerning relief status is made public in the *Social Security Bulletin*. Information on automobile registration comes from the various state governments and the Department of Commerce, while figures showing the changing proportion of telephone subscribers are reported from time to time.

The scope of the census is constantly being expanded; the 1940 census will obtain more information than the 1930 census. As the length of the census questionnaire grows, the task of recording answers for each individual in the entire United States increases. In this connection, it is interesting to note that part of the information obtained by the 1940 census will be obtained through sampling—that is, certain questions will not be asked of everyone, but of every twentieth person only.

If surveys are to check accurately against elections, if they are to analyze the sentiment of the voting public, they must guard against the bias of participation and non-participation. For although disfranchised groups have valuable ideas and opinions, it is the voting public—the people who actually go to the polls and cast their vote—who remain the decisive factor.

This increases the difficulty of establishing the political cross section. The estimates of the total population given in the census figures must always be used in combination with information about how many people can and do vote. Eligible voters may quickly be determined by reference to state voting requirements. Actual voters can be studied in a series of elections, by checking them against the eligible voters. But the problem becomes more complex when we try to estimate the proportion of each group and class in the total voting public. In certain districts in Weimar, Germany, the votes of men and women were separately tabulated in successive elections. This made it comparatively easy to see what proportion of men and women went to the polls. But in the United States, where no such election practice exists, and where all votes—of men and women, old and young, rich and poor—look the same in the ballot box, a better knowledge of voting participation can come only through continued research in this field.

Extremely valuable and original work in studying voting variations from group to group in certain areas has been done by such American social scientists as Gosnell, Merriam, Pollock, the Swedish student Tingsten, and others. The polls of public opinion have also made a contribution to the study of voting behavior. A large part of the information used by the American Institute has come from its recurrent surveys. Every ballot sent out by the Institute since experimental sampling started at the end of 1933 brings in more and more knowledge of voting behavior. It is becoming clear that voting participation differs according to certain principal factors: (1) *The type of election:* In general, the heaviest vote occurs in presidential elections, although this is not true in some of the Southern states, where the Democratic primary election really determines the winner. In some Southern states, the vote in the Democratic primary for Senator or governor exceeds the vote in that state in the general election for presidential candidates. Voting is lightest in elections on bond issues or other specific referendums, as differentiated from votes on candidates. (2) *Geographic areas:* Voting participation varies widely between different states, counties, and even between local voting precincts, within a given area. In recent years, seven times as large a proportion of the inhabitants of Indiana voted for President as voted in the states of South Carolina and Mississippi. (3) *Sex:* Since the advent of women's suffrage, women have neither registered nor, according to the Institute's experience, voted to the same extent as men. (4) *Income levels:* Studies by the Institute staff have shown that voting participation varies according to income group. While different localities generally vary a good deal, the people in the lower-income levels do not vote in such a high proportion as those in the middle and upper groups. (5) Other important variables include age, color, and nationality, but, as the polling process continues, more precise relationships between political behavior and other variable factors are likely to be discovered.

II. *The Size of the Cross Section*

The second major premise for the successful study and measurement of public opinion lies in the adequacy of the sample. The number of voters included in the cross section must be large enough to offset sizable variations due to chance factors. But both experience and statistical theory point to the conclusion that *no major poll in the history of this country ever went wrong because too few persons were reached.*

Until 1936, *The Literary Digest* symbolized accuracy in the public mind, and its millions of ballots were regarded as insurance against error. But modern surveys clearly reveal that accurate results can be obtained with a small sample, provided it is carefully selected. Polls today have convincingly demonstrated that quality is far more important than quantity.

In studies on national issues, the Institute has used from

3000 to 60,000 interviews, depending on the closeness of the contest and the degree of accuracy desired. Thus, when the maximum number of persons is polled—60,000—the chances that any one eligible voter in the United States will be polled are about 1 in 1000. When the minimum number of interviews is taken, the chances are 1 in 20,000. On general studies of opinion on issues, small samples of from 3000 to 9000 cases have been found reliable.

A survey which predicts an election within 5 per cent is generally regarded as "amazingly accurate." *Yet this degree of accuracy can be attained with from 600 to 900 ballots.* A valuable table giving the size of sample necessary for accuracy within specified limits in random sampling has been worked out by Professor Theodore Brown of Harvard University. Professor Brown shows that the mathematical chances are 997 in 1000 that a random sample of 900 cases will be accurate within 5 per cent where opinion divides evenly. Where opinion divides in the ratio of 80 to 20, 576 cases are enough to secure this degree of accuracy. The table further indicates that where opinion divides evenly, only 2500 cases are needed in a random sample to secure accuracy within 3 per cent, and 10,000 cases to secure accuracy within 1.5 per cent. After that point, the addition of tens of thousands or hundreds of thousands of cases brings only fractional increases in precision. Thus by means of careful sampling, a highly reliable result can be obtained from a relatively small number of cases.

The laws of probable error have long been known. These laws have been tested by a great variety of experiments ranging from an analysis of height and weight data to throwing dice or tossing coins many thousands of times. They are laws which no government can repeal.

By permission of the President and Fellows of Harvard

College, Professor Brown's table of probable error due to size of sample is reproduced below.

Size of Sample Necessary to Be Practically Sure of Accuracy
(i.e., on the Basis of Three Standard Deviations)
Within Predetermined Limits [1]

Range of Error: (3σ)	Where Opinion Divides Percentagewise As Follows						
	20% 80	25% 75	30% 70	35% 65	40% 60	45% 55	50% 50
0.1%	1,440,000	1,687,500	1,890,000	2,047,500	2,160,000	2,227,500	2,250,000
0.2	360,000	421,875	472,500	511,875	540,000	556,875	562,500
0.3	160,000	187,500	210,000	227,500	240,000	247,500	250,000
0.4	90,000	105,469	118,125	127,969	135,000	139,219	140,625
0.5	57,600	67,500	75,600	81,900	86,400	89,100	90,000
0.6	40,000	46,875	52,500	56,875	60,000	61,875	62,500
0.7	29,388	34,439	38,571	41,786	44,082	45,459	45,918
0.8	22,500	26,367	29,531	31,992	33,750	34,805	35,156
0.9	17,778	20,833	23,333	25,278	26,667	27,500	27,778
1.0	14,400	16,875	18,900	20,475	21,600	22,275	22,500
1.5	6,400	7,500	8,400	9,100	9,600	9,900	10,000
2.0	3,600	4,219	4,725	5,119	5,400	5,569	5,625
2.5	2,304	2,700	3,024	3,276	3,456	3,564	3,600
3.0	1,600	1,875	2,100	2,275	2,400	2,475	2,500
3.5	1,176	1,378	1,543	1,671	1,763	1,818	1,837
4.0	900	1,055	1,181	1,280	1,350	1,392	1,406
4.5	711	833	933	1,011	1,067	1,100	1,111
5.0	576	675	756	819	864	891	900
6.0	400	469	525	569	600	619	625
7.0	294	344	386	418	441	455	459
8.0	225	264	295	320	338	348	352
9.0	178	208	233	253	267	275	278
10.0	144	169	189	205	216	223	225
15.0	64	75	84	91	96	99	100
20.0	36	42	47	51	54	56	56
25.0	23	27	30	33	35	36	36
30.0	16	19	21	23	24	25	25
35.0	12	14	15	17	18	18	18
40.0	9	11	12	13	14	14	14

[1] Table copyrighted, 1932, by the President and Fellows of Harvard College.

NOTE: The table is worked out on the basis of three standard deviations. This means the chances are 997 in 1,000 that the range of error for each sample size will be as shown in the column to the left.

It may be mentioned that, according to the same statistical laws, all the samples given could be cut in half and yet the results would still be equally accurate 962 times in 1,000.

Of these two major determinants of reliability—the character and size of the cross section—the former is, by all odds, the most important. If the cross section is carefully selected, a sample of only a few thousand will give accuracy within limits of 3 or 4 per cent. On the other hand, if a cross section is badly chosen, no amount of mere case piling will eliminate the error. As a general principle, a controlled sample of a given size is even more likely to be accurate than a random sample of the same size.

It is highly significant that less than one tenth of one per cent of *The Literary Digest's* 19-point error in 1936 could reasonably be due to the *size* of sample. One tenth of one per cent is the range of error which can be expected with practical certainty in a sample of 2,227,500 cases, as can be seen in the table, where opinion divides in the ratio of 55 to 45. The *Digest's* final report, showing Landon with 57 per cent to 43 per cent for Roosevelt, was based on 2,376,523 ballots. Virtually all of the *Digest's* error was undoubtedly due to two other factors which determine accuracy in this field of opinion research—cross section and timing.

The statistical requirements for size of sample vary according to the issues involved, the detail of analysis desired, and the division of opinion. When opinion divides evenly, the practical limit of error due to size of sample runs from 2.7 per cent for 3000 cases to 0.7 per cent for 50,000, as Professor Brown's table shows. These limits of error are reduced still further as opinion becomes more one-sided.

In most instances, analysis of the results can be made in such a way as to show the extent to which stability is improved by increasing the size of the sample. Studying the results emphasizes the needlessness of piling up a large number of additional cases after a sample has achieved stability.

Consider, for example, the Institute's study of opinion on the N.R.A. In 1936, a survey of 30,000 ballots asked the question: "Would you like to see the N.R.A. revived?" The first 500 cases showed a "no" vote of 54.9 per cent. The complete sample of 30,000 cases returned a "no" vote of 55.5 per cent. In other words, the addition of 29,500 cases to the first 500 cases in this instance made a difference of six tenths of one per cent in the national findings. Here are the figures:

Number of Cases	Per cent Voting Against Reviving the N.R.A.
First 500 ballots	54.9
First 1,000 ballots	53.9
First 5,000 ballots	55.4
First 10,000 ballots	55.4
All 30,000 ballots	55.5

With this conclusion about the size of the sample, Emil Hurja's experience fully agrees. "I have taken a handful of reports," Hurja writes, "from a poll totalling 6,000 answers, and the analysis of the handful containing 109 ballots has given me the same answer, within less than 1%, revealed by detailed examination of the entire 6,000 ballots. Once a sample of 419 ballots received too late to include in a general classification gave me the same answer within 5%, of that which was revealed by analysis of 150,000 cards."

Such an outline indicates that a truly accurate picture of public opinion can be obtained with a small sample, *provided the cases selected are representative of all the major groups within the population.* It was on this basis that the modern surveys proceeded in their first experimental test in the presidential election of 1936. The Crossley poll, the *Fortune* Survey, and the poll conducted by the American Institute of Public Opinion took care to cover the major subgroups in the population as fairly and completely as possible. Their superiority over the "gigantic sampling" of *The Literary Digest* came from a common reliance on the principles of controlled sampling.

In building their miniature electorates for the election of 1936, the three modern polls selected geographic district, urban-rural balance, economic status, age, and sex, as the basic factors controlling the divisions of political opinion. The Crossley and Institute polls took the state as the geographic unit, while the *Fortune* Survey modeled its sampling on the nine major census areas of the United States. To control the proportion of votes from cities and farms, from the various economic classes and age groups, and from men and women, quotas were established for each of these major groups to mirror the actual divisions in the population as a whole. In the case of the *Fortune* Survey, the allocation of ballots to different areas and groups was made on the basis of the total population, and each important race group was given full weighting. The inclusion of many Southern Negroes in the Survey meant that a careful distinction between "political" and "social" cross section was not made in 1936, although later *Fortune* Surveys have distinguished between these two types. The Crossley and Institute polls, on the other hand, established their quotas on the basis of estimates of probable voting participation, and ballots were selected from each group in accordance with estimates of actual voting. The Institute used the additional check of controlling the political composition of its sample by obtaining Democratic voters, Republican voters, and third-party voters in the same proportion as the citizens of each state declared themselves in the previous presidential election in 1932.[1]

All the modern polls used much smaller samples than *The Literary Digest*. The *Fortune* Survey's estimate in 1936, which so closely paralleled the division of the national popular vote, was based on only 4500 cases, collected by a very small staff of trained interviewers. Crossley's sampling plan in 1936 called for 15,000 weekly family interviews, and since the published reports were based on returns totaled every two weeks, the numerical size of each sample averaged about 30,000 family interviews. The Institute's successive samples in 1936 averaged from 25,000 to 40,000 replies, and in states where the campaign promised to be close, the proportion of ballots was increased. Most of the Institute's ballots were collected by mail in 1936, augmented by direct interviews from groups which failed to respond to mailed ballots. In contrast to the *Digest*'s practice of cumulating its returns throughout the campaign, each of the more flexible modern surveys conducted spaced polls at intervals, thus obtaining a measure of the shifts in sentiment.

Thus, in contrast to the *Digest*'s dependence on an enormous number of ballots, and its neglect of reliable sampling procedures, the three modern nation-wide polls took precautions to control the composition of the cross section. While they differed from each other on minor points in their application of these sampling principles, the newer methods were in fundamental opposition to the *Digest*'s system. In theory and in practice, the modern methods

---

[1] For an account of the various methods used in 1936, see: Crossley, A. M., "Straw Polls in 1936," *Public Opinion Quarterly*, October, 1936.

represented a new epoch in the history of public-opinion measurement. To this transition, various factors contributed their share. Singleness of purpose characterized the modern polls. They had but one concern: to get a true picture of public opinion. They derived their income solely from their editorial budgets. The *Digest* tried to combine measuring opinion with increasing its own circulation, a dual policy which inevitably led to mass balloting. The modern polls, on the other hand, reduced ballot distribution to a minimum, and concentrated on getting as accurate a cross section as possible. The *Digest* tried to be representative by taking a large sample; the modern polls relied on a quota system so that each class voted in the proportion that it formed of the whole voting public. The *Digest* followed a fixed, prearranged plan, and did not attempt modifications. The modern polls allowed for flexibility. They kept adjusting their returns by checking them against the proper quotas. The *Digest* cumulated all its returns, and thus submerged short-term changes in the total result; the Crossley, *Fortune,* and Institute polls, on the other hand, took samples at frequent intervals.

Apart from minor differences in size of sample, methods of ballot collection, and the categories used to control the sample, all the modern surveys relied on the same principles of controlled sampling. This use of careful methods provided the basic reason for the relative success of the new polls in 1936. The research which had been proceeding since 1932 had built up certain determinable rules of polling conduct which the *Digest* did not follow. The 1936 election gave a glimpse of how accurate the new science of public-opinion measurement might become. But further tests had to be made before the sampling referendum could finally take its place as a reliable method of measurement. The modern history of these opinion surveys is built on the lessons learned in the incubation period from 1933-36, and in the successive tests of the last four years.

★

CHAPTER SIX

★

Experiments in Accuracy

THE 1936 presidential election made possible the first experimental test of this new method in a nation-wide laboratory. Sampling machinery received a working trial in the course of an actual election, and the experience gained provided the starting point for later adjustments and improvements.

One of the clearest lessons was the key importance of the time factor. Even though the most accurate polls took periodic measurements in 1936, all of them probably stopped polling too soon. In the Institute's survey, for example, anywhere from ten to twenty days elapsed between the date when the final surveys were conducted and Election Day. Later study showed that when the Roosevelt-Landon curves for individual states were projected in accordance with the previous trend, the Institute's figure came remarkably close to the actual division of the vote officially recorded in the election.

The Institute also learned in 1936 that direct interviews were superior to mailed ballots. In its own survey, the Institute relied on a combination of the two methods, generally using the mails to reach the upper- and middle-income groups and depending on personal interviews to cover most of the lower-income groups and to acquire supplementary information about farm voters. The experience

77

of the Institute showed that mail ballots provided a fairly satisfactory coverage of upper-income groups and a good, although not completely satisfactory, coverage of the middle levels. Mail ballots, however, proved less reliable among the lower-income groups, and direct interviews were used to offset this possible source of bias. The response to mail questionnaires varied considerably from group to group. In the light of this experience, the Institute discontinued mail ballots, and since 1936 has relied, in its normal survey work, entirely on personal interviews.

As a result of the 1936 election, the data on voting participation, on the key areas to be sampled, and on the quotas for the different income and age groups were carefully revised. It was apparent that the controls which had been used were by no means to be considered as fixed or final for all time. Indeed the knowledge of which controls are best for building the cross section must rest on continued research in many different types of elections, and on a wide variety of issues. In measuring public opinion toward foreign countries, for example, racial derivation is an important control whereas on other issues it does not appear to have any special significance. Religion occasionally plays an important part in political campaigns; it also influences opinion on such issues as birth control. And on other issues, education proves the determining factor.

One thing, however, must not be overlooked. Assuming that such basic controls as economic class, geographic district, and political affiliation have been carefully checked, other factors such as race, religion, and education almost always correspond to the proportions in which these factors exist in the population as a whole. This point has been empirically tested by the Institute. From time to time, questions concerning racial derivation, religious affiliation, and education are placed on ballots which test opinion in elections and on issues. Comparison of the sample returns with census statistics on these factors reveals an extremely close correspondence, and provides an additional check against the danger of overlooking some important conditioning factor in future tests of sentiment.

Opinion surveyors do not know in advance all the factors which determine the individual's vote. It would take a psychoanalyst to make such a study, and even he might well be puzzled. What the surveys do is to deal with certain objective controlling factors which may conceivably wield an influence on large numbers of people, and which can be accurately identified. The cross section does not call for controlling the proportion of people with blue eyes, or people with rimless spectacles, because, so far as it is possible to determine, such characteristics bear no relationship to basic attitudes. The controls which are used, then, are those which are considered the main determinants of public opinion.

"The failure of a sample to take account of all possible distinctions," a statistician has written, "by no means proves that it is a biased sample. It is only a question of omitting *essential distinctions* that renders a sample inadequate, and it is not always evident in advance which characteristics will turn out to be essential." [1] More precise knowledge of which controls are most relevant can be gained only through the experience and observation of actual polling work.

Thus the controls which modern surveys are now using may be changed in the light of future developments. Today, the economic class and income group to which a person belongs seem to determine his political opinion,

[1] Levinson, N. C., *Your Chance to Win*, New York, 1939.

although some years ago this was not true. Controls of political-party affiliation are not fixed and unchangeable. The party labels, "Democrat" and "Republican," are fairly useful guides in the present day, but if and when political interests begin to shift within these old categories, surveyors will have to devise new controls, based not on the old party labels, but on the new political alignments.

The cross section, then, is not a geometrical puzzle. Its construction calls for more common sense than mathematical subtlety. It can be created only by digging away at facts, census reports, income-distribution reports, studies of voting affiliation and participation. It is never fixed, once and for all; it may demand adjustments from time to time as new information becomes available. The cross sections used by contemporary surveys vary from poll to poll. But although modern surveyors may disagree from time to time as to how the job can best be done, they have one common objective—to build the best possible cross section.

The key to the improvement of the cross section and the solution of other problems of polling technique depends on the continued practice of matching the sample against the voting population in successive elections. Each new election study in which the Institute has engaged since 1936 has furnished a signpost to greater accuracy.

Why, it is sometimes asked, do the public-opinion polls go "out on the limb" from time to time and make predictions of the political future? The press and public want an objective scoreboard during the excitement of a political race. Imagine how meaningless and uninteresting a football game would be for the spectator if he could not learn how the teams stood at half time, or if the question "Who is leading?" were left solely to the guesswork or imagination of players and partisans. For the same reason, the game of politics takes on added interest when an impartial scorekeeper charts the divisions of sentiment during a closely fought campaign.

But pre-election tests of sentiment and political predictions are important not because they tell people what is probably going to happen before it actually happens. Pre-election tests are important because they enable surveyors to put this new method of measuring public opinion through its most exacting test. From time to time sampling methods must be placed alongside the yardstick of an election, for the closeness of the estimates made by the polls to the actual count of local, state, or national elections is the best objective check on validity and accuracy.

But no election, it must be observed, is a perfect check on polling accuracy. If American elections were supervised by a dictator who decreed heavy penalties for nonvoting, and if every eligible voter consequently marched off to the polls on Election Day, the problem of getting a true sample of these voters would be greatly simplified. But in a democracy, every election is itself a "sample," since every eligible voter does not cast his vote. In this sense, a pre-election survey must be regarded as a sample of a sample.

There may be many factors which distort an election as a test of poll accuracy. The weather, for instance, may draw voters in unequal proportions from urban and rural areas. Thus, in some elections the careful opinion surveyor might have to co-operate with the Meteorological Bureau before his prediction could be sound. The power of the political machine and its ability to "get out the vote" is another variable which might, in close elections, determine the outcome. In extreme cases, political corruption could operate to vitiate the findings of a public-opinion poll. In some elections, sudden opinion changes may occur at such a late date that they cannot be caught by public-opinion polls. Finally, a rather small fraction, sometimes less than one third of the registered voters, actually takes part in voting. In such instances, the poll may provide a more accurate picture of popular sentiment than the actual vote.

In spite of these difficulties, the Institute has consistently shown its belief in the accuracy of its own sampling procedures by making successive predictions in elections of various types. Since its presidential-election predictions in 1936, the Institute has published election forecasts of eleven state and national contests. In these surveys the polls have estimated the actual results with an average error of 3.5 per cent. Experimental studies have also been made in over forty state elections as further tests of cross-section and sampling procedures.

Following the 1936 election, the Institute predicted the Detroit mayoralty election in November, 1937, within 2 percentage points; the re-election of Mayor LaGuardia of New York within 4 points. A few days before Maine's referendum on the sales tax in August, 1937, a survey showed the Maine public against the tax by 72 per cent. At the actual election, the sales tax was defeated by a vote of 67 per cent. In December, 1937, the Institute conducted a survey among unemployed persons to determine how many had responded to the Federal unemployment census of the preceding month. It found that 26 per cent had failed to send in their cards. A checkup taken by the government later showed that 28 per cent of the unemployed had failed to register.

In the Maine Republican gubernatorial primary election of 1938, the Institute predicted that Governor Barrows would win with 78 per cent of the vote, which was within 3 percentage points of his winning majority of 75 per cent.

When, in 1938, Governor Albert Benjamin (Happy) Chandler contested the Democratic senatorial primary election in Kentucky with Alben W. Barkley, the Institute's final pre-election prediction indicated that Senator Barkley would win with 58 per cent of the vote. In the primary election, he received 56.6 per cent.

In the summer of 1938, President Roosevelt startled close observers of politics by declaring the need for "purging" the Democratic party of reactionaries. In successive speeches, the President urged the rank and file of the party to vote for "liberal" Democratic candidates, defining a "liberal" as "one who opposes a moratorium on reform."

Preparatory to his swing through the West and South, the President declared he would not oppose a candidate in a Democratic primary merely because of that candidate's vote "on any single issue"—meaning, to most observers, the candidate's position on the Supreme Court plan. Of more importance, said the President, was the candidate's general attitude toward present-day problems.

Opinion studies showed that if the President were to base his purge on the Court issue alone, such action might well have a boomerang effect. To Democratic voters throughout the country, interviewers put the question:

"Do you think the Roosevelt administration should try to defeat Democratic Senators who opposed the President's plan to enlarge the Supreme Court?"

A majority of Democratic voters, 69 per cent of those interviewed, indicated that they would oppose any effort to defeat Democratic candidates who were against the President on the Court bill. The rival symbols which later became slogans in the primary elections were evident in this early study. "Senators have a right to voice their own opinions and should voice them," held the opponents of the purge; while the President's supporters proclaimed that "The New Deal needs a united front!"

Thus the polls revealed the divisions of public opinion in various states where Democratic primaries were to be held, long before the elections, and even before the President had singled out Senators George, Smith, and Tydings as special targets. In a speech at Barnesville, Georgia, the President criticized Senator George as a bitter opponent of the New Deal. A little later in a speech at Greenville, South Carolina, the President marked Senator Smith as an early target for the purge, by referring to him as "one who thinks in the past," and later on went to Maryland to deliver a speech in behalf of Congressman David Lewis, New Deal opponent of Senator Tydings.

As the battle between the New Deal forces and conservative Democrats headed for the final election showdown, the Institute called on interviewers in each of these states to test the sentiment of the voting public.

The South Carolina primary election came first. In that election the final sampling forecast indicated that Senator Smith would be renominated with 57 per cent of the vote to 43 per cent for Governor Johnston, his New Deal opponent. In the actual election returns, Senator Smith received 56 per cent to Johnston's 44 per cent.

When the President criticized Senator Walter F. George as a "reactionary," the Institute sent telegrams to seventeen field correspondents in Georgia, requesting them to test public sentiment on the President's speech at Barnesville, Georgia, and to wire their returns. Voters throughout the state were asked:

"Do you think President Roosevelt should have made the Barnesville speech criticizing Senator George?"

Voters indicated their disapproval by an overwhelming margin of three to one. Even though the Georgia race was complicated by the candidacy of the strongly anti-New Dealer, Eugene Talmadge, the Institute surveys showed Senator George to have a substantial lead over both former Governor Talmadge and the New Dealer, Lawrence Camp. An interesting side light showed that, in spite of the unwillingness of the average Southern Democratic voter to follow the President in his purge program, President Roosevelt continued to retain his tremendous popularity among the rank and file of Georgia Democrats.

The following table shows how the final prediction of the popular vote compared with the actual results in the Democratic senatorial primary in Georgia:

	Institute Prediction	Popular Vote Results
George	46%	44%
Talmadge	28	32
Camp	25	24
McRae	1	Withdrew just before the election

In the Maryland primary, the Institute predicted the re-election of Senator Tydings with 57 per cent to the 43 per cent of David J. Lewis. In the election, Senator Tydings was re-elected with 58 per cent of the total vote.

In the Congressional elections of 1938, the Institute forecast the first decline in Democratic strength, as registered by Congressional votes, since the New Deal began. The Institute's final pre-election prediction was that Republicans would be likely to gain 75 seats, over the 1936 results, in the House of Representatives.

Here is a comparison of the Institute's estimates of the way in which the membership of the House would be divided as compared with the official results of the election:

	Congressional Seats	
	Institute Prediction	*1938 Election Results*
Democrats	264	262
Republicans	165	170
Third parties	6	3

The Institute's surveys indicated that the chief Republican Congressional gains would come in the industrial East and particularly in Ohio, Illinois, Pennsylvania, Indiana, Michigan, and New Jersey. As a matter of fact, the chief Republican gains were made in Ohio, Pennsylvania, Michigan, New Jersey, and Indiana.

Finally, the Institute declared that the Republican upturn would have an effect on succeeding state elections, and that the Republicans stood to gain a half dozen of the most important governorships that year. The Republicans gained eight additional Senate seats and won governorships in such key states as Massachusetts, Connecticut, Pennsylvania, Ohio, Michigan, Wisconsin, and Minnesota.

During the same month in which the Institute conducted this nation-wide test of its methods, the Dewey-Lehman campaign for Governor of New York State provided still another test of polling accuracy. After a series of checkups and preliminary surveys, poll returns showed that the race was going to be an extremely close one, for only one or two percentage points separated the two candidates in the earlier returns. Four days preceding the election, President Roosevelt delivered a radio talk in which he commended Governor Lehman to the New York State voters. Aware that such a talk, delivered at this cru-

cial point of the campaign, might cause a slight shift sufficiently powerful to sway the delicate balance of political
forces, a last-minute survey was taken before the final estimate was made. On the basis of this last-minute check, the
Institute forecast that Governor Lehman would be elected
with about 50.2 per cent of that vote. Governor Lehman
actually received 50.7 per cent.

The Institute made one prediction concerning the
November, 1938, elections which fell far short of the accuracy established in the Congressional or the New York
State gubernatorial predictions. Just before the election, it
was estimated that the "ham-and-eggs" pension movement
in California would be defeated by about 2 to 1. In the
election in California, the pension proposal polled about 45
per cent of the total vote. Extensive postelection analysis
revealed that the main reason for the Institute's error lay in
the fact that the opponents of the pension scheme had conducted a campaign of ridicule in an effort to laugh the plan
into defeat. Apparently, this campaign led many of the
plan's supporters to conceal their true voting intentions. In
succeeding unpublished studies which the Institute made
in connection with the 1939 election, this factor was controlled. In general, there is little doubt that greater accuracy has followed on the heels of continued polling experience.

Some political observers prophesy that sooner or later
the modern polls will "flop" on an election, and follow
The Literary Digest to the limbo. Postmaster James Farley,
in his book *Behind the Ballots,* wags a knowing finger at
those engaged in polling public opinion. "Just you wait and
see," Mr. Farley writes. "Polls go wrong, and that's all
there is to it." To the question, "Can the polls go wrong?"

the answer is this. Just as careful polls will be correct to within a few percentage points most of the time, so they *may* go wrong some of the time. The same laws of probability that enable the polls to be accurate 95 times in 100 mean that they will be inaccurate 5 times in 100. For the laws of chance operate inevitably, and in close elections, where opinion tends to divide evenly, it might not always be possible to predict the actual winner by the polling method.

The goal of present-day surveys is to keep within three to four percentage points of the correct division of the total vote. With accumulating experience and continued research, this batting average may be improved, but, even then, a poll must expect to strike out occasionally. A small degree of error in a few specific instances may cause a poll to mispredict the actual winner, but the accuracy of polls must be judged on the basis of their closeness to election returns in a high percentage of election predictions.

Election predictions are, for the general public, the spectacular and dramatic side of public-opinion polls. They enable the casual observer on the side lines to see for himself the accuracy which careful sampling makes possible, and they help to focus the attention of the public on the fact that an election is taking place which is of vital concern to the people themselves. But there are far more important reasons for the continuation of studies of public opinion during elections.

In the first place, such pre-election polls are an objective check on accuracy, in the sense that they permit the intensive study of various influences which determine the direction of the popular vote during the course of a campaign.

Secondly, pre-election polls contribute to our knowledge of the voting behavior of individuals and groups in real-life situations, by supplying a body of concrete facts against which guesswork and impression may be checked. For the student of politics, the polls can provide systematic information on the way in which opinion crystallizes during an election campaign. The problem of whether political propaganda is really an effective method of getting votes, or whether, as some people insist, elections are won or lost before they start, can be thoroughly analyzed only by actual field study of trends in sentiment throughout the course of a series of campaigns. Observers of politics have not infrequently based many of their "theories" on traditional assumptions. Do major last-minute switches occur frequently? On what issues and under what conditions can we expect such movements of opinion to take place? Are there "surface currents" and "ground swells" in public opinion during an exciting political campaign? How effective are the rival propagandas? What is the public attitude to the competing parties? Frequent polling in various situations will help to answer these questions. The answers will be based not on speculation, but on repeated observations in different elections.

Because of the controls which are used, it may be possible to give this answer in specific terms. The polls help to identify different opinion alignments by economic class, age, sex, political affiliation, and geographic section, and to locate the various shades of opinion in the attitudes of conflicting groups of real people. Finally, sampling techniques throw light on actual voting behavior and the degree of voting participation in different groups.

In this sense, the polls play a part in the objective study of various phases of the public-opinion process, and, by operating in realistic rather than hypothetical situations, add materially to our store of political knowledge. They contribute one more precision instrument which may increase our understanding of how the democratic experiment actually works. We can agree with Walter Lippmann who has said, "The social scientist will acquire his dignity and his strength when he has worked out his method. He will do that by turning into opportunity the need among directing men of the Great Society for instruments of analysis by which an invisible and most stupendously difficult environment can be made intelligible." [1] It is only when our knowledge of existing conditions has been thoroughly checked that we can take the next step and work for future improvements.

Elections, then, are the laboratory in which the polls are tested, and in which new facts and problems continually come to light. But the practical value of the polls lies in the fact that they indicate the main trends of sentiment on issues about which elections often tell us nothing. The polls must ultimately be judged on the basis of their contribution to a better knowledge of what the public thinks about the various questions of the day. The first stage of testing has demonstrated clearly that the polls can mirror the sentiment of large groups of individuals in concrete election situations. The second stage of practical application shows that the polls can also help to chart the main divisions of sentiment on issues, and so make possible continuous measurements of public opinion.

---

[1] Lippmann, Walter, *Public Opinion*, p. 373.

CHAPTER SEVEN

★

Behind the Scenes

POLLS of public opinion command interest because they articulate what the mass of the common people thinks about the headline issues of everyday life. Over the last few years, interviewers have continuously questioned voters throughout the nation to discover and chart public reactions to hundreds of important questions ranging from the structure of the Supreme Court to the problem of unemployment, from the war in Europe, to new plans for old-age pensions. The picture that is being built up from week to week reflects the impact of events and propagandas springing from a wide range of sources. Pre-election surveys are essentially tests of method. The modern application of this method lies in measuring public opinion on issues as they arise from the stream of conflicting interests, objectives, and ideals.

With the growing conviction that sampling methods, carefully applied, can provide a useful tool of analysis, many more questions have been raised concerning the other phases of polling procedure. The various stages will emerge in clearer focus in the course of a rapid tour of inspection of the polls at work. The interested observer will want to know how a typical survey is conducted. Who selects the issues for public decision? On what basis are these issues chosen? What checks are used to guard against biased questions? Who are the interviewers? How are they chosen? How do we know they are honest? What are the pitfalls and snags in the process of measuring opinion? At what stages and by what methods could the machinery be made more accurate?

Selecting Issues

The opinion surveyor's first job is to select the issues which appear to be most interesting and vital to the greatest number of people. Theoretically the ideal director of a public-opinion poll would need to combine in himself the best qualities of the journalist and the political scientist. Not only must he know what topics are of current interest, he must also try to anticipate the issues which will probably develop into subjects of mass attention and discussion. He needs always to be "on top of the news" in order to pick questions of topical, national significance; but he must also be aware of the difficulties involved in mapping the attitudes of the ordinary citizen. He must try to see the relations between different issues, and take a long-term view of his tasks and responsibilities.

Choosing issues and wording questions are simple only to the uninitiated. The expert knows the possibilities of error. Bias may intrude at various stages, and bias is the eternal foe of the conscientious poll director since it would instantly vitiate his measurements.

Clearly the first place where bias might enter lies in the selection of the issues. For to select the issues is to determine what is important. Now, it is a well-known fact that people's ideas of "what is important" vary with their personal problems, their interests, and their political objectives. To the farmer, crop yields, grain and livestock prices, transportation and farm subsidies rank high in importance; to the industrialist, the major issues may be commodity prices, labor costs, taxes, and markets; while the factory worker's main interests are likely to be centered on his weekly pay check, the affairs of his union, and the problem of unemployment. The issues which are vital to old people may be pensions and security; while to the young, they will perhaps deal with education, conscription, and sport. The biases of the staunch Democrat or Republican lead them to place emphasis on different aspects of foreign and domestic policy.

Confronted with these opposed conceptions of "what is important," the first task of the opinion surveyor is to avoid identifying the vital issues of the day with the interests of any social group or class. Political extremists are bad observers of public opinion because they are tempted to confuse their private world with the public world. The surveyor's goal must be to maintain an impartial, objective attitude to contemporary conflicts and claims. Measuring public opinion calls for a certain "laboratory" attitude of mind. It needs people trained in the scientific method, who approach their job in the full realization that personal biases may exist, and that objectivity can be gained only through constant vigilance, self-questioning, and experiment. Naturally, the selection of issues for public-opinion study will depend on the nature of the investigation and the type of organization which is conducting the study. For polls dealing primarily with national issues, like those conducted by the American Institute of Public Opinion, certain broad guiding principles must be borne in mind:

1. The issues must deal with all possible aspects of the contemporary scene, and cover political, economic, social, and moral issues of common concern.

2. The issues must be of direct interest to the mass of the public, and involve questions on which large sections of

the people may be expected to have formed an opinion. People, for example, are not conversant with details of government finance or the nuances of diplomatic negotiations.

3. The issues selected must be of current, topical interest. In many cases, it is difficult to elicit attitudes related to events which are rooted in the distant past, or events so far in the future that public attitudes have not had the chance to form.

4. The issues must try to impinge closely on the everyday life experiences of ordinary people and must avoid being too remote and hypothetical. They need not be "profound," but may deal with manners as well as with politics.

Such general guiding principles need particular methods of application. The American Institute, for example, conducts week-to-week conferences of editorial and research executives. These persons follow the news culled from a wide range of sources; they chart political trends and social tendencies; they discuss past events and future possibilities; and finally they draft a lengthy series of issues which appear to be uppermost in public discussion. Since public opinion is a phenomenon of temporary surface currents, as well as long-term ground swells, some of the issues never really dominate popular attention, while others, unforeseen in the regular week-to-week conference, may suddenly "break," and call for special telegraphic surveys. For this reason, the average Institute ballot which is drawn up at the question conference shows a mortality rate of as high as 40 per cent on issues which never become dominant. On the other hand, special supplementary questions may have to be added to cover new events such as the bombing of the *Panay* or the sinking of the *Athenia*. The range of issues covered by the modern polls, when placed against a chronology of domestic and political events, indi-

cates that the exploration of the public's attitudes has pro-
ceeded consistently on a wide front. Since the birth of the
Institute, over 1000 issues have been submitted to the
American public.[1]

Wording the Questions

When issues have been chosen to satisfy the criteria of
(1) inclusiveness, (2) widespread public interest, (3) timeliness, and (4) concreteness, the stage is set for the next
problem of wording the questions as clearly as possible.

It is age-old knowledge that questions can be worded in
such a way as to bias the response. The plebiscites which
dictators employ to obtain popular ratification of their
policies are generally of the "Am I right?" or "Am I right?"
variety, and the response which they get usually contains
no element of surprise. In the second German Reichstag
election of November 12, 1933, voters were asked to express
their attitudes in a plebiscite proposal which read:

> Dost thou, German man or German woman, approve the
> policy of thy Reich government, and art thou ready to ac-
> knowledge this policy as the expression of thine own view-
> point and will, and solemnly pledge thyself to it?

The fact that 40,588,804 German voters supported the
proposal cannot truly be called a perfect expression of
public opinion. For, in the first place, the instructions to
the voters read:

> The voter in the plebiscite shall mark his cross on the
> green ballot under the printed "Yes." The circle "No" shall
> be left free.[2]

---

[1] Reprints of many Institute questions and results may be found in the
Public Opinion Quarterly, published by the School of Public Affairs of
Princeton University.

[2] Brooks, Robert C., *Deliver Us from Dictators*, 1935, p. 117.

While quite apart from the instructions, the question itself contained emotional words, used ancient forms of personal address calculated to arouse basic patriotic sentiments, and, moreover, strongly discouraged a real expression of dissent.

Similar biases in a public-opinion poll would instantly disturb the results. Fortunately, the obvious forms of intentional propaganda are not too hard to detect. The modern public is steadily being educated by psychologists and students of propaganda into a growing awareness of the power of stereotyped words, symbols, and catch phrases which are laden with emotional content.[1] People are suspicious, and rightly so, of the demagogue who inveighs against the "Reds," the "capitalists," or the "international bankers," and whose slogans, clichés, and weasel words transform the gaudy variety of political life into mutually exclusive categories of black and white. No expert eye is needed to detect the propaganda content in the question:

"Do you favor the hateful exploitation of the many for the sole benefit of the greedy few?" which the Communist-party comrade might want to ask the public; or in the question:

"Don't you think that the New Deal dictatorship should stop persecuting business?" which some extreme exponent of big business might like to pose. Both questions would constitute equally flagrant examples of biased wording and would be instantly rejected by a critical public.

While a poll may be misleading because the questions contain "colored" words, it may also have little value if the question fails to provide a·clear set of alternatives. An

---

[1] On this question see: Menefee, S. C., "Stereotyped Phrases in Public Opinion," *American Journal of Sociology*, Vol. XLIII, No. 4, Feb., 1938; Studenski, Paul, "How Polls Can Mislead," *Harpers*, December, 1939.

interesting study of this kind of flaw appeared in a poll conducted in 1937 by the Council of Action in Great Britain, a political pressure group. In that year the Council decided to organize a ballot in four constituencies with a large government majority in order to make a rapid test of the public's attitude in those districts to the crisis created by the resignation of Mr. Anthony Eden from the post of Foreign Secretary. The Council asked for an answer to the question:

> Do you approve of Mr. Anthony Eden's stand for good faith in international affairs and will you support his demand for the re-establishment of peace and security through the League of Nations?

Critical members of the public, following the time-honored British custom of venting their wrath in the columns of the London *Times,* swarmed to the attack. The following excerpt from one of many letters which poured into *The Times* points to the alertness of the public in detecting badly-phrased questions:

> If the Council of Action desires a real test of public opinion, a question so worded will never obtain it for them. I have had something to do with the framing of questionnaires for scientific purposes. The first criterion in any questionnaire is that the answer shall not be suggested by the question. None can say that this criterion has been fulfilled by the Council of Action. Further, if a decision between two views is required, both must be given. Instead the voter is to be presented with what amounts to an ultimatum which may be paraphrased "Vote for Mr. Eden's view or proclaim yourself against good faith in international affairs and against the League of Nations." No statistician would regard as valid replies to a question framed on these lines. Moreover, it places any supporter of Mr. Chamberlain in an entirely false position, unable to answer the question at all.[1]

---

[1] London *Times,* March 7, 1939.

It is obvious that when the question fails to allow for the expression of opinion on both sides of an issue, it immediately loses much of its validity. But such glaring examples of partisan phrasing are generally self-exposing.

We can be sure that faulty wording does not always arise from a deliberate attempt to influence public opinion. The road to hell and the road to inaccurate polling results are both paved with good intentions. Unintentional biases are more dangerous than intentional propaganda because they are frequently more difficult to detect. The same word or phrase may mean different things to different people, and surveyors must be continually on the alert against the use of misleading language. To eliminate such bias, the Institute conducts constant preliminary testing and retesting of the questions which are being considered as ballot possibilities.

A staff of experienced, competent persons experimentally tests each question on a proposed ballot. Questions are not tested separately and individually, but are included on a typed ballot in the form and position which tentatively seem to be logical. This experimental ballot includes all questions which are likely to be used on the subsequent printed ballot.

Testing differs from actual interviewing. The purpose of interviewing is to record accurately the opinions or "no opinions" of respondents on issues of current interest; the purpose of pretesting is to determine whether the question is clear. The test interviewer is not interested primarily in recording opinions; he is concerned with making certain, first, that most poll voters have some understanding of the issue and, second, with detecting any flaws in the question. This means that the competent question tester must be constantly probing to discover whether the respondent really understands the question. He should be alert to detect puzzling words and phrases, and ingenious enough to devise substitute phraseology which he can then proceed to check on other respondents.

He must adopt a severely critical attitude toward all questions, and his criticism must be based on actual test interviews, not on "armchair" judgments. It is clear, of course, that awkwardly phrased questions or questions that are confusing, inadvertently "loaded," or over the heads of respondents will distort the results of the poll.

As an extreme example of the way flaws in questions are detected by testing, consider the case of this innocuous-looking query:

"Do you think the United States will have to fight Japan within your lifetime?"

This apparently is a simple issue, concisely stated. It is speculative, to be sure, but speculation is not barred from the realm of public opinion. However, after running the gauntlet of test interviews, this question was found deficient on three counts: first, it confused the respondents; they were somewhat alarmed by the suggestion of compulsion and, before attempting to answer the question, wanted to know if it meant that Japan might actually invade this country, might attempt to seize the Hawaiian Islands or Alaska, or might in some other way force the United States into war.

The second fault of the question was that the phrase "within your lifetime" meant different things to different people, depending on their current state of health and their normal life expectancy.

The third strike on the question was the fact that people generally dislike questions which seem to require consultation with a crystal ball or a bearded prophet; they ordinarily do not want to project their thoughts into the remote future.

Another illustration of the value of experimentation with questions concerned this issue: "Do you think liquor advertising should be prohibited?" Test interviews revealed that respondents thought the word "prohibited" referred to the use of liquor and beer rather than to advertisements of the beverages.

A recent question conference framed a question to this effect: "If England and France pay something on the war debts they now owe us, should we lend them money to buy war supplies in this country?"

The question seemed satisfactory, as do most questions in the formulative stage, but preliminary tests in the field quickly revealed its flaw, namely, that respondents were confused by the pronoun "we." Did the question refer to government loans or to private loans?

The difficulty was easily obviated by rephrasing the question to read: "If England and France pay something on the war debts they now owe us, should the *United States government* lend them money to buy war supplies in this country?" The difference in wording may seem insignificant, yet if the question in its original form had gone on the ballot, the results would probably have been somewhat different from those which were recorded.

Pretesting, then, is an essential. But in the last analysis the ultimate test of the worth of a ballot question must rest with the concrete field experience of the interviewers, each of whom contacts a small segment of the American cross section. Interviews are made in every section of the country, and some amazing accents, colloquialisms, and interpretations of the king's English are peculiar to some regions. If a ballot question successfully runs the gauntlet of thousands of interviews with representative American citizens, it may be considered reliable. Not infrequently the most careful testing will fail to reveal question flaws which are not detected until interviewers in the field make their usual reports after each assignment, listing the "most interesting," "least interesting," and "least understood" questions, the reasons for their choices, as well as suggested rewordings. These supplementary reports are invaluable guides to the construction of future ballots and indirectly as a check on the interviewer's ability and perception.

The Institute's experience with many different types of questions indicates that the following criteria are most significant:

1. The questions should be as brief and to the point as possible. Long conditional or dependent clauses tend to confuse people.
2. The words and phrases should be simple and in common day-to-day use, among all groups in the community.
3. The questions should not include words which have a strong emotional content.
4. The questions must avoid all possible bias or suggestion in favor of or against a particular point of view.
5. The questions should include all the important alternatives which may emerge on a given issue.
6. Where the individual is being asked to choose between different alternatives, this choice of alternatives must be given as early in the question as possible.
7. In cases where the choices in a question are lengthy or numerous, it is preferable to list these on a card which the respondent can read. The average person is not likely to be successful in retaining a long list of alternatives, or complex questions, in his mind.

To these preliminary "checks" and "balances," the Institute has added an objective technique to detect bias in its questions. Where the wording of a question is in doubt, valid differences are often discovered through a "split-ballot" technique. In these cases, two wordings of the questions are placed on separate ballot forms. One form, the "A" form, is put to half of the voters in the cross section, while the "B" form goes to the opposite half containing the same types of voters. Tabulation soon reveals what difference, if any, can be ascribed to the wording of the questions.

The effect of wording will obviously not be similar on all questions. On many issues public attitudes are fixed, and these remain the same despite small word changes. When the Institute polled on the question of prohibition, for example, the "A" form of the question ran:

"If the question of national prohibition should come up again, would you vote to make the country dry?" while the "B" form was reworded:

"If the question of national prohibition should come up again, would you vote for prohibition or against it?"

These two forms of the question were used in two successive polls, and in all four studies, conducted on the basis of four comparable samples, the result in each case was a constant figure of 66 per cent opposed to prohibition.

The effect of changes in word form is receiving increased attention. Certain generalizations have stood the test of polling experience. When an opinion is deeply held, when it is a question on which people have formed convictions, the wording of the question is of relatively minor importance. On opinions concerning the Supreme Court fight, or on basic American attitudes to the present European conflict, slight variations in the form of the question, assuming the meaning is kept constant, do not produce appreciable differences in the results.

Immediately before the outbreak of war in Europe, the

Institute asked three questions dealing with Germany's demands on Poland. The questions and results were as follows:

	Yes	No
A. Would you like to see England, France, and Poland agree to Germany's demands regarding Danzig?	12%	88%
B. Do you think Hitler's claims to Danzig are justified?	13%	87%
C. Do you think Hitler's claims to the Polish Corridor are justified?	14%	86%

While it is doubtless true that many of those interviewed might not have been able to distinguish Danzig from the Polish Corridor on a map, there was no doubt about their general attitude to the German action, as can be seen from the consistency of their replies.

The historic debate on American neutrality policy in November, 1939, provided the occasion for another test of this point. In studying the attitudes of the public, the Institute asked the question:

"Do you think the United States should do everything possible to help England and France win the war, except go to war ourselves?" The result here was: *Yes,* 62%; *No,* 38%. When the question was reversed to read:

"Do you think the United States should do everything possible to help England and France win the war, even at the risk of getting into the war ourselves?" the result was:

Yes (even at risk of getting in): 34%.
No (not at risk of getting in): 66%.

The attitudes revealed by these questions set the limits within which American public opinion considered the proposal to change the embargo provisions of the Neutrality Act. In October, 1939, the Institute asked the question, on the "A" ballot form:

"Do you think Congress should make changes in the Neutrality laws so that England and France, or any other nation, can buy war supplies here?" The result: *Yes, 62%; No, 38%*.

The Institute's question caused considerable discussion. Representative Karl E. Mundt, Congressman from South Dakota, amongst others, suggested that the question had been incorrectly phrased. He argued that the Institute's question contained the phrase "war supplies," but that it failed to specify "arms, ammunition, and implements of war," such as airplanes and munitions. Institute tests showed, however, that the inclusion of the phrase "arms and airplanes" did not substantially change the result of the question, for on the "B" form which went to an identical cross section of voters:

"Do you think Congress should make changes in the Neutrality Law so that England and France or any other nation can buy war supplies, *including arms and airplanes,* in the United States?" the result showed: *Yes, 60%; No, 40%*.

The question form here apparently had little effect on the response—owing largely to the settled nature of the convictions on this issue.

In using the "A" and "B" split-ballot forms, the Institute has found significant differences in only a small fraction of the cases. The basic reason for this lies in the pretesting which is done to eliminate bias in the question before it is placed on the ballot.

But it would be a great error to assume that the only

worry of the surveyor is the fear of being "unneutral" in wording questions. Of even greater importance is the danger of being unintelligible. A question may lack clarity either because the issue with which it deals is too technical or because the phrasing is itself obscure. The mass of ordinary people do not have an opinion on all subjects. They are generally not interested in the specific details of domestic or foreign policies, or in the minutiae of governmental affairs. They are not specialists in economics, or history, or psychology; they are frequently more interested in football scores than in Congressional debates.

The issues and questions selected, then, must not be too specialized or too difficult for the ordinary person. The polls will show a high "no-opinion" vote when they ask ordinary citizens to give their views on the details of monetary policy, the military aspects of defense problems, or the conduct of foreign trade negotiations. Inevitably, in the day-to-day work of the Institute, it has been difficult to find the target of common understanding with every shot. At times, the questions asked have been too specialized for all the members of the general public to answer. In January, 1940, the Institute asked the questions:

What is your understanding of the term, "reciprocal trade treaties?"

Do you think Congress should give Secretary Hull the power to make more such treaties?

The replies obtained from voters throughout the country indicated that, of all those interviewed, only one person in ten, on the average, indicated by his reply that he understood the principles on which reciprocal trade agreements rest, while almost 90 per cent expressed ignorance of the phrase "reciprocal trade treaties." In other words, when either the Republicans or the Democrats attempt to make a popular issue out of Mr. Hull's agreements, they are, in reality, addressing only about six million of the nation's sixty million eligible voters.

Questions can be unintelligible, not only because the issue itself is too specialized, but also because the wording may be too difficult. Phrasing a public-opinion ballot has been called "a nightmare in semantics." But gradually, through the process of continuous questioning, the Institute is building up a neutral vocabulary—a public-opinion glossary—within the comprehension of the mass of people.

Public-opinion surveys at times indicate that the American electorate reacts to popular symbols without understanding the meaning of those symbols. A case in point is the great hue and cry about balancing the Federal budget. Careful tests have shown that the term "balance the budget" is not generally understood; many respondents confuse budget balancing with retirement of the national debt; some in the lower-income brackets have the hazy notion that a balanced budget has something to do with larger cash benefits for the indigent. Phrases like "constitutionality," "security regulation," "appropriations," "presidential powers," "collective bargaining," "union shops," or questions involving the difference between municipal, state, and Federal judges, the details of labor-employer relations, of taxation proposals, the political role of various cabinet members, the geography and history of countries outside the United States, and even the names of important and widely publicized domestic agencies, like the National Labor Relations Board and the Dies Committee, are frequently unfamiliar to many people approached in public-opinion surveys.

In this sense, the polls are charting virtually unexplored sectors of the public mind, discovering where the contours are sharp and jagged, and where they are covered in mist and fog. The job of mapping the areas of ignorance is every bit as important as mapping the areas of specialized knowledge, for both elements go to make up the conglomerate which is public opinion.

★

CHAPTER EIGHT

★

Meeting the People

IN THE application of every instrument there is a constant human equation. The task of constructing and applying the public-opinion poll depends on the effort and co-operation of many individuals at each stage of the total process. The observer on his tour of inspection must turn from selecting issues and wording questions to seeing how the opinions of the people who go to make up the total cross section are actually obtained.

When the final ballots are prepared on the basis of the pretested questions, the send-out is mailed, with detailed information regarding interviewing procedure and cross-section assignment, to interviewers in every state of the country. The interviewer then becomes the vital link between the two processes of question planning and final tabulation. He is the advance guard of the modern surveys of public opinion. If the field work is careless or inaccurate, the final picture will be imperfect. How can the polls guarantee that the interviewers will carry out their job conscientiously and well?

Three main checks have been devised for this purpose: careful selection of the interviewing personnel, regular contact between the interviewer and the central office, and objective checks on the validity of the completed ballots which each interviewer returns. Interviewers are selected

on general grounds of intelligence, experience, education,
and their interest in public-opinion study. They begin their
investigations either after direct application or on recom-
mendation from educators, lawyers, or other responsible
people. In most cases, a strong research incentive stimulates
students to seek interview work on a part-time basis. Appli-
cations are filled out regarding education, age, past experience, political and religious affiliation, nationality, and the
like, and the selected applicants are given detailed information describing the interviewing procedure to be followed.
The necessity of adhering strictly to the assigned cross section is explained, and these applicants then receive trial
assignments to test their suitability for the work.

At the moment of writing there are about 1000 members
of the field corps who interview on Institute ballots. Because of cross-section requirements, it is necessary to have
a staff of this size, but obviously every individual interviewer does not receive an assignment on each send-out. A
recent survey indicates that of this total, 68 per cent are
men, 32 per cent women; that the median age of this group,
both for men and women, is 30; that 90 per cent are college
trained; that 48 per cent of the interviewers are professional
men and women—teachers, high-school principals, lawyers,
and ministers, as well as a large body of students.

The political backgrounds and sympathies of the members of this field corps are highly interesting, indicating
an even balance between the supporters of the major parties
and those who give "no preference" or some third party as
their political preference. While 23 per cent of the interviewers claim to have "no preference," 35 per cent are
Democratic in sympathy, 37 per cent are Republican, and
5 per cent declare themselves in favor of some third party.
The even character of this distribution is one of many pro-

tections against possible political bias. Since most of the interviewers are students and professional people, many with training in field research, and since their sympathies are distributed about equally between the two major parties, the dangers of prejudiced or indifferent interviewing are minimized.

From the office in Princeton, the interviewer receives an assignment specifying the number of each of the various types of voters to be interviewed in his particular area, in order to fit the requirements of the total cross section for each state—how many "on-relief," "poor," "poor-plus," "average," "average-plus," or "wealthy" voters he needs to fill each of the major economic, age, sex, and color categories.

Interviewers make a selection of economic types for their assigned cross section on the basis of the following general economic classifications:

Wealthy: Respondents in this classification are represented in the top 1 to 3 per cent of the population. Such voters normally have an income of $6500 a year or more.

Average plus: These are people who form about 14 per cent of the voting public. Their incomes fall between $2200 and $6500.

Average: This is a large sector of the great "middle class," comprising 28 per cent of the voting population. The income range is roughly from $1285 to $2220.

Poor plus: These people comprise 20 per cent of the voters. The income scale of this group falls between $930 and $1285.

Poor: This is the poorest class which is not actually supported by the government. Although these people are self-supporting, they are usually not far above the relief level.

Old-age assistance: These are the voters receiving old-age-assistance pensions from the state government. A part of the money is usually obtained from the Federal government.

On relief or W.P.A.: The wage earner in such families is employed as a laborer, sewing-room worker, or in some similar capacity on W.P.A. projects. This group, of course, does not include foremen, timekeepers, and administrators receiving well above the average level of relief wages.

The voters classified as "poor," "on relief," or "old-age assistance" make up the remaining 36 per cent, and their average incomes go up to $930 yearly.

Interviewers either estimate the ages of respondents or, as is most frequently the case, simply ask: "Would you mind telling me your approximate age?" Virtually all respondents state their ages without hesitation. Most men are co-operative on this point, but occasionally the interviewer has to use considerable tact to assess the age of the reticent matron who exercises the traditional female prerogative of understatement. Interviewers make it a point to obtain a good distribution of age groups, including in particular the 21-to-30 and the over-50 groups. The "too-young-to-vote" category includes people of 21 to 24 years old who were too young to vote in the 1936 presidential election, but who will be eligible in 1940.

A continuous up-to-date check on factors which control the cross section is maintained by analyzing all the ballots of every survey. These analyses provide an accurate check on age, sex, occupational groups, and the broad economic categories, while factors like the proportion of telephone subscribers and automobile owners can be closely checked against existing data.

Some people imagine that to secure a sample of Democratic voters, for example, the interviewers employ special lists containing the names of registered Democratic voters, or that lists containing the names of "relief" candidates are used as the basis for selecting voters in this group. The Institute does not use lists of names in interviewing a cross section of the voting public. Not only would the cost in time and money be prohibitive, not only would the use of names tend to destroy the "anonymous" character of the interview; practical experience has shown that such a method is unnecessary for polling accuracy. In all cases, the interviewer himself selects at random the types on the basis of the quota requirements and his own observation in his district.

Occasionally the question is raised: "Do interviewers question the same people each week?" The answer is no. Each successive ballot is based on the replies of different individuals who are representative of a general type. Interviewers are advised not to interview the same individual more frequently than once a year. The interviewer must study the quotas which tell him what types of voters are required to make up his own cross section. The cross section covered by any one interviewer in any one state will not *by itself* be representative of that state, but his ballots, together with those of all the other interviewers from the same state, will constitute a miniature electorate which includes in correct proportion the main divisions of the population within the state as a whole.

First of all, let us say, the interviewer wants some representatives of the "poor" income group. He will know that he can meet typical individuals in this group by visiting the poorer areas of the city or by talking to semiskilled laborers on the job or at home. In some cases, it will be easier to get interviews in the evening than in the daytime, although experience will soon tell him that no one is eager to be interviewed when supper is waiting on the table. At eight o'clock, then, the interviewer approaches a middle-aged man, dressed in working clothes, who is sitting on the front porch of a house classified as "poor." The interview might go something like this:

INTERVIEWER: I am interviewing people to get their views for the American Institute of Public Opinion—the Gallup poll. Every week, in every state, we ask representative people their opinions on questions of national importance. I'd be glad to have your ideas on a few questions. I don't want your name—just your opinions.

RESPONDENT: I don't believe my opinions are worth much.

INTERVIEWER: That's where you're wrong! In this poll we get the opinions of wealthy and poor, old and young, men and women, Democrats and Republicans—we take a cross section of the country. The results of these surveys are published by newspapers throughout the country. You may have seen these reports in your own daily paper.

RESPONDENT: Well, come to think of it, I believe I have.

INTERVIEWER: Do you plan to vote in the next election here?

RESPONDENT: Yes, I'll probably vote.[1]

INTERVIEWER: Should the Constitution be changed to require a vote of the people before Congress could draft men for war overseas?

RESPONDENT: I think it should. Most of the people in my shop don't want to get mixed up in a war, and they'd soon tell those politicians in Washington so.

INTERVIEWER: Should we send our Army and Navy abroad to fight Germany?

RESPONDENT: Hell, no—look what happened last time. We learned our lesson.

INTERVIEWER: If England and France were being defeated, would you favor sending our Army and Navy to fight Germany?

RESPONDENT: Well, maybe. But I'm not sure about that one—it's too far away.

---

[1] Voters in Institute surveys must be residents of the community assigned to the interviewer and must be eligible to vote, except in those cases where a social cross section is used.

INTERVIEWER: If you're not sure, I'll mark it "no opinion."
Is that right?

RESPONDENT: Yes, that'll do.

INTERVIEWER: Would you prefer to see the Democrats or
the Republicans win the presidential election this year?

RESPONDENT: I'm not certain. I think I'll wait to see who's
running.

INTERVIEWER: Did you vote in the 1936 presidential election?

RESPONDENT: Yes, I did.

INTERVIEWER: Did you vote for Lemke, Roosevelt, Thomas,
or Landon?

RESPONDENT: Well, I voted for Roosevelt.

INTERVIEWER: Now—just one or two short questions. Do
you have a telephone in your home? Do you own an automobile? What is your specific occupation, your work? I have to
estimate your age. I'd say 39. What! 46? I'd never have
guessed it. Thanks very much, sir. When the final returns
appear, you can see how the rest of the country feels about
some of the questions you've just answered.

To get "upper-income" ballots, the interviewer may
travel to the wealthier residential section of town, or he may
make street, store, or office interviews during the day to fill
the quotas for "average" or "average-plus" men. He will
find women at home or in shopping centers. He will meet
young people in colleges, in business offices or workshops,
or as they grab a bite of lunch at the corner drugstore. If
he is an interviewer in a rural area, he will need a car and
may have to go into fields to get farmers to take time out
from hay pitching or fence mending.

In many cases, the section of the city or the type of resi-
dence will provide a useful first clue to the individual's
economic status. But questions which deal with automobile
ownership, use or access to a telephone, and the specific
occupation of the individual interviewed furnish a very
necessary check on the interviewer's first impressions. While

it is comparatively simple in most cases to select the various types on sight according to the broad income categories—it is not difficult, for example, to separate the income groups in which a New York taxi driver or an elderly dowager in a chauffeur-driven limousine are to be placed—there are instances where simple inspection does not accurately determine economic status, and where the value of these objective checks becomes obvious.

An interviewer's story illustrates the dangers of relying solely on judging an individual's income group by his appearance:

> A big, burly Irishman, about fifty years of age, and very shabbily dressed in laborer's clothing, was idly standing on a corner in a very poor section of a large city. He was agreeable to my interviewing him. Before approaching him, I had classified him in my own mind, as "poor," "poor plus," or possibly "on relief," and as a Democrat. I was consequently quite surprised when he suddenly laughed, and said, "I bet you took me for a laborer in these old clothes. I'm a state morals investigator." And he was a Republican to boot.

Objective checks on occupation, then, are necessary at all times. Many interviewers have solved the problem of getting their quotas of "on-relief" voters by going directly to the relief offices in their communities and talking to the applicants as they stand in line. One interviewer tells the story of how the public-welfare officials became suspicious of a strange young person who was forever asking questions in the office, and finally asked her to desist. With considerable ingenuity, she hit upon the technique of getting her "cases" in a local grocery store not far distant, because its sign, RELIEF CHECKS ACCEPTED HERE, attracted many persons from the relief office. Interviewing methods are not rigid; they may be adjusted according to the interviewer's own set of local problems within the general limits of his week-to-week assignment.

When the interviewer has completed the assignment, he makes out a report in which he analyzes the public's reaction to the various questions on the ballot, and then mails the completed returns to the office in Princeton, New Jersey. Ordinarily, a national survey takes two weeks to complete, although special polls can be rushed through by telegraph and preliminary results obtained in forty-eight hours.

When the ballots have been returned, a final check on careless or inaccurate interviewing is made. The experience of handling interview reports over a period of years has given those in charge of the field-staff departments a sound general knowledge of the earmarks of good and bad interviewing. An experienced person can study the ballots and detect those which have been carelessly done or falsified. Another check in the interests of polling accuracy is obtained by comparing the interviewer's returns in his area with those from similar districts, and by checking his results with such objective controls as telephone and automobile ownership. The Institute at times relies on a "flying squad" of seasoned interviewers who can be used for rapid preliminary surveys, or sent into areas where an additional check on the results of field interviewers seems advisable.

A combination of these techniques is used to secure reliable interviewers, to inform them fully of the purpose of the survey and the interviewing procedure to be adopted, and to check their results when ballots have been completed and mailed to the central office.

There is one final reason for such safeguards. As we shall presently see, the interviewers can and do make an invaluable contribution to the knowledge of how people think and how well the polls are performing their task. They are in daily contact with voters throughout the nation. In the course of countless interviews many new problems come to light, and suggestions are continually being sent in to the central office, where they are later incorporated into succeeding surveys. Along with the raw statements of attitude according to "yes," "no," and "no opinion," interviewers seek to get from the people they meet free comments on why they hold the opinions they do. These background comments, which form the soil in which political and social attitudes develop, are later analyzed at the Institute. In a real sense, the problems which interviewers meet in their daily round act as guides for further research in the never-ending job of improving the machinery of opinion measurement.

That they have done their job faithfully and well, and have consistently maintained a high caliber of performance, may be seen in the accuracy of dozens of pre-election studies in which these interviewers have co-operated. Much of the responsibility for the success of the sampling surveys must go to the unsung group of men and women who take these week-by-week soundings of public opinion. The interviewers meet the people of America. Their experiences form an exciting chapter in the history of the effort to measure the pulse of democracy. They provide the human case material against which the "people's own story," as told in their own words, can be more fully understood.

When the completed ballots have been returned to the institute, they are tabulated by means of Hollerith cards and mechanical sorters, which make it possible to total opinions at the rate of 400 a minute. Analysis of the results, or breakdowns according to sex, age, economic status, political affiliation, geographic area, and dozens of other variables, are then compiled. The final figures are sent to the editorial staff which works in collaboration with the Institute director to prepare a regular release for the newspapers on the basis of the returns.

It has been estimated that the triweekly reports of what America thinks are made to about 8,000,000 readers through the medium of leading American newspapers. At the present time, over one hundred newspapers provide all the funds necessary to support this new effort to measure objectively the opinions of the mass of common people. These newspapers are located in every section of the country and represent every shade of political opinion. A recent compilation showed that 26 subscribing newspapers classified themselves as Republican or Independent Republican, 32 as Democratic or Independent Democratic, and 48 as Independent.[1] It is a tribute to these newspapers and to those who make them that, in spite of wide differences in the policies advocated in their editorial columns, they have impartially reported the surveys even when the results conflicted violently with their own editorial opinions. With each of these subscribing newspapers, the Institute's agreement stipulates that no changes can be made in the results or interpretation of these results. It is significant that in the four years of this experiment in opinion reporting, there has not been a single case in which an editor has attempted to distort Institute reports by manipulating the results to suit editorial policy.

Among the publishers or editors of newspapers underwriting the poll are seven directors of the Associated Press; while eight Scripps-Howard newspapers are sustaining

[1] For a classification of the newspapers which publish the Institute's findings, see p. 323 in Appendix.

members. Newspapers as different in their editorial attitudes and policies as the *Atlanta Constitution* and the *Chicago Daily News,* as distant as the *Honolulu Star-Bulletin* and the *Portland* (Maine) *Telegram;* publishers as opposed politically as Frank Gannett of the *Rochester Democrat-Chronicle* and Barry Bingham of the *Louisville Courier Journal* have stood by the polls, and made possible ever more accurate knowledge of the trends in American public opinion.

Why do newspapers support the public-opinion polls? It is clear that the present-day polls sponsored by the newspapers are related to the old-fashioned straw votes conducted by newspapers and magazines in the past. The new elements in the present situation are improved accuracy and greater timeliness. The contrast emerges clearly in comparing *The Literary Digest* poll with the polls conducted by the Institute or the *Fortune* Survey. The polls conducted by the *Digest* were operated at the enormous cost of a half million dollars for each major nation-wide survey. Because of the great expense involved, the *Digest* poll could not measure public opinion more frequently than once every two to four years. Not only do the modern polls, based on a small, carefully selected cross section, provide more accurate measurements; they can be applied to give continuous and rapid measurements of public opinion at all times.

Ten years ago, this time factor was not so important as it is today. For issues which, like prohibition, went through a time cycle of twelve years, there was no vital need for checking opinion trends at frequent intervals. But the slow-working machinery of the *Digest* failed to match the tempo of a swift-moving age. An issue like the proposal to change the composition of the Supreme Court was proposed, debated, and decided within a period of three or four months. The *Digest* poll could never have gone into action in time to make a national poll on the Supreme Court reorganization plan before the whole debate was over and the issue settled. Events like the wave of sit-down strikes in 1937, the purge of conservative Senators in 1938, the outbreak of war, and the need for defining American neutrality in 1939 emerge with dramatic suddenness. Improved techniques for disseminating news—the telegraph, the radio, the wirephoto—have made it possible for public opinion to form almost overnight.

To conduct a continuous audit of the reaction of the public, the modern polls have had to speed up their investigations and reports of the trends of public opinion. The *Fortune* Survey, with its quarterly studies, was a step forward. In 1938, *Fortune* began to report trends at monthly intervals. The American Institute began its series of studies at first on a weekly basis and later accelerated its sampling machinery to cover publication of the surveys three times a week. The cost of a single *Digest* "sample" has been spread over a series of smaller representative samples, and these have proved to be at once more accurate and more timely in their results. In supporting the Institute's rapid type of opinion reporting, the newspapers have thus kept pace with the changed conditions of 1940 by adding factual and more up-to-date news of what people think to their improved modern facilities for collecting news about what people do.

To news about events, pictures about events, and editorial comment about events, the polls of public opinion have added a fourth dimension of modern reporting. They describe the reactions of public opinion to the events themselves. Newspapers underwrite this new development in public-opinion measurement because what people think is news, and important news in our swift-moving world. In making the polls possible, they also fulfill their historic function as the guarantor of a free public opinion.

PART II

★   ★

EXPLORATIONS
IN PUBLIC
OPINION

★   ★

★

★

CHAPTER NINE

The Fourth Stage of Democracy

HÁLF a century before the present era of public-opinion polls, James Bryce sketched the evolutionary setting of rule by public opinion. In the first stage, public opinion is static and passive, acquiescing in the exercise of unquestioned political authority by the dominant group. A second stage is reached, he suggested, when conflicts arise between this ruling group and the people, in which the people gradually awaken to a sense of their abilities and power. In the third stage, public opinion becomes an active and controlling force influencing the course of public policy through the periodic election of representatives who act for the people.

In visualizing the future, Bryce made a statement of prophetic import:

"A fourth stage would be reached," he wrote, *"if the will of the majority of citizens were to become ascertainable at all times."*

The introduction of the sampling referendum, operating continuously to assess public opinion on all the major issues of the day, has been hailed by some students as a step toward this fourth stage. "If this discovery lives up to its present promise," writes Robert Updegraff in his study of the public-opinion polls, "it will mean an advance in human relationships, and a forward step in the technique of self-government, which in practical social importance will rank it with the original conception of government by the people."

Have the polls of public opinion really helped democracy work better? The answer to this question can best be given by judging the polls on a purely utilitarian basis. In our pragmatic age, the value of frequent public-opinion polls must be viewed in relation to the need for more accurate information about public opinion, and the way in which polls have operated to meet these needs.

The first part of this study described the machinery of the polls. We shall now see how this machinery operates in the actual setting of American public life.

During the past few years, the polls have measured public opinion on scores of important issues. The next eight chapters do not cover all of them; each chapter confines itself to a case study of one representative issue. Therefore, these chapters do not offer a complete history of the public-opinion poll, neither are they arranged in chronological order. Their purpose is to show how past surveys reveal certain trends in public opinion. They describe the polls as they help to define the mandate which a group gives to its leaders. They chart the interest and preferences of public opinion toward rival candidates and measure the true strength of pressure groups. One study tells how the polls have helped to reveal how easily a weak democracy can breed the germs of dictatorship, while another describes how people could express their views about living standards and the economic divisions in modern society. Still another study tells how the polls went directly to the public and exploded the social myth that discussion of venereal disease was taboo. The last two examples show the polls measuring British public opinion in wartime and American opinion concerning the war, describing the foundations on which a democratic foreign policy is based.

The issues with which these case studies deal cover the kind of problems on which the polls can fill the gaps in the existing democratic structure. The need for real-life studies of how people think supplies an essential corrective to the vast amount of wishful thinking and speculation which has shrouded much of the discussion about the nature of public opinion. One thing is certain: the modern substitution of candid-camera studies of opinion for impressionistic and florid descriptions is vitally necessary. As the reserve force in democratic politics, public opinion can play its part only if the common run of people are continually encouraged to take an interest in the broad lines of public policy, in their own opinions, and in those of their fellows, and if clear channels exist through which these opinions can become known.

CHAPTER TEN

Defining the Mandate

IN 1888, when Franklin D. Roosevelt was a boy of six, Bryce described in *The American Commonwealth* a situation remarkably similar to the Supreme Court enlargement plan which rocked the country in the fifth year of the New Deal. Bryce wrote:

> Suppose a Congress and President were bent on doing something which the Supreme Court deems contrary to the Constitution. They pass a statute. A case arises under it. The Court on the hearing of the case unanimously declares the statute to be null, as being beyond the powers of Congress. Congress forthwith passes and the President signs another statute more than doubling the number of justices. The new justices outvote the old ones: the statute is held valid: the security provided for the protection of the Constitution is gone like a morning mist.
>
> What prevents such assaults on the fundamental law—assaults which, however immoral in substance, would be perfectly legal in form? Not the mechanism of government, for all its checks have been evaded. Not the conscience of the legislature and the President, for heated combatants seldom shrink from justifying the means by the end. Nothing but the fear of the people, whose broad good sense and attachment to the great principles of the Constitution may generally be relied on to condemn such a perversion of its forms. . . . To the people we come sooner or later.

During the first three years of the Roosevelt Administration (1933-36), the Supreme Court "deemed contrary to the Constitution" one New Deal measure after another. It killed the N.R.A., the A.A.A., the Railroad Pension Act, the "hot-oil" control act, the Frazier-Lemke mortgage moratorium. It ruled against minimum-wage legislation. With each adverse decision, the New Dealers grew more angry. They felt, in the words of the President, that the Court was taking the country back to "the horse-and-buggy days." They believed something had to be done.

Accordingly, one bleak day in February, 1937, President Roosevelt opened fire on the Supreme Court. He announced a plan remarkably similar to the one described by James Bryce forty-nine years before. The plan sought to increase the size of the Court by providing that for each justice over seventy years of age who did not retire, a new justice should be appointed. As there were six judges over seventy at the time, the scheme called for a maximum of six new appointments, or a Court of fifteen members, assuming that none of the older justices resigned.

The President declared his plan was necessary in order to infuse "new blood" into the Court and to speed up the judicial machinery. As Bryce had pointed out, the scheme was perfectly legal, since the Constitution gives Congress the power to determine the size of the Court. In fact, the highly conservative American Bar Association, in its annual convention of 1921, had come out for a bench of eleven members.[1] And changes in the size of the Court had been made six times before, in the administrations of Jefferson, Van Buren, Lincoln, Johnson, and Grant.

It soon became apparent, however, that the President

---

[1] When the Bar Association submitted the President's plan to a vote of its members in a poll in May, 1937, the outcome was 4 to 1 against the proposal.

had touched off a bombshell. Commentators kept up a steady drumfire of opposition. To Walter Lippmann the "pernicious" Court plan was "the greatest issue since slavery." The attacks boiled down to two main arguments: (1) that the plan would undermine the power, freedom, and prestige of the Court by making it subservient to the executive, and (2) that the President had played false with the public by concealing the real motive for the change, which was not to speed up the judicial machinery, but to secure a Court whose members would rubber-stamp New Deal laws.

The President's defenders replied that the Court was behind the times in its social philosophy, that its members were out of step with the other two branches of government, which represented the people. *And besides, cried the New Dealers, hadn't the President just been given*—the year was 1937—*a rousing mandate at the polls by no less than 27,000,000 American voters?*

There lay the rub. What did the President's landslide victory of November, 1936, mean? Was it a mandate to curb the Court? Since the people had seen for themselves that the President and the Court were at loggerheads, did a vote for Roosevelt mean a repudiation of the Court? No analysis of the election figures could possibly show the answer. In fact, curbing the Court's power had not even been a campaign issue.

The controversy gave opinion research an early opportunity to demonstrate its value. On two occasions, once before and once after the 1936 election, the Institute had applied its yardstick to public opinion on the Supreme Court.

Both times the results made it plain that the majority did not wish to curb the Court. Many voters did say that the Court should be more liberal in reviewing New Deal legis-

lation. But when the Institute asked in November, 1935—
sixteen months before the actual proposal—whether the
power to declare legislation unconstitutional should be
curbed, a majority of approximately 60 per cent replied in
the negative. Significantly enough, this sentiment was not
changed by the smashing New Deal victory in the 1936
election. A survey one month after this election found
almost the same percentage against tampering with the
Court's powers.

In view of the results of the two polls, it seems obvious
that the election did not constitute a vote to alter the Court's
composition. In fact, on October 24, nine days before the
election, the Institute declared in print that a victory for
Roosevelt would not mean any Court-curbing mandate.
The general attitude of the public was plain: the majority
of voters opposed any basic change in the function or power
of the judiciary, although they believed that individual
judges on the bench should take a more liberal attitude
toward the New Deal. The basic desire was for a change in
the spirit, rather than the structure, of the Court.

Within a few hours after the President announced his
Court-reform plan, on February 5, 1937, the Institute began to test the opinions of a cross section of voters in city,
town, and country, by asking the question: "Should Congress pass the President's Supreme Court plan?"

The immediate objective was, of course, to find out
quickly and accurately what people thought of the Court
plan—by states, by groups, by income levels. Obviously the
results would also show one other thing: how much the
President's personal championship of the Court plan had
influenced those 60 per cent of the voters who, in previous
Institute polls, had always opposed curbing the Court. The
President was riding the crest of a new wave of postelection

popularity. Would he now be able to swing public opinion around to his side on the Court issue?

The first poll returns encouraged the New Dealers. They showed the country about evenly divided. The actual results were 47 per cent in favor of the President's plan, 53 per cent opposed.

That was in late February. Then came a series of events which gradually reduced public support for the plan. First, the Court handed down a decision sustaining the constitutionality of the Wagner Labor Relations Act. This decision made Court reform seem less necessary in the eyes of some voters. Next, Associate Justice Van Devanter, one of the conservative members of the Court, announced he would retire. This meant the President would have his long-cherished opportunity to appoint a liberal to the Court. Finally, on the last day of the term, the Court upheld the constitutionality of the immensely popular Social Security Act. To many people this showed that the Court was not irreconcilably anti-New Deal. With each of these developments, the Institute's successive surveys found a drop in the number of voters favoring the Court plan. By the time the fight had ended, approximately 60 per cent of the voters were opposed to the plan—the same proportion that had championed the Court's power before the controversy started.

The difficulty of defining mandates has been a major shortcoming of democracy. The meaning of the 1936 election in relation to Court reform is but one example of the problem. Elections are seldom clear-cut votes on significant issues. When the noise of battle and drumbeating is over, the bewildered voter is often left to ask himself, "What did my vote really mean?"

He is even more confused when new issues arise that he did not foresee when he voted. When the successful candidate interprets his victory to mean that his supporters will approve of everything he does about all issues and under all circumstances, the voter can only stand and wonder. Elected officials claim a mandate from the people, yet the people seldom have an opportunity to be heard.

The seriousness of this situation in a democratic country is inescapable. In England the opposition can always displace the government of the day if it wins a majority in the House of Commons, a state of affairs that encourages public interest in politics between elections. In America, there is a real danger of a dwindling public interest during non-election years, with consequences that might threaten the very existence of the democratic state. Frequent surveys of public opinion can help to focus popular attention on vital issues.

Since the American Institute was founded in 1935, it has continuously reported on the popularity of President Roosevelt and his program. While the President's standing with the people has varied from time to time, the Institute has shown that a majority, and for the most part an overwhelming majority, has always supported him. Yet despite his tremendous personal popularity, the people have not blindly endorsed every New Deal measure. They were for the C.C.C., for social security, for wages-and-hours legislation; but they voted against the N.R.A. and the the A.A.A. shortly before these laws were declared unconstitutional, and they steadfastly refused to go along on Supreme Court change. It is only by means of such referendums that programs can be separated from personalities, and the mandates of the leaders clearly defined.

★

★

CHAPTER ELEVEN

Airing the Smoke-Filled Rooms

FEW American political institutions have aroused more caustic criticism than the national political conventions which fill the highest executive office in the nation. Presidential nominating conventions have been bitterly attacked as ". . . super market places for political deals and bargains, trades and treachery." The spectacle of more than a thousand cheering delegates combines the noise and excitement of a three-ring circus with the passion of an old-time religious revival. But behind this façade a small group of politicians and party managers make the real decisions in the "smoke-filled rooms," thus moving countless observers to criticism and occasionally to constructive action.

Herbert Agar has drawn a graphic picture of the nominating conventions of 1936 and of the "function" of the attending delegates. With minor variations in dates and personalities, the description could serve to cover many similar conventions in the past:

> There was no choice, in the way of badness, between the Republican and the Democratic conventions. Both were unworthy spectacles which might have been invented by a Fascist satirist to illustrate the degradation of democracy. There was more enthusiasm at the Democratic convention; but, if possible, there was more vulgarity. . . .
> The delegates even showed signs of being ashamed of their own immoderate antics. They wondered whether the

way to run a great political party is to get drunk and ride
donkeys into hotel lobbies, or to scream hideously for half
an hour because the chairman has just announced (what
everyone has known for a month) that Senator Joe Robinson
(or Senator Steiwer) is about to make a speech. The delegates knew there was something deeply wrong. They knew
they ought to be doing serious work. Yet there was no serious
work to do, so they took refuge in idiocy.

The delegates should not be blamed for the raucous farce.
They were the usual collection of local party workers, of
postmasters and ex-postmasters, with a scattering of more
disinterested citizens. Had they been asked to help make
anything in keeping with the high-flown language that was
being used by the speakers, they would have tried to respond.
But the position of the average delegate at a national convention has neither dignity nor sense. . . .

. . . The lesson of the 1936 conventions is that the professional politician must devise some new machinery for
doing the necessary work of organization. . . . The time has
come when the national convention as now conducted breeds
a vicious cynicism both in the participants and in the be-
holders. Such a mood is a threat to the democratic system.
For the wages of cynicism is death.[1]

Here is a political problem to challenge the inventiveness
of every student of contemporary politics. The existing
nominating-convention system is not an integral part of the
written Constitution: it cannot be regarded as sacrosanct;
it is merely an interesting survival of an earlier day. In the
past, Americans created new methods of self-government
whenever the old methods obviously worked badly. The
methods for selecting the President have evolved from a
continuous quest for improved measures of democratic
control.

The system of nominating conventions was invented by
Andrew Jackson to replace the undemocratic system of

---

[1] Agar, Herbert, *Pursuit of Happiness*, p. 129.

selection by caucus under which earlier Presidents had been chosen. "After a long struggle," Louise Overacker writes, "King Caucus was dethroned in the national field and representative assemblages supplanted legislative caucuses everywhere. The 'plain people' had triumphed over the 'aristocracy.' Jacksonian democracy was triumphant." Yet almost from the date of the first nominating convention, the new system began to develop characteristics as undesirable as those it was designed to replace. In 1832, Jackson called the first convention to place the rubber stamp of approval on his decision to make Martin Van Buren's candidacy for Vice-President binding on the whole party machine. He called the second convention in 1835—eighteen months before the election—because he wished to maintain and consolidate his grip on the party. As Herbert Agar writes, "Jackson claimed that the delegates to this convention were fresh from the people, representing the considered opinions of the electorate. As a matter of fact, they were an outrageous collection of party hacks, representing nothing except the orders which the local machines had received from Washington."

Through the years, the convention system continued to reveal the impotence of public opinion to control the party machines and the political bosses. The proportion of party voters who voted for the convention delegates was never large. As the voting population increased with successive franchise extensions, the number of delegates transformed the convention into a mass meeting, and gave greater scope to the manipulative power of the insiders. The lack of power of the delegates, and the people whom they were supposed to represent, left a gap which was quickly filled by the active minority of politicians and officeholders who made their nominations almost in private session and later an-

nounced their decisions for a clamoring group of delegates
to ratify.

It was this system of remote popular control that became
the target of reformist attack at the turn of the century. In
the growing wave of reform that followed the Progressivism
of such leaders as Robert M. La Follette and Theodore
Roosevelt, the movement for direct presidential primaries
expressed a widespread desire to democratize the nominating process. In 1903, La Follette became the spearhead of
the assault on the party bosses. He urged that good government was swiftly vitiated by bad nominations:

> The life principle of representative government is that
> those chosen to govern shall faithfully represent the governed.
> To insure this the representative must be chosen by those
> whom he is to represent . . . to secure this every complica-
> tion of detail and method, in any system behind which such
> intruding power or authority might be concealed must be
> torn down and cast aside. The voter and the candidate for
> nomination who desires to represent the voter must be
> brought within reaching distance of each other and must
> stand face to face.[1]

Theodore Roosevelt expressed the same democratic
philosophy: "The right of popular government is incom-
plete," he wrote, "unless it includes the right of the voters
not merely to choose between candidates when they have
been nominated, but also the right to determine whom these
candidates shall be." [2] Behind this new drive for direct
primaries was the intention to give the people themselves
the right to make their voices heard in the nominations.
The advocates of direct primaries hoped that the aspiring
candidates would enter their names in the state primaries

---

[1] Quoted in Smith, C. W., *Public Opinion in a Democracy*, p. 382.
[2] Odegard, P., arid Helms, E. A., *American Politics*, p. 499.

where the mass of the voters would express their preferences, and thus guide the delegates at the convention.

Yet the evidence suggests that the presidential-primary system has failed to dislodge the political machines. Louise Overacker has studied the successive nominating contests in both parties since the introduction of the primary system.[1] In only three cases—in the nomination of James M. Cox in 1920, Alfred E. Smith in 1928, and of Franklin D. Roosevelt in 1932—did the Democratic-convention choice parallel the majorities secured in the primaries.

In 1916 and 1936, Wilson and Franklin D. Roosevelt were obviously marked for renomination, and their endorsement by the primaries had no significance. In 1912, Wilson received more primary votes than any of his opponents, but his vote was exceeded by the combined vote of Clark and Harmon, and more Clark than Wilson delegates were elected. In nominating John W. Davis in 1924, the convention ignored the primary verdict for McAdoo.

The record of the Republican conventions is even more disillusioning. In 1912, Theodore Roosevelt ran into the disparity between the theory and practice when he received 1,165,000 primary votes against 766,000 for President Taft and 327,000 for La Follette. But Taft controlled the organization, especially with the Southern delegates lined up in his favor, and therefore won the nomination. In 1920, the Republican leaders rejected Hiram Johnson with 900,000 primary votes, General Leonard Wood with 725,000 votes, Frank Lowden with 375,000, and Herbert Hoover with 350,000 in favor of Warren G. Harding, who had entered his name in only two primary states and obtained 150,000 votes, barely carrying his own state. Hoover lost most of the

[1] Overacker, Louise, in *The American Political Scene*, Ch. VII, ed. by E. B. Logan, 1938.

primaries in 1928, but obtained the nomination, while in
1932 his renomination was so obvious that the primaries did
not mean much. In 1916, Hughes did not enter the primaries. Only in 1924, with the nomination of Coolidge, did
the candidate favored in the Republican primaries receive
the nomination.

Of course the direct primaries have made an indirect
contribution to the final decisions of the conventions but
they have not yet achieved their primary purpose of ensuring democratic control over nominations as well as over
elections. Indeed, the goal toward which La Follette looked
—of bringing the voter and the candidate for nomination
face to face—is even more remote than it was in his day. In
1913, at the height of the campaign for the extension of the
presidential primary, its supporters declared that primaries
were destined to sweep the country like wildfire, and insisted that the new system had only to be tried to be copied
by every state in the Union. Yet the intervening years have
witnessed not an advance but a retreat.

At one time twenty-six states authorized preferential
primaries, but by 1940 the number had dropped to sixteen.
The primary system even in only sixteen states might still
provide a fairly good indication of public sentiment if the
potential nominees of both parties entered all the primaries.
But this seldom happens. Reluctant to face this test, the
candidates generally go into the primaries only when they
think they can make the best possible showing. As a result, only a small proportion of voters have an opportunity
to express their choice for the guidance of convention
delegates.

Moreover, even when primaries are held, the number of
voters who go to the polls is likely to be small. Statistics

compiled by Louise Overacker show that in 1916, the peak
year of presidential primaries, the vote cast in all states with
primaries was less than a third as large as the vote cast by
the same states in the general election. A similar ratio was
found in 1920 and 1924.

When we consider that thirty-two states have no presidential primaries, that the leading candidates do not generally enter more than a handful of the remaining sixteen
primaries, and that, even if they do, the vote is likely to be
small, it is little wonder that the convention system still
affords the machine leaders every opportunity for manipu-
lation and control.

With the introduction of the public-opinion polls, however, a new factor has appeared. It may even be that in the
future such systematic soundings of public opinion among
the rank and file of the nation's voters may perform the
service which the presidential primaries were designed to
do. The polls can help measure the political preferences of
ordinary voters not merely in a few states, as in the case of
the primaries, but throughout the entire country. Although
the primaries give the public a choice between only those
candidates who happen to enter the primary, the public-
opinion surveys record preferences on all candidates. No
longer need there be any doubt which candidates are the
popular choices. Months and months before convention
time, the polls begin to conduct surveys of political sentiment. Recurring tests at successive intervals indicate the
trend of sentiment, the emergence of new candidates, the
impact of events on candidate popularity. The surveys can
even indicate with a fair degree of accuracy *why* people
favor the candidates they do.

In 1936 there was never any doubt that Landon was the

popular choice of the Republican rank and file. The proof did not lie in the primaries. On the contrary, although Landon had won many of the primaries, he had only eighty-eight delegates pledged to him as a result of primary elections. His nation-wide popularity had demonstrated itself in the Institute's polls. As early as December, 1935, he took the lead with 33 per cent of the votes of those expressing a choice. The proportion rose steadily until by May 31, 1936—eleven days before the nomination—he was the choice of 55 per cent, as compared with 18 per cent for his nearest rival, Senator Borah. In this instance, the choice of the rank and file proved to be the choice of the convention, for Landon polled 986 votes on the first ballot and was unanimously nominated on the second. But that one instance is scarcely enough to alter the well-recognized fact that conventions do not always nominate the most popular man.

After 1936 the Institute's studies found Senator Arthur Vandenberg taking the lead as popular choice for 1940. He maintained this lead until November, 1938, when Thomas E. Dewey jumped into front rank, largely because of the strong race he ran for governor of New York. From 1939 onward the popular Republican trio has consisted of Dewey, Vandenberg, and Taft. The month-to-month measurement of their popularity up to convention time will give future students of politics the facts with which to compare the choices of the mass of party voters with the choices of the convention.

It goes without saying that the polls, by conducting these trial heats, are in no way attempting to predict which candidate stands most chance of being nominated by the party conventions. All the polls can do is to map the divisions of popular sentiment on the merits of rival candidates, and to describe how this sentiment changes with the march of events. It follows from this that measurements of popularity, or a statement of particular order among candidates, can in no way be taken as a final reading, since fluctuations may occur from week to week. Through the medium of frequent opinion studies, the polls can help to provide a better guide to the politicians in making their selections. They will show which groups support each candidate. They will tell leaders and party strategists which candidate is more likely to appeal to youth, which candidate is more likely to attract Southern voters, which candidate has the widest following among the working class. And it is equally important to remember that the polls will give information to the opposite party, which can adjust its plans accordingly.

No one can seriously predict that the country would have better Presidents if the nominating were done by the people. It has never been tried. Perhaps the people's choices would be no better than the choices of party leaders in smoke-filled rooms. The point is that the original purpose of the presidential primary was to give the people a voice in the nominations, and this aim is being better fulfilled today through the public-opinion surveys than by any other means. Perhaps a combination of sampling referendums and preferential primaries will in the long run result in a better method of selecting the best type of democratic leadership.

"The troubles of representative government," Walter Lippmann has written, "go back to the failure of self-governing people to translate their experience and their prejudice by inventing, creating, and organizing a machinery of knowledge."

Continuous polls can constitute a kind of public-intelligence service in the field of social groups and opinion, and will indicate in a measurable way tendencies which would otherwise be the subject of speculation and guesswork. In the light of this knowledge, existing institutions may be better able to perform the democratic purposes to which they are dedicated.

By focusing the attention of the mass of the people during the periods between elections on the fact that nominations and election *are* coming off, by drawing attention to the different candidates, and by stimulating discussion of possibilities and chances, the public-opinion polls are performing a valuable function in reminding the citizens of a democratic state that they have responsibility for their own leadership.

★

CHAPTER TWELVE

★

The Real Strength of Pressure Groups

ONE of the most sacred individual rights in a democracy is the right of petition. Alone, or in company with other individuals, a citizen of the United States may call upon his elected representatives to advocate particular courses of action. It is only when the petitions of one national group conflict with the desires of another group that an impasse arises and a need for conciliation and perhaps for compromise appears. But when aggressive minorities are on the march, how is the Congressman to decide where the truth— or where the greater truth—lies, especially when, as so often happens, the minority represents itself as the majority?

As Kenneth Crawford points out in *The Pressure Boys,* American legislative halls have long been the happy hunting grounds of the pressure groups. Another observer has singled out over twenty important group interests which are constantly represented on Capitol Hill.

The legislator obviously owes a duty to his home district to legislate in its best interest. But he also owes a duty to legislate in the best interests of the nation. How can he learn what the wishes of his constituents are, and whether they agree or disagree with the wishes of the nation at large?

The sampling referendum offers a gauge of strength for the claims and counterclaims which reach the American

144

legislator, whether he lives in the great echo chamber of Washington, D.C., or in his own state capital. Consider, for example, the course of two important "minority" movements in recent years—the demand for large-scale old-age pensions to be financed out of "transaction taxes," and the demand of new groups of American labor for a larger share of the national income.

The most famous of all the pension plans is the Townsend Plan, fathered by a retired California physician who was moved to action by the insecurity of elderly Americans in his own state. Details of the plan had varied from year to year, but in 1934, when it first emerged from the Golden West into the national spotlight, the plan proposed to give every person sixty years or over $200 a month. All the recipients had to do was to retire from active labor—if any—and to agree to spend the entire $200 in a month's time. The plan envisaged a transaction tax on every exchange involving money, a tax which was expected to accumulate $24,000,000,000 a year.

Critics of the plan urged that Townsendism would confiscate almost one half the national income for the immediate benefit of the sixty-year-olds, while leaving the average annual income for everyone else at about $210.

In the spring of 1935, Congress rejected the plan by an overwhelming vote. But the Townsendites were not easily silenced. They began to organize for political action. Townsend Clubs were formed all over the country, in every state and in most Congressional districts. They collected large sums of money through innumerable small contributions. They were determined to become the most powerful bloc of voters wedded to a single legislative proposal since the days of the Anti-Saloon League.

There was a real basis for their self-interest. Congress had not yet enacted the Social Security Act of 1935, and even when that Act was passed many aged persons found that the payments either did not apply to them or were pitifully small. But Townsendism combined the fervor of a religious revival with the assurance of an earthly heaven.

As the Townsend Clubs became increasingly vocal, promising to unseat Congressmen who opposed their measure, the legislators became increasingly concerned. The Clubs sent questionnaires to every member of Congress: "Will you vote for the Townsend Plan?" Thirty-nine hastily made promises of support. Some Congressmen who had first opposed the plan turned political somersaults. Others made hurried trips to Washington during the off season to offer the Townsendites their co-operation. "Congressmen shivered in their boots," wrote an observer, "fearful of the strength of this incorporated octopus in pursuit of the millennium."

The question was, would this fantastic movement sweep the country and force the hand of the national legislature? Townsend and his cohorts cried a vociferous "Yes." Speeches, placards, and politicians asserted that victory was imminent. "After 1936," they cried, "we will have our own President in the White House and full control over Congress."

The Institute decided to send interviewers through the country to test the strength of this movement, which so confidently claimed that "public opinion" was on its side. Of thousands of people in every walk of life, in every section of the country, these interviewers asked the question:

"Are you in favor of government old-age pensions for needy persons?" and further:

"How much do you think should be paid monthly to each person?" By sweeping majorities of 9 to 1, voters approved the principle of government old-age pensions. But to the Townsend Plan as a method of achieving this objective, most of the people were firmly opposed. Even in the hotbeds of Townsendism—Oregon, California, and Washington— the percentage of $200-a-month Townsendites was small. On the Pacific Coast, the intellectual and spiritual home of the movement, only 16 per cent voted for this sum, and in the country as a whole only 3.8 per cent named the $200 figure.

Thus the people of the country with virtual unanimity rejected the Townsend proposals as they stood at that time. This revelation of Dr. Townsend's true strength in the country, made possible by careful polling, was followed by a Congressional investigation and a conservative revision of their claims by the Townsendites. Did the failure of this enticing scheme mean that the people did not want old-age pensions? By no means; indeed, the voters favored the principle of old-age pensions by a 9-to-1 majority. What amounts, then, did they think would be adequate?

When asked what sum they favored as a monthly pension for the aged, the largest single number of voters suggested $30 for the individual and $50 for husband and wife, amounts that came much closer to the administration's social-security legislation than they did to the Townsend Plan's $200 a month. An interesting side light indicated that the voters preferred the retirement age of sixty years advanced in the Townsend Plan to the administration's limit of sixty-five.

Thus the polls showed the strength and direction of pension sentiment. They illustrated how widely the claims of a pressure group might diverge from the real support its program commanded throughout the country. One can see, too, how polls might indicate which aspects of particular proposals enjoyed public support and which did not. It was clear that the people favored government old-age pensions as well as the retirement age suggested in the Townsend Plan, but it was equally clear that they disagreed with the amounts.

Repeated studies of public attitudes on the question of old-age pensions have sketched the same general picture. As successive "new" schemes have emerged, notably the "ham-and-eggs" plan which disturbed the Californian horizon, the Institute has continually tested public sentiment toward them. Whether the idea of the moment has called for "Two Hundred Dollars a Month at Sixty," or "Thirty Dollars a Week at Fifty," the polls have tried to get an accurate picture of popular approval or disapproval. And in each case the average American has favored a much more moderate plan than the propaganda would indicate. Recent surveys show that the figure the public prefers for old-age-pension plans averages about $40 a month for single persons and $65 a month for married couples. The problem of the old and needy has been widely discussed. Most people acknowledge the responsibility of a liberal society to care of the aged. But at the same time, public opinion has consistently seen through the claims made by some pressure groups, and has consistently advocated workable methods of operation.

When minorities become deafened by the sound of their own voices, the polls focus attention on the popular attitudes toward means and ends. The mass of voters may express themselves in different language, depending on their education and their habitual ways of thought. But where the question can be understood, where it touches familiar symbols in the individual's thinking, there is frequently no difference in the basic intellectual process involved, whether the respondent be a stockbroker or a tenant farmer. For instance, a New England interviewer who was trying to find out how people in different parts of the country were reacting to the Californian "ham-and-eggs" pension plan of "Thirty Dollars Every Thursday" turned in two ballots, one from a charwoman and one from a professor of economics. The professor replied at length on the plan's economic implications and concluded that it was "absolutely unsound." But his basic conclusion did not differ much from the old lady's who answered: "How I'd love to have thirty dollars every Thursday, just to spend as I wanted to . . . but I don't think it could ever be done in this world. If they gave that to me and everybody like me, a lot of other people would be doing without. I'm for raising the present pensions just a little. Then maybe it'd be righter for everybody."

It is better for Congress to measure the claims of strident minorities than to rely exclusively on the claims themselves. One other example will show how necessary it is to extend this knowledge.

The drive of John L. Lewis and the C.I.O. for the organization of workers in the mass-productions industries, bringing with it the sit-down strikes of 1937 and the continuing split between the C.I.O. and the American Federation of Labor, posed new questions to Congress and to American public opinion.

Did the American public approve of labor unions? The Wagner Act of 1935 had definitely recognized labor's right to organize into unions, but did the public support this guarantee or not?

Would the public accept the sit-down strike as a legitimate new weapon in labor's arsenal?

How far would the public support labor's claims to a greater influence in national affairs?

Popular attention was focused on a dramatic series of sit-down strikes. Labor found that it could halt production more effectively by sitting down than it had previously done by walking out and forming picket lines. The automobile industry, with its assembly lines and its delicate machinery, was specially vulnerable. As more than one union man told Institute interviewers: "They can't use scabs while we're *in* there!"

The Institute's surveys quickly indicated the lines the public's reaction had taken. An overwhelming majority of the voters—7 to 3—favored labor unions, but many voters declared they had become less sympathetic since the outbreak of the sit-downs. Opposition was especially strong among the upper- and middle-income groups and throughout the farm population generally. The majority of voters called for government regulation of strikes and a system of Federal mediation.

Not only did a majority oppose sit-down strikes; there was even a majority willing to authorize the use of force against the sit-downers. The Institute asked: "Do you think that state and local authorities should use force in removing sit-down strikers?" The wording was intentionally severe, because the Institute wanted to measure how deeply public opinion had been challenged by the new strike method. Sixty-five per cent of the voters replied that they would approve the use of force if necessary, with middle-class voters and farmers leading the opposition. The greatest sympathy for the sit-down principle came from the lower-income groups of the large cities. The voting followed by only a few days the forcible eviction of sit-down strikers from the big Hershey chocolate factories in the middle of

Pennsylvania, and it showed clearly that the Hershey incident might have been duplicated in many parts of the United States.

These soundings were warning signals to labor, and there is evidence that responsible labor leaders made sharp attempts to curb the use of the sit-down themselves. William Green of the A.F. of L. blasted the technique publicly and declared that public opinion would not support it. Spokesmen for John L. Lewis reported that the C.I.O. leader was much concerned, and Lewis himself was careful never to endorse the sit-down method.

Here is a chart of the public's reaction to this new weapon and to labor's militant campaign in 1937-38:

	Lower Group	Middle and Upper Groups
In Favor of Labor Unions	81%	74%
Favor Government Regulation of Labor Unions	67	71
Favor Incorporation of Unions	83	87
Favor Making Sit-Downs Illegal	58	72
Favor Using Force to Remove Sit-Down Strikers	51	71
Favor Calling Out Militia When Strike Trouble Threatens	51	60

In the years immediately ahead American democracy will need to accommodate many conflicting group and sectional interests to the total interests of the nation. This can be done, perhaps, if legislators and citizens know and recognize the desires of the American people and the desires of important minority groups. What may be fatal to national understanding, and to the legitimate needs of the special minorities themselves, is a failure to recognize what the public will approve and what it will not approve.

In February, 1940, *The New Republic,* spokesman for
liberal and progressive causes for a quarter of a century,
editorialized on the lag—even in the minds of the most
intelligent leaders of labor—which separates judgment and
reality: "In general," *The New Republic* editor wrote,
"I suspect that Mr. Lewis's sources of information as to
what is going on in this country are not so good. I question
whether he realizes how bitter, even after all this time, is the
anti-union feeling of important elements in the community."

If the new measurements of public opinion had no other
usefulness, their possible use as barometers of public tolerance for the marching minorities would justify the further
work of students and research men.

★

★

CHAPTER THIRTEEN

When Elections Fail

"Nothing is so likely to interfere with fundamental American rights," said Supreme Court Justice Frank Murphy, "as frauds in the handling of votes. At any time, the subject is of vital import for the nation, but at this moment, in view of world affairs affecting the democracies, it is essential that any practices tending to weaken the American system be vigorously uprooted." [1]

Elections fail when a powerful political machine obtains a strangle hold on the voting machinery through which the will of the people is expressed. When votes can be bought and sold, the election result does not represent a free expression of public opinion, but merely the work of a small group of active politicians who "interpret" the rules under which political decision can take place. Occasionally this "interpretation" includes stealing ballot boxes in wards where the vote is assumed to be unfavorable to the machine.

Such conditions destroy people's faith not only in elections, but in the idea of democratic decision itself. When voters cease to feel that they can freely and honestly choose their own leaders, when the result of elections becomes a foregone conclusion, democracy moves slowly but relentlessly toward dictatorship. In cases where corruption affects

---

[1] Kane, Harnett V., "The Kingdom of the Kingfish," *New Orleans Item-Tribune,* December 10, 1939.

the official election returns and subverts their usefulness as expressions of public opinion, the polls provide an unofficial way of going beyond the politicians to the people. By interviewing the voters themselves and asking them how they feel about the conduct of elections in their own community, such direct studies of public opinion may even provide a better index of the true state of opinion than the results of an election where the voters feel that dishonesty and corruption are to be expected. Such conditions demand exposure, as the first step to removing them.

In recent times, the United States District Attorney's department has been digging hard to find out the basis for the widespread belief that elections held in the state of Louisiana have been corrupt and dishonest. With O. John Rogge as spearhead of the campaign, the department has been busy investigating the charges of past election frauds and political corruption in that state. Even before the sudden death of Huey P. Long, critics described Louisiana politics as a major blot on the nation's reputation for open and honest elections. Raymond Daniell has drawn a colorful picture of the desperate state of some sections of Louisiana public opinion. "Long's death," he wrote, "left a state on the verge of civil war. The Square Deal Association and other bands of enemies were drilling with wooden guns, against the day when they would rise up and, with real firearms and ammunition to be supplied from some mysterious source, seize the capital and drive him and his henchmen into political exile. Organizations of minute men met secretly in the rural parishes, and, in the cities, men gathered in hotels and private homes to plot the overthrow of the dictator. Talk of assassination was a common thing wherever the enemies of the Kingfish got together. The atmosphere was like that of a banana republic on the brink of revolution." [1] After Huey's death, his "heirs" continued to hold sway, acting in accordance with the belief that it was "the duty of Long's followers to complete his programs and perpetuate themselves in office."

Many months before the primary election of January 17, 1940, the discontent that had been smoldering against the Long machine broke out in the form of opposition to the candidacy of Earl Long, recent successor to the late Huey's throne. Four candidates arose to challenge the old order: Attorney Sam Jones, an Independent candidate with business backing; James Noe, former Huey Long supporter but opponent of the Earl Long faction; Vincent K. Moseley, a Harvard law graduate, and James H. Morrison.

In the course of a violent campaign, candidates Noe and Morrison charged the Earl Long machine with corruption and dishonesty in previous elections. Noe carried his attack to the highest state tribunal and finally won a nine-month fight during which he was forced to go to the Supreme Court of Louisiana to get permission to photograph the parish books in the district of Orleans, which, he claimed, "revealed whole pages of forged names," with many different voters listed in the same handwriting.[2] Candidate Morrison added his voice to "challenge this blockade of corruption," demanded a vote "for democracy and honesty in government," and urged that "there must be no intimidation at the polls and there must be no stealing of the ballot boxes." [3] In the course of this excitement, a citizens' Committee Against Dummy Candidates and For Honest Elections was formed. The slogans of the campaign revolved

---

[1] Daniell, Raymond, "Huey's Heirs," *The Saturday Evening Post*, July, 1939.

[2] *New Orleans Item-Tribune*, December 13, 1939.

[3] *Times-Picayune*, December 13, 1939.

around charges and countercharges concerning the honesty of the rival forces and the elections in Louisiana.

In the midst of this electoral jamboree, the Institute decided to try to find out what Louisiana voters themselves thought about the state of their democracy. In December, 1939, resident interviewers, augmented by picked crews of field investigators, saw people in parishes from the delta of the Mississippi to the upcountry parishes along the Arkansas line. The investigation covered 31 of the state's 64 parishes and interviewers talked to more than 2500 citizens in all walks of life. The attempt was made to try to find out *what the people themselves thought* about Louisiana elections and politics, by asking such questions as:

1. Do you think elections in Louisiana in recent years have been honestly conducted?	*Honest*	25%
	Dishonest	60
	No Opinion	15
2. Do you think that if the present state administration is returned to office next year it will "clean house" in the state government?	*Clean House*	30%
	Not Clean House	51
	No Opinion	19
3. Do you think the state courts of Louisiana are honest?	*Honest*	36%
	Dishonest	40
	No Opinion	24

In all its years of polling experience the Institute had never encountered such an amazing political situation in any other state. Faced with an impending state election, a majority of voters interviewed declared their belief that state elections in recent years had not been honestly conducted, fully half the voters had no faith that the Earl Long regime would "clean house" if returned to power, and a substantial group felt that the state courts of Louisiana were dishonest!

Analysis revealed that the greatest differences were found in the opinions of the various income levels:

1. Elections Honestly Conducted?

	Yes	No	No Opinion
Upper Group	22%	65%	13%
Middle Group	22	62	16
Lower Group	31	54	15

2. Administration Clean House?

	Yes	No	No Opinion
Upper Group	20%	64%	16%
Middle Group	27	54	19
Lower Group	37	41	22

3. State Courts Honest?

	Yes	No	No Opinion
Upper Group	30%	52%	18%
Middle Group	33	44	23
Lower Group	43	31	26

Thus the Institute's analysis by income groups showed wide degrees of variation in the opinions of people in different income groups. The least criticism of the Long regime came from voters in the lowest-income levels, while sharpest criticism came from the business groups and the middle- and upper-income groups. The polls thus indicated the stratifications in the Louisiana voting public and distinguished the social groups who supported the administration from those who were its strong opponents.

Paradoxically enough, although many voters polled in Louisiana were critical of the administration and tactics of Earl Long, a majority continued to revere the memory of the famed Kingfish. During the investigation, the question was asked:

"Taking everything into consideration, do you think

that Huey P. Long was a bad or a good influence in Louisiana?"

The results were:

Good Influence	55%
Bad Influence	22
Both Good and Bad	14
No Opinion	9

If such facts about public opinion were of striking interest, the problems which faced the interviewers in Louisiana were equally significant. In the early days, many people suspected the opinion surveys and feared to express their views. But with the growing acceptance of opinion polls, cases of fear and unwillingness to co-operate became rare, except in Louisiana where interviewers ran into almost as much "resistance" as they might face in a dictatorship. People were guarded in their replies for fear of reprisals and coercion. Time and again, both in New Orleans and in upstate Louisiana, investigators found doors narrowed to slits or slammed shut as soon as the interviewer disclosed his purpose. Fear of expressing an opinion on state politics was more common in the poorer districts, and men proved to be even more apprehensive than women, although some women, in the absence of their husbands, said: "My husband has told me not to talk to anybody about state politics." In the city of New Orleans an average of one person in every five (20 per cent) indicated that he was afraid to talk for fear of political reprisals or for other reasons, even though voters were given every assurance as to the confidential character of the interview. The proportion of people who "wouldn't talk" in the outstate parishes, however, was much smaller.

A typical statement came from a New Orleans woman living in a poor side street:

Huey Long was the bestest man we ever had, but don't you go writing any of this down. My husband will kill me if ever I told anything. There was a man here the other day—an' bigger than you—and he told my husband plenty. We're all for Long on this street—every one of us—so don't go askin' me any more.

More than once investigators were threatened with shotguns or held for the local sheriff. A local investigator reported as follows:

I saw a farm off the road a piece. I got out of the car and approached the door. When I reached the porch stairs the front door flew open, and a tall man strode out cocking a double-barreled shotgun: "I don't know what you want," he said, "but I'll give you just ten seconds to get back through that there gate."

To the introductory question in which voters were asked whether they thought the influence of Huey Long in Louisiana had been good or bad, one man answered:

Good. Huey was a fine man. He did more for us poor folks in a day than all the others did in all the years. What did they say in them other houses?

Told that some said good, some bad, he exploded:

Why those cheatin'— They never any of 'em had a job exceptin' for Huey Long and his brother. I wish you'd show me the ones that says he was a bad influence! I'll report them tomorrow and they'll sure lose their jobs fast.

You [indicating the interviewer] are probably a Long man, and you'll probably report 'em before I can, but I sure wish you'd let me do it.

The Institute thus discovered that most people were skeptical about the honesty of past Louisiana elections, and that many Louisiana voters were afraid to talk, fearing the possibility of political reprisals.

In such a situation, it was realized that a pre-election prediction would be most difficult. Such polls can be accurate, as we have seen, only where the people vote without coercion or special inducement, and where full confidence exists that the ordinary electoral process of counting noses will be fairly conducted. The opinion survey of the attitudes toward candidates in the Louisiana Democratic primary, then, did not constitute a reliable basis for a forecast, it merely indicated the general attitudes toward the various candidates as of the month of December.

This survey found Long and Jones running neck and neck in the choice of state voters, with the other candidates lagging behind. Here are the Institute's figures:

Long	34%
Jones	34
Noe	20
Morrison	10
Moseley	2

Such estimates suggested that while the figures could in no sense be taken to represent a prediction, there was a chance that Earl Long might fail to secure the needed majority of the popular vote over all other candidates to avoid a run-off election. The *New Orleans Item-Tribune*, of December 13, made the point clearly: "We no more claim that the Gallup poll is going to be correct," the editorial ran, "than that our postal poll of city precincts is going to materialize in the ballot boxes. There are so many factors in the Louisiana election that considerable changes can take place between now and election day."

If the polls and newspaper editors were cautious about predicting the election result, the candidates themselves suffered from no such shyness. As in all elections, the "elation complex" functioned in the sweeping predictions made by each candidate. All the leading political rivals delivered messages of conquest and victory. From Earl Long's headquarters came the announcement:

> The Long strength is growing by leaps and bounds all over the state. The wave of acclaim for the Long ticket is sweeping through Louisiana with the fierce intensity of a prairie fire, from the swamps and bayous of the Gulf to the red clay hills along the Arkansas line.[1]

This description of public opinion was intended to throw the rival camps into consternation:

> With the election a little more than six weeks off and the Earl Long Landslide growing by leaps and bounds from day to day, the three opposition camps become frantic as they see the handwriting on the wall.

But Earl Long was not the only candidate who saw his victory as imminent. Both James Noe and Sam Jones had equal confidence in being elected. On December 17, in a speech at Plaquemine, Noe declared: "We are moving into the lead every day of the race," while during the famous camera study of the Orleans register, he said:

> Photographing the books means an honest election, and that means that I will be high in New Orleans.[2]

But according to the *New Orleans Item-Tribune*, Jones also claimed victory in New Orleans:

> From Jones himself came the statement that Governor Long is slipping so fast in New Orleans, that I am perfectly confident of carrying the city.[3]

The Institute's survey was not warmly received by the Long supporters. The official Long newspaper, *The Amer-*

---

[1] *The American Progress*, December 1, 1939.

[2] *Times-Picayune*, December 13, 1939.

[3] December 10, 1939.

ican Progress, was eloquent in its condemnation of the poll: [1]

Three months ago a half dozen post-graduate "Social Science Workers" from Princeton University, augmented by seven or eight East Side New Yorkers who had never in their lives seen a possum, tasted a sweet potato or chewed a plug of tobacco, arrived in New Orleans to conduct a so-called "survey of public opinion."

After taking a few sight-seeing trips, getting some fancy grub at the famous restaurants in New Orleans, looking at some swamps and sending picture post-cards back home, they then wrote some mystic figures in their little black books and hurried back to their boss, a low-ceiling guy with bifocal glasses who sits enthroned way up there in Princeton, New Jersey, like the Wizard of Oz and peers owlishly at figures all day long until he looks like a left-handed figure "4".

And out of this hocus-pocus of numbers and dope sheets and form charts, lo and behold, if up didn't jump the Gallup Poll. . . . Of all the jackassery we have ever seen this bull-shooting windbag Gallup Poll takes the first prize. . . . In Louisiana there are more than 600,000 voters with the banner registration of this year and the free poll taxes. Now let's see what per cent of the voters in Louisiana the Gallup wizards "interviewed". 2500 out of 600,000 *represents less than one-half of one per cent.* Working it out to decimal places it reveals that the Gallup people only claim to have "interviewed" .00416 per cent, *or only about four people in every thousand.*

Here is this man Gallup, who calls himself an "Institute," and gives the front elevation of "Doctor" to his name, way up there in New Jersey, having the effrontery to try and say with authority what the people of Louisiana are going to do and basing his prognostication on what 1 out of 250 people are reported to have told him. We have heard recently of the Gallup investigation. A friend up in Bienville Parish wrote us that he was visited by a smart aleck Harlem nigger wearing a double-breasted suit and talking with a Harvard "a",

[1] December 29, 1939.

who wanted to find out how people were going to vote. Our friends thought the nigger was a Sam Jones man, but now it seems he must have been a Gallup wizard.

Brother Gallup is wasting his time. What he should do is to go over to Europe and settle the war. He could probably poll some Siberian wastes, a few towns on the Rhone River and catch a fish in Scapa Flow, climb the Eiffel Tower and presto the war would be over. What a man!

Such a colorful description was obviously less concerned with evaluating the uses or abuses of opinion polls than with condemning a specific result which appeared to contradict the Long party's election claims.

In the primary election itself, although Long got a higher proportion of the Louisiana vote than the Institute's survey indicated, he failed to get the absolute majority of the popular vote necessary to avoid a run-off election. Here is a comparison of the poll estimates and the results of both the primary election held in January and the run-off election between Jones and Long held a month later:

FIRST PRIMARY: January 17, 1940

	Institute: December Survey	Election Result	Percentage Deviation
	City		
Jones	27%	25%	+2%
Long	44	50	—6
Noe	21	19	+2
Morrison	6	5	+1
Moseley	2	1	+1
	Country		
Jones	37	28	+9
Long	29	38	—9
Noe	20	22	—2
Morrison	12	10	+2
Moseley	2	2	0

City and Country

Jones	34	28	+6
Long	34	41	—7
Noe	20	21	—1
Morrison	10	9	+1
Moseley	2	1	+1

SECOND PRIMARY: February 20, 1940

City

Jones	47	45	+2
Long	53	55	—2

Country

Jones	62	54	+8
Long	38	46	—8

City and Country

Jones	58	52	+6
Long	42	48	—6

Thus, on February 20, 1940, the voters of Louisiana made their choice for Sam Houston Jones, and repudiated what one writer called "the continuation of a Louisiana hay-ride through the Kingdom of the Kingfish's apprentice."

Since the Louisiana elections, strong charges have been made that votes were stolen by the tens of thousands in both the first and second primaries. Sam Jones, James Noe, and other interested persons have declared that theft took place in wholesale fashion both in New Orleans and in the country districts. O. John Rogge, investigating for the United States District Attorney's office, declared that in the first count "the investigations have disclosed a number of irregularities and several possible violations of the mail fraud statute of the federal criminal code. The postoffice inspectors have received evidence that fraudulent ballots were placed in the boxes of the second precinct of the

Ninth ward of Plaquemines parish and in the first precinct
of the Fifth ward of New Orleans." [1]

In the second primary, Federal officials received similar
evidence. In addition, the government charged three men—
a city policeman and two minor Long officials—with violat-
ing the Federal civil-liberty statute by beating a Jones
photographer who was attempting to photograph an al-
leged scheme to spy on those marking their ballots, and
then signal to officials inside to spoil Jones ballots.

The successful candidate, Sam Jones, even charged that
he actually won the city of New Orleans, but that 25,000
to 50,000 votes were, in his opinion, stolen from him. Some
Jones men have placed the figure even higher.

Whether or not corruption was actually at work in the
Louisiana elections, the Institute's survey of the voters' attitude toward past elections, and of their preferences in
the 1940 primary, revealed political conditions which were
badly in need of ventilation. In the first place, the survey
illustrates concretely how easily biasing factors may operate in certain elections to warp the true expression of public opinion. When a powerful machine holds the reins of
office, a poll of public opinion, based on a carefully chosen
cross section of the voting public, may prove more representative than the election itself. The Institute obviously had
no basis for checking the validity or honesty of past election results. This was in no sense the purpose of the survey.
What the survey tried to find out was whether or not the
people of Louisiana themselves thought that past elections
had been honestly conducted. The discovery that large
sections of Louisiana voters had apparently lost faith in
the old administration and in the possibility of registering

---

[1] *New Orleans Item-Tribune,* February 25, 1940.

a true verdict so long as the old machine remained in power pointed to serious defects in the working of the democratic process in that state. The widespread fear of expressing an opinion on political questions reflected the suspicion that the interviewers were in reality checking up on the machine or its opponents. The violent reaction of the administration newspapers to the conduct of an impartial opinion study gave further indication of the fear of a free expression of public opinion.

Politics has two fundamental aspects: it deals with political power and with *means*, just as it deals with political ideals and with *ends*. Sometimes the ends themselves are forgotten or become merely the private objectives of those in power. In such circumstances ordinary processes of democratic decision may fail to represent the will of the people. The polls can help to indicate where the pulse of democracy is faint and uncertain, and, by so doing, point to the need for applying restoratives which will strengthen that pulse.

★

★

CHAPTER FOURTEEN

Thirty Dollars a Week

THE average person in any community cannot fail to notice how sharply different levels of income and comfort cut
across the American social scene. He is aware of the plight
of families on relief, of the middle-class families struggling
to make ends meet, and of the people who are well to do
and economically secure. Through the movies and the
daily newspapers he comes to know about the Joads and
café society. How does he react to the economic and social
differences he sees about him? Is America becoming "class-
conscious," as the proletarian writers of the last few dec-
ades have confidently predicted? What does the ordinary
citizen think "the American standard of living" should be?

As America enters a strange new decade, public-opinion
research already provides some tentative answers to these
questions. The subject will figure conspicuously in future
public-opinion studies—studies which will have weather-
vane significance for the kind of country America is to be.
Let us look at the present indicators.

As far as the economic reality is concerned, the picture is clear. Even in the boom of 1929, only about 6 million families had incomes of $3000 a year or more; the
great majority earned far less. Eighteen million families—
more than half the population of the United States—earned
less than $1500. Then came the cataclysm, and within

two or three years the national income of the United States had dwindled to almost half what it had been in 1929, dragging living standards downward all along the line. Especially hard hit were the 18 million families who had been getting along on less than $1500 a year. The shrinkage in family income provided little chance to build even a small reserve against such hazards as unemployment, old age, and sickness.

The economic protest of these sectors of the population was translated into political terms in 1932. In the presidential election of that year, American voters cast 23,-000,000 ballots for Franklin D. Roosevelt. It just equaled the total Democratic vote cast for Al Smith in 1928 together with the total Democratic vote obtained by John W. Davis in 1924. It was the largest vote any presidential candidate had ever polled, and it announced the beginning of political action among the millions of American families with small incomes. Even in 1937 the underlying problem of insecurity among the lower economic levels still existed. Standing in the Washington rain to deliver his Second Inaugural, on January 20, 1937, President Roosevelt declared that the need to solve it was the greatest challenge to American democracy. "In this nation," he said, "I see tens of millions of its citizens—a substantial part of the whole population—who at this very moment are denied the greater part of what the very lowest standards today call the necessities of life. I see," he summarized, "one third of a nation ill-housed, ill-clad, and ill-nourished."

Many Americans are concerned over the same picture which the President painted. But despite the inequalities of life at different levels of the economic pyramid, there is little evidence that the people themselves are dividing into self-conscious class blocs. If there are problems to solve, the dominant attitude is still that they will be solved not through the impact of hostile classes, but through unified national effort. The historian Charles A. Beard placed his finger on the central reason for this when he wrote of the "subjective consciousness" of the American people, a consciousness not solely of immediate economic surroundings such as unemployment and scanty diet, but also of common membership in a "middle class" which has a future as well as a past. The extent of this consciousness of belonging to the middle class—culturally and socially—was clearly indicated in an Institute survey conducted in 1939.

"To what social class in this country do you think you belong," voters were asked, "the middle class, the upper, or the lower?" It made little difference whether the voter was a Democrat or a Republican, whether he lived in a city or in the country, whether he worked in a factory or owned the factory himself. In all cases, nearly nine Americans in ten said they viewed themselves as members of the middle class:

Upper Class	6%
Middle Class	88
Lower Class	6

With the sense of belonging to the middle class goes a whole pattern of thought. The average American believes in most of the traditional accompaniments of middle-class life. He believes in the value of education. If he could have more of it, he would like to have more training in business subjects and English. He believes in "opportunity"—although not quite as firmly as he once did—and he believes in property and in owning some himself if he can manage it.

Side by side with his subjective belief in a middle-class

status, however, the average American has a sharp realization that his life is not secure. The facts here were revealed in another 1939 survey in which the Institute asked: "If you lost your present job (or business) and could not find another, how long do you think you could hold out before you would have to apply for relief?" The survey found seventeen persons in every hundred *already* on relief or on one of the Federal government's work projects. Nineteen out of a hundred said they could hold out one month or less, sixteen could hold out one to six months, thirteen could hold out six months to three years, and thirty-five thought they could hold out three years or more. *If the groups who say they could hold out for six months or less are added to those persons now on relief, the total includes a majority of the people of the entire country.*

The study showed that, although skilled and unskilled laborers suffer from the greatest insecurity, many members of the white-collar classes—clerks, office workers, and people in the service trades—fear the future too. Indeed, nearly a quarter of these people told interviewers they would exhaust their reserves within a month's time.

When the same poll asked to what *income group* people felt they belonged, nearly a third said "the lower class":

Upper-Income Group	1%
Upper Middle	6
Middle	41
Lower Middle	21
Lower	31

It is not strange, then, that American elections have seen a noticeable class factor at work ever since the early 'thirties. Millions of lower- and middle-income voters crossed over to the Democratic party in 1932 and have remained there since. During this period, the Republican party has had its center of gravity in the upper-income levels, while the Democratic center of gravity has been among the "lower third" and voters on relief.

Simple proof of this growing relationship between economic insecurity and the political alignments of recent years can be found in the survey breakdowns of this insecurity question asked in 1939:

	For Roosevelt	Against Roosevelt
Persons now on relief	81%	19%
Those who could hold out one month or less	61	39
One month to six months	58	42
Six months to three years	56	44
Three years or more	55	45

The key to why people now vote Democratic or Republican lies in the economic stratification of the American people. At the extremes of the economic scale, political positions are coherent and, to a large extent, predictable. But between the extremes lies the middle-income group which is likely to become an increasingly decisive factor in future elections.

All through the first and second administrations of President Roosevelt the Institute has found this middle group holding the balance of power—on issues as well as in elections. What income characterizes this group? If you put that question at random to a few well-to-do brokers and bankers they are likely to tell you, "About $5000 a year" —just as Mr. Morgan identified the middle class, before a Senate committee, as those families which could afford to have a servant. *But actually the middle-income group in the United States, numbering nearly one half of the whole voting population, averages between $1000 and $2000 a year per family.*

John Jones is a typical member of this group. He lives in a small Eastern city. He works for a hardware store. He has a wife and two children. He earns $30 a week. Nearly every dollar he earns goes for immediate necessities such as rent, food, clothing, and carfare. Yet, whether he knows it or not, he is a "typical" member of the middle-income group, and on his vote the course of American political life probably depends.

What is an adequate standard of living for the average American family? The Great Depression first focused attention on this vital question, and provoked response from many economists, experts, and welfare associations. A few years ago the government considered that the average family of four required at least $2500 a year for continued subsistence. Certain New Deal planners like Mordecai Ezekiel set an objective of $2400 or $2500 for a family of this size. William Green, of the American Federation of Labor, has named a goal of $3600 for the skilled workman and his dependents.

The Institute therefore felt it would be valuable to let the people express themselves on the question of income standards, and to add the view of the general public to the estimates of the theorists and social planners.

Five hundred interviewers covered voters in every state and every income group in the country and found almost all persons interviewed eager to express their own ideas. People in all walks of life were asked:

"What is the smallest weekly amount a family of four must have to live decently?"

And:

"How much income a year do you think the average family of four needs for health and comfort?"

No sums were suggested. The voters wrote in whatever
sums they chose. Their aggregate answers to the first question established for the first time a nation-wide consensus
on what the minimum standard of "decency" should be.
The sum averaged $30 a week—approximately $1560 a year
for the typical family of four—among all those interviewed.

Professional workers, businessmen, and skilled laborers
named a higher figure for decency than other groups.
Farmers, who frequently enjoy a noncash income in farm
produce and other things, named a lower figure. Similarly,
city dwellers named a higher amount than residents in
small towns and rural districts.

Typical persons living in the "ill-housed, ill-clad, and
ill-nourished" lower third gave $23 as the weekly sum
needed, or approximately $1200 a year.

Here are median amounts named by important population groups throughout the United States:

In the Opinion of:	Median Weekly Amount for Decency (In Dollars)	Same on Yearly Basis (In Dollars)
Profession and white-collar workers	35	1820
Merchants and businessmen	35	1820
Skilled laborers	35	1820
Farmers	25	1300
"Lower third"	23	1196
U. S. average (median)	30	1560

What would public opinion's idea of the "decency"
standard of $30 a week mean? Undoubtedly it would con-
tinue to mean a very modest standard of living. The typical family spends about 33 cents out of every dollar for
food today, and a $30-a-week income allows about $10 a
week to feed four persons. The next largest amount goes

for the home, including rent, light, heating, and furniture. The family with $30 a week has about $9 a week to spend on its home. This leaves 10 or 12 cents out of every dollar for clothing and 10 or 12 cents for transportation. When these slices have been taken out, a family with a $30 income has between $4.50 and $6 for everything else—for medicine and doctor's bills, for books and education, for entertainment and insurance and savings. When the second question was asked to find out what voters thought would be necessary for a "health-and-comfort" standard, the median figure set was $38 a week, or $1950 a year. According to the surveys, almost two thirds of all American families in 1937 were living well below the health-and-comfort standard set by public opinion. The difference between the two standards in real terms would be a difference of quality in food, perhaps a bit more for rent and for comforts, labor-saving devices, and recreation.

Across the United States there is, of course, the widest variation in cost of living. It is not surprising, therefore, to find that voters in the Institute's income-standard survey tended to set somewhat different money standards depending on where they lived.

In the South, public opinion set a $20 median as the decency standard, but the paradox is explained by the fact that the South includes millions of Negroes living at depressed standards who expressed their delight at the thought of getting $12 or $15 a week. When the Institute's investigators talked with Negro men and women, many of them replied that they could "get along" on four or five dollars. The average sum these Southern Negroes named was only $12, which is far below the minimum standards set by both public opinion and income economists. With Negroes ex-

cluded, the average income wanted by white Southern
families was $25 a week.

The farm states of the Middle West asked less than the
figure of the national average, while the Pacific Coast states
and the industrial states of the Middle Atlantic area asked
more. States in the Great Lakes area (East Central) and
those in the Rocky Mountain section voted for $30.

The following table shows how much money the voters
of the different sections considered necessary (1) for minimum decency, and (2) for health and comfort:

Sections	Decency Standard (Per week)	Health-and-Comfort Standard (Per week)
New England states	$30	$39
Middle Atlantic states	35	39
East Central states	30	38
West Central states	25	33
South (excl. Negroes)	25	33
Rocky Mountain states	30	38
Pacific Coast states	35	38
U. S. average (median)	30	38
Southern Negroes	12	—

How did this picture of "what ought to be" compare
with the actual state of affairs? Government-research studies on the division of the national income indicate that
the typical family of four lives on far less than the amount
which public opinion feels to be essential for a "decency"
minimum standard. The research figures for income vary
with different estimates. But the main lines of the income-
distribution study conducted by the Brookings Institution
for 1929 still hold good. And in that year the Institution
found that nearly 6 million families had less than $1000
and that 12 million families, or more than 42 per cent, had
less than $1500.

Such studies of income distribution, whether condensed
in the official estimates or in the stories people tell of their
own insecurity, acquire profound importance when measured against what public opinion thinks the standards ought
to be. So long as this chasm remains between what people
have and what they think they need, protest movements
and welfare legislation are bound to have a real basis in
our democracy. The discovery that, while 88 per cent of
the American people feel themselves members of the middle social class, 31 per. cent place themselves in the lower
economic class illuminates one of the grave social facts of
our times. But such discrepancies between aspirations and
actualities must first be brought to light before they can
be solved. The people's own story, as told through such
surveys of public opinion, may one day play a part in the
ultimate solution.

CHAPTER FIFTEEN

★

★

Upsetting Some Taboos

POLLS of public opinion have not dealt exclusively with attitudes toward political and economic issues. Emphasis has frequently been given to questions which are not "political" or "economic" in the narrow sense, but which are equally significant for the continued "pursuit of happiness." The growing interdependence of large-scale society has increased the number of supposedly "private" problems. In our own day, the merging of "private" and "public" affairs is increasingly evident in all those spheres where large groups of people are affected by the behavior of their fellow men.

Nothing reveals this merging of private and public questions more clearly than the increasing concern which the modern state has shown in the health of its citizens. The individual's physical well-being is today a public problem, and governmental agencies have subsidized medical research, set up health bureaus, and stimulated health experts to prevent and cure disease. The growth of the idea that the state is responsible for the health of its citizens has helped medical science to grow from immaturity into one of our most highly developed techniques. Diseases hitherto thought incurable are now amenable to treatment, yet the costs of sickness and disease, in human as well as economic terms, remain enormous. Since we now possess expert knowledge, this question arises: is the public prepared to receive and act on the basis of this new information which could transform the health of the nation if it were widely disseminated and applied?

More than once, public-opinion research has dissipated hobgoblins in this field. In 1938, for instance, the surveys uncovered the fact that more than four out of every ten Americans have had to forgo medical care at some time because of the costs of treatment. They found that a majority of Americans would be willing to pay some fixed charge by the month or year if they could be assured of complete medical and hospital care. Interestingly enough, most of these voters said they were willing to pay $2 a month per person—a figure which health associations agree is an entirely reasonable charge. This revealed a large potential market for a new principle in medical care, and one which may have a wider and wider adoption in the 1940's—the principle of group health insurance.

At the same time, the survey showed that the public now accepts the responsibility of the Federal government to provide medical care for those Americans who cannot possibly pay for it themselves, even under a lenient group-insurance plan. Increased unemployment, diminishing income, and the difficulty of collecting payments have caused many physicians to accept the same view themselves. Indeed, the Institute has found surprisingly widespread agreement among doctors and physicians as to the advantages of voluntary health insurance and government aid where necessary.

Cancer and tuberculosis have long headed the list of public-health enemies. The surveys have indicated additional points of attack on these twin plagues but have also revealed many misconceptions among the very groups where their incidence has been greatest. Of all the diseases and ills of mankind, certain types, like syphilis and other venereal diseases, have been particularly stubborn in their resistance to control.

Backwardness here was not due to inadequate knowledge, for the medical profession had gone far in isolating and controlling the dread bacilli which lay at the root of these disorders. Men like Ehrlich and Wassermann discovered how to detect and fight these diseases.

Nor was action delayed because the diseases themselves were of little importance. Estimates suggested that there are approximately 12,000,000 cases of syphilis in the United States, with immeasurable attendant costs in sickness, misery, and death. Dr. Thomas Parran, United States Surgeon General, has estimated that, "if all the conditions due to syphilis were reported as such, it would be found to be the leading cause of death." In spite of the seriousness of this scourge, the experience of the Scandinavian countries where elaborate public-health measures had been introduced bore witness to the ultimate victory which awaited a united attack. Could the same progress be made in America in combating this social scourge? Two factors were present and known:

1. That the problem was vital, that ignoring it would be disastrous, that the disease must be stamped out.
2. That scientists and doctors had worked out reliable methods of diagnosis and prevention.

But one final factor, without which the other two could accomplish nothing, was lacking. One question needed to be answered: what about the attitude of the American people?

It was in answering this question that the polls performed a real public service. There is little doubt that the taboo in some sections of polite society toward discussion of these diseases underlay the inaction which, for years, had dominated both government and health authorities. Dr. Parran has written:

> It cannot be repeated too often that first and foremost among American handicaps to syphilis control is the widespread belief, from which we are only partially emerging, that nice people don't talk about syphilis, nice people don't have syphilis, and nice people shouldn't do anything about those who do have syphilis.

Not many years ago it would probably have been considered impossible for students of public opinion to ask typical Americans what they were willing to do about the care of syphilis. Probably it would not have occurred to the students to ask, for the whole subject was beyond the pale of popular discussion. It was improper. It was taboo. It was impolite. Some individuals declaimed that "the stupidity of the people" and "the inertia of the masses" would block any effort to get action. Fatalists took the view that social diseases were sent "to plague mankind," and argued from this that mankind could and should do nothing about them. Moralists smugly insinuated that the victim must "pay for his sins," forgetting that these diseases strike the innocent as well as the guilty.

Loudest of all the groups who urged that nothing could be done were those who agreed "in principle" that the idea of eliminating syphilis was a good one, but insisted that the stupid majority would block it. People were heard to argue: "It's a good idea, but the people just aren't ready for it. You'll never be able to get their co-operation in a large-scale scheme for isolating the disease." "Sure, I know that doctors and a small educated minority understand the cause and cure and know how to fight it successfully. But the majority will always resist new information and new ideas. Look at what they did to Galileo when he dared to suggest that the earth was not the center of the universe." "No, it's a good idea in theory, but you'll never be able to get action. The mass of people will be against you every time."

In the past, variations on such old themes had dominated discussions of venereal disease. The veil of secrecy was in part created by individuals and pressure groups and therefore the American public had been treated like children. Although newspapers ran many stories about tuberculosis and cancer, most editors were afraid to "offend" their readers by printing discussions of the cure of social diseases, and radio chains ruled such subjects off the air. "Fear of offending the public," said Dr. Parran, "is first and foremost among human handicaps in progress against syphilis."

A vital need existed to get the movement of control under way. The popular stereotype, then, was that the public would emphatically refuse to tolerate discussion of these problems and that references to syphilis and gonorrhea would be considered "shameful" and "disgusting."

The utter falseness of this view was proved by a series of polls conducted by the American Institute beginning in December, 1937, on questions related to venereal disease. Having been assured that "the people were reactionary and uninformed" on this matter, the Institute had its field interviewers ask a representative cross section of Americans:

"Would you be in favor of a government bureau to distribute information concerning venereal diseases?"

The response was favorable beyond the wildest hopes of the most thoroughgoing advocate of the antidisease movement. Ninety per cent of those interviewed said "yes" to the question, while only 10 per cent were opposed. The overwhelming mass of the people, then, supported educational

measures to disseminate information about these diseases.
The people were further asked:

"Should this bureau set up clinics for the treatment of
venereal diseases?"

Favorable response here was equally overwhelming, for
88 per cent said they favored a system of clinics. On both
these points, sentiment throughout the country was widespread in favor of controlling the disease. It was highest
among poor voters. Persons on relief were 95 per cent in
favor of government clinics, possibly because they believed
such clinics might give free treatment:

	Per Cent Favoring Bureau	*Per Cent Favoring Government Clinics*
Women	91	91
Young Persons	93	92
Reliefers	93	95
Farmers	88	86
Small towns	88	85
Big cities	91	89

Small-town residents and farmers appeared to be slightly
less interested, perhaps because the disease rate is lower in
many of those areas. But the response from all adult groups
in all sections of the country was so overwhelming that it
focused attention on the problem. Nobody shied away from
the questions put by the interviewers. Only two or three
voters out of every 100 failed to express an opinion.

Members of the field staff reported that the voters themselves said the questions were among the most interesting
ever put before them. Often voters were not content with a
"yes" and "no" answer, but would volunteer explanations.
"Yes," they remarked frequently, "I'm in favor of any steps

at all that would help to control the disease. Nothing the government could do would be too drastic." Others told interviewers: "I wish this had been done long ago."

Many voters took the position that as long as infection is prevalent in a large section of the population, "no person is safe." With others, control of syphilis was just a matter of "good business." A filling-station operator in a small Ohio city probably summed up this point as well as anyone: "The money spent to control syphilis now," he said, "would empty half our state institutions inside a generation." From person to person, opinion differed as to just how much money syphilis is costing the country every year in the care of incompetents and delinquents. But the burden on the state and on the individual certainly influenced many of the opinions.

Thus the polls of public opinion revealed that with 12,000,000 cases estimated in the United States, adult voters by majorities of nine to one favored the establishment of two of the preconditions for successful treatment: education and medical clinical facilities. Following publication of these results, some progressive sections of the press took up the issue and launched an educational campaign.

Later in the same year, New Hampshire legislators voted to require a premarital test for venereal diseases for all persons seeking marriage licenses. Other states had similar laws, and the Institute wanted to find out if the voters supported such legislation where it was actually in effect, and how the voters felt in states that had not yet taken such action. To find the answer, the question was posed:

New Hampshire legislators have voted to require a test for venereal diseases for all persons seeking marriage licenses. Would you favor such a law in this state?

Ninety-two per cent said "yes." The budget-balancing American was even willing to spend cash to control the disease:

Should Congress appropriate $25,000,000 to help control venereal disease?

Seventy-nine per cent said "yes."

In August, 1937, Chicago public-health officials, with state aid and the help of the United States Public Health Service, decided to try to find out how many people would actually take advantage of the facilities for therapy which they intended to build. More than a million ballots were mailed to Chicago families to find out how many would be willing to take free blood tests in order to permit accurate diagnosis. The first published reports showed 93 per cent favoring the step, thus making it possible to plan the conditions for large-scale detection and treatment. The Institute decided to extend such an inquiry to cover the country as a whole. To a nation-wide cross section of voters interviewers put the same question which appeared on the Chicago ballot:

In strict confidence and at no expense to you, would you like to be given by your physician a blood test for syphilis?

A further question was then added:

"How would you vote if you received this ballot?"

The response from the national cross section was along the lines of the earlier general Institute ballots on education and the provision of clinical facilities. Eighty-seven per cent said "yes." All the subgroups within the Institute's general sample were over 80 per cent in favor of submitting to pre-marital tests. The Chicago figure is interesting, in the sample breakdown, since it illustrates the close correspondence of the results obtained by the sample method with those obtained in the Chicago public-health study by a complete enumeration of families:

Official Chicago Poll (incomplete)	93%
Institute poll (Chicago only)	95%

The response from voters between the ages of twenty and thirty was even more warmly in favor than the other groups. Since most of the probable candidates for treatment would likely be recruited from the ranks of the young, this response was particularly encouraging. On the basis of translating the Institute percentage figure into the whole country, the poll might be interpreted to indicate the willingness of over 60,000,000 Americans to undergo such an examination.

All the referendums conducted on this question supplied facts about public opinion which encouraged doctors and research scientists to expand their war against syphilis. The overwhelming support given to these questions indicated plainly that the general public was in sympathy with the ideas held by men like Dr. Thomas Parran. Today, growing numbers of private physicians are searching out syphilis and reporting cases for treatment. In the last few years, newspapers in almost all our large cities have published articles on the subject, and the old taboo against the word syphilis in news columns is on the way out. Newspapers are beginning to discuss the subject as they do pneumonia or any other disease. Magazines, too, have opened their pages to articles about it; and they are finding overwhelming approval from their readers.

Undeniably, the polls helped open the publicity channels for the drive against venereal disease. Rather than sit back and make armchair assumptions about public opinion, the polls provided facts which gave the lie to old-fashioned

stereotypes. Further, such surveys helped to provide rough
quantitative data for doctors and administrators who
wanted to eradicate this disease and needed to know how
many people might be involved in a large-scale scheme of
education and control.

The taboos about which so much had been heard were
almost totally destroyed when it was found that the people
were as eager for intelligent action as the doctors and educa-
tionists. Without a device like the poll of public opinion,
the real attitude of the people might have remained hidden
much longer under the pressure-group claims and hoary
ideas of a bygone prudish age. Such surveys demonstrate
that it is not always correct to urge that "history can be
written as the record of the errors of majorities." Here is
one case where the majority, once it had been made articulate, was instantly and unerringly on the side of medical
and social progress. Who knows but that a sampling referendum taken several years ago might have shown the people equally eager for a public-health movement against
venereal disease, and thus dissipated earlier the prejudices
that have retarded this much-needed advance?

★

CHAPTER SIXTEEN

★

A Nation at War

THE years preceding the outbreak of war in September, 1939, were punctuated by sharp tensions in public opinion in all the countries nearest the danger zone. The swift moves of Japanese armies in the Far East, the rise to power of the National Socialist party in Germany, the successive hammer strokes against the European structure laid down at Versailles, and the spasmodic attacks on small and weak nations were closely followed not only by the various foreign offices, but also by the mass of the people. Interest was directly related to proximity to the scene of potential conflict. The intense absorption of the public in foreign affairs symbolized the common realization that vital questions of war and peace did not concern the diplomats alone, but directly involved the common people who would ultimately be called upon to do the fighting and the suffering.

How did the British public react to the impact of events in Europe? What did the average British voter feel was worth fighting for? Did British public opinion favor a policy of isolation, or a policy of acting jointly with other nations to resist aggression? Beginning in 1938, the British Institute of Public Opinion began to publish a regular series of sampling surveys in which the people expressed their own views on these questions.

Such scientific studies, like their American prototype,

were prefaced by cruder methods of assessing public opinion. Back in November, 1934, one of the first-large scale tests of British public opinion was conducted. In some quarters the decline of confidence in the League of Nations as the guarantor of European peace had followed swiftly on the emergence of armed force as the decisive influence in world politics. Lord Robert Cecil, one of the early founders of the League system, was firmly convinced that the mass of the British people strongly supported the principles of collective security. In order to demonstrate this, a mammoth Peace Ballot was organized by the British League of Nations Union. "For the first time in history," the official account declared, "the British people had the opportunity of making themselves heard on a first-class issue other than, and above, party politics, and free from the atmosphere and rivalries of a General Election."

The issues on the Peace Ballot were drafted in the form of five questions to be answered by a "yes," or "no":

1. Should Great Britain remain a Member of the League of Nations?
2. Are you in favor of an all-round reduction of armaments by international agreement?
3. Are you in favor of the all-round abolition of national and naval aircraft by international agreement?
4. Should the manufacture and sale of armaments for private profit be prohibited by international agreement?
5. Do you consider that, if a nation insists on attacking another, the other nations should combine to compel it to stop by—
   a. Economic and nonmilitary measures?
   b. If necessary, military measures?

The Peace Ballot was conducted on a nation-wide basis, local committees being formed in each constituency for the purpose of collecting votes from all individuals over

eighteen years of age who would co-operate. The final
returns, including the "abstentions" and the "doubtful"
voters, were sent to the central committee for tabulation
and analysis. Voluntary workers delivered ballots from
house to house, and tried to get everyone over the age of
eighteen to fill them out. Sometimes several ballots were
left with the householder and collected several weeks later.
Toward the end of the collection campaign, ballots were
even printed in various newspapers for the convenience of
readers who had not been reached earlier. Such methods of
obtaining opinions afforded little protection against possible bias due to the unwillingness of opponents of the ballot
to respond, and there were few guarantees against duplica-
tion of ballots on the part of intense advocates of collective
security. The collection of these ballots took nine months,
and voting continued from November, 1934, to June, 1935.
During this time, the Peace Ballot was attacked by the
extreme Conservative wing in Great Britain and was even
termed by the small but vocal Isolationist press, a "Ballot
of Blood." Others declared that such questions were "too
difficult" to be decided by public opinion, and suggested
that such a poll was a "useless undertaking." In the course
of an enormous publicity campaign, which stimulated wide
interest in press, political, and public circles, some
11,539,165 ballots were gathered—the largest unofficial poll
of public opinion in recent history. The total number of
votes cast represented more than 38 per cent of the entire
list of voters over the age of eighteen in Great Britain and
Northern Ireland.

The tremendous size of the total vote was overshadowed
by the size of the affirmative majorities which were secured
on the various questions. On the first four questions, the
vote ranged from 20 to 1 to 10 to 1 in favor of the affirmative

side, while on the side of economic sanctions it was about
16 to 1. The vote for military sanctions obtained majorities
of about 3 to 2, including abstentions. The enormous balloting, and the support of such a large section of the British
people, led Sir Samuel Hoare, in his Geneva speech of September 11, 1935, to proclaim that British policy was to rest
solidly on the League's principles: "The attitude of the
British nation in the last few weeks," the Foreign Secretary
declared, "has clearly demonstrated the fact that this is no
variable sentiment, but a principle of international conduct
to which they and their government hold with firm, endur-
ing, and universal persistence." There is little doubt that
the Peace Ballot had great effect on the declarations of the
British government in that year. It acted as a weathercock
to provide a clear warning long beforehand of the storm of
public protest that followed the Hoare-Laval Abyssinian
proposals in December, 1935, and that resulted in the resignation of the Foreign Secretary.

The Peace Ballot of 1934-35 was an enormous undertaking. Yet in spite of the "gigantic sampling," there were
weaknesses in the technique which to some extent distorted
the results as an expression of the various streams of public
opinion. In the first place, the purpose of the Peace Ballot
was not only to measure the various tendencies objectively,
but to justify a particular view of policy: "The first object
of the Ballot," the official history points out, "was to demonstrate that the British people were behind the Government's
expressed object of making 'the support and extension of
the authority of the League of Nations a cardinal point' in
Great Britain's policy." For this reason, as well as because
the enterprise was sponsored by the League of Nations
Union, the vote represented the collective-security adherents, but probably failed to include the views of people

who were suspicious of the aims of the groups behind the Peace Ballot. Because of the aims of its sponsors, and the method of collecting the ballots, those who held a contrary view of policy may well have boycotted the poll. The Peace Ballot thus became a general test of collective-security sentiment, but did not provide a true statistical sample of public opinion. Secondly, the Peace Ballot took over nine months to complete, required the enlistment of hundreds of thousands of voluntary workers, and cost the headquarters alone the sum of £12,000. Because it took so long to conduct, the factor of changing sentiment over time probably operated as well.

The Peace Ballot, then, while the most enormous sampling on record, cannot be accepted as an impartial and representative test of public opinion. It was a tremendous but solitary effort, and when it had done its work, knowledge of British public opinion on other issues again became the prey of guesswork and wishful thinking.

Successive crises, such as the Spanish Civil War, the resignation of the Foreign Secretary, Anthony Eden, the invasion of Austria, and the annexation of Bohemia and Moravia, all contributed to the growing tension in international affairs, which vitally affected the lives of all people in Europe. An undoubted need existed to get a better measure of the reactions of the British public to these events by a method at once more rapid, more regular, and more representative than the technique of the Peace Ballot. For there was a fundamental truth in the statement that preceded the official story of the Ballot:

> The weathercock of articulate opinion whirled in the winds of contrary propagandas, and the still small voice of John Smith and Mary Brown remained inaudible.

Obviously the thing to do was to ask John Smith and Mary

Brown. It was so obvious, so audaciously simple, that nobody had ever thought of doing it.

If our democracy is a true democracy, John Smith and Mary Brown, and the sum of their opinions, are the things that matter. They are the rock upon which the fabric of our Government is based. Upon their response all advance ultimately depends.[1]

To meet this need, the British Institute of Public Opinion was formed in 1936, to act on the basis of the methods that had been built up in the United States. From 1936 to 1938, the Institute conducted a series of tests of its sampling methods in successive by-elections: West Fulham (1937), Oxford (1938), West Lewisham (1938), East Norfolk, Batley and Morley, and Hallam (1939), and predicted their outcome with an average error of only 2 per cent.[2] In 1938, the London *News Chronicle* began the publication of the returns of the Institute's polls. During the fateful year of crisis and international tension which led up to the days in early September, 1939, the polls did continuous service in mapping the reactions of the British people to such events as the Munich Agreement, Mr. Neville Chamberlain's policy of "appeasement," the march of the German troops into Prague on March 15, 1939, the abortive Franco-British discussions with Russia, and scores of other issues, covering a wide range of domestic as well as foreign affairs.

Some studies dealt with questions of fact, rather than questions of opinion. Back in December, 1937, for example, the British people were asked:

| Have you taken any precautions against air raids? | Yes | 7.5% |
| | No | 92.5 |

1 *The Peace Ballot: An Official History.*

2 This average error of 2 per cent includes the error of 6 per cent in the British Institute's Batley and Morley poll, due largely to the failure to continue polling through to the last possible moment before the by-election.

In December, 1938:

Have you volunteered for any form of national service?	Yes	19%
	No	81

In June, 1939:

If there were any air raid today (June, '39) while you were at home, could you, by foot, reach a shelter in seven minutes?	Public shelter	12%
	Own shelter	12
	Arranged private shelter	4
	None	72

Such questions of fact served to focus attention on the state of the nation's preparedness, and to indicate where gaps and deficiencies existed. The results indicated, in a sense, the effects and future reference points of the government's preparedness campaign. Frequent studies of public opinion made it possible to know how the British people felt and what they were prepared to do. The changed conditions involved in preparing a nation for modern war placed renewed emphasis on public opinion. Civil defense, air-raid precautions, and practice "blackouts" signified that the Home Front might become the fighting front, and pointed to the need for getting better information about their effect on civilian morale. The polls helped the government obtain a measure of how the British public was making the adjustment to the strange, new, even frightening conditions. Paper proposals and elaborate bureaucratic schemes supplied half the picture. But the other half could only be supplied by the people themselves.

On September first, the German armies invaded Poland, and the transition from peace to war was irrevocably made. Did the fact that Britain was at war mean that the polls of public opinion would cease? Soon after the outbreak of war, an editorial in the *News Chronicle* showed that the need for frequent and reliable measurement of public opinion was not a peacetime fad, but a wartime necessity:

> In time of war the value of this system of testing public opinion becomes greater than ever. First, in a nation at war, for the survival of free democracy, it is vital that liberty of expression of opinion shall, within proper limits, flourish. Secondly, if the will and effort of the people are to be sustained at the highest level, it is important that some regular and consecutive guide to the trend of public opinion shall be made available to those who frame and direct the nation's policy.
>
> It is hoped and intended that through the continuance of the surveys of public opinion during the coming months, an index to the views of the people will be provided in war as it has been in peace.

Despite the vital conflict in which Great Britain is engaged, the British Institute of Public Opinion has conducted surveys on many controversial issues connected with the war. The results have been published without censorship even when they showed sharp divisions of public sentiment and revealed opposition to political leaders and governmental policies. There is awareness of the fact that the free expression of public opinion is necessary even in a period of crisis in the British government's attitude toward the polls.

A good example of how the polls find out where "the shoe is pinching" may be seen in the following question, arising from the fact that deaths due to traffic accidents had risen steadily since the introduction of the "blackout."

"Are you in favor of the blackout being made less strict?" People voted 3 to 1 to make the regulation less rigid. Many other problems created by the war—the evacuation of children, the government's food-rationing scheme, the effect of rising prices—have seen the British Institute's interviewers talking to people in England, Scotland, and Wales to see how people were taking to the regulations prescribed by crisis conditions.

Throughout its regular surveys, and continued through the wartime effort, the polls have conducted tests of Mr. Chamberlain's personal popularity with the electorate. Month by month the question has been asked:

"In general do you approve or disapprove of Mr. Chamberlain as Prime Minister?"

Surveys conducted shortly after Munich found the Chamberlain curve sloping downward, reaching a low of 55 per cent in December, 1938. A brief rise followed until March, 1939, when Hitler's swift invasion of Prague raised a flurry of criticism in England against "appeasement" of the dictator powers, and the Prime Minister's popularity again began to decline. The trend was abruptly halted by the Polish crisis and the declaration of war against Germany. Just before the declaration of war in September, 59 per cent said they approved of Chamberlain as Prime Minister. Since the outbreak of war, the popularity of the Prime Minister rose steadily to 71 per cent in December, 1939. From then on, however, Chamberlain's popularity declined, sinking to 61 per cent as of April, 1940, and then collapsing to 35 per cent in early May, as shown by a telegraphic survey after the British withdrawal from southern Norway.

The British public has also spoken up on its attitude to other political leaders: in May, 1939, for example, when the question was asked:

"Are you in favor of Mr. Winston Churchill being invited to join the cabinet?"

A slight majority of 56 per cent said "yes." Since then Mr. Churchill as First Lord of the Admiralty, the man responsible for the conduct of Britain's war at sea, has been much in the public eye. The question was asked:

"If you had the choice between Mr. Chamberlain and Mr. Churchill which would you have as Prime Minister?" The results showed:

Chamberlain	52%
Churchill	30
No Opinion	18

The majorities in support of the British Prime Minister perhaps compare unfavorably with the published majorities of the contemporary dictators. But at least they represent real convictions and beliefs, and not "official" pronouncements.

One question which the British Institute asked of voters has aroused wide comment. The results were released in Great Britain on December 13, 1939, after that country had been at war with Germany since early September. The question was:

"Are you satisfied or dissatisfied with the government's conduct of the war?"

British voters divided as follows:

Satisfied	61%
Dissatisfied	18
Stop the War	11
No Opinion	10

While voters favoring the Chamberlain government expressed satisfaction with the conduct of the war by a vote of more than 7 to 3, supporters of the opposition parties were evenly divided in sentiment, less than half saying they were satisfied:

	Government Voters	Opposition Voters
Satisfied	74%	46%
Dissatisfied	10	31
Stop the War	5	14
No Opinion	11	9

Many people expressed amazement that the British government should permit the publication of a survey which, although it showed support from 60 per cent of those interviewed, revealed 1 voter in 5 as dissatisfied with the conduct of the war and a further 11 per cent eager to "stop the war." Surely, they argued, a nation at war must take every step to suppress critical opinion in order to avoid the appearance of disunity?

Such a view has many adherents. It is often claimed that criticism must be suspended in wartime, and that public opinion must give up its right to oppose the government of the day.

Yet there are real weaknesses in this case, and real sources of strength in the apparent "disunity" presented by a nation which seeks to maintain the spirit and the practice of criticism within itself even at war. The grave danger involved in limiting the right of public opinion to express itself clearly, even in wartime, lies in the assumption that the civil and military leaders responsible for the conduct of the war are infallible and that they cannot make mistakes. But it is precisely this view—that the citizen should abdicate his right to criticize and present the government of the day with a blank check to act as it pleases—which is the central assumption of dictatorship. Pursued to its logical conclusion it would heighten the powers of bureaucracy, drive the government of the day into increasingly rigid measures of censorship and suppression, and render the people unfit to play their part in understanding the objects for which the war is being fought, or the purposes ultimately to be embodied in the peace.

Past history points to the fact that, even in wartime, a free public opinion is a measure of strength. Obviously this does not mean that the polls should be free to ask questions on the details of military action, or questions which might reveal information useful to the enemy. An army, it has been said, cannot be run like a debating society, and the right to criticize must inevitably be tempered by military exigencies. But democratic governments are today aware of one fundamental fact: mature nations cannot be run like a kindergarten.

"War-time unity of outlook," as Harold Laski writes in *Liberty and the Modern State,* "is never worth the cost of prohibitions." Undoubtedly there is real value in the maintenance of a free public opinion in the midst of a crisis. In the last war, President Wilson's Fourteen Points were, by implication, critical of Allied policy, yet they also acted to waken liberal opinion to a sense of its responsibilities.

Publication of the fact that the people are not completely unanimously behind a wartime government need not cause alarm. A *New York Times* editorial of December 15, 1939, has clearly emphasized this point in commenting on Britain's wartime surveys:

> No doubt somewhat similar results might have been obtained in any country at war during the past century or century and a half. No nation is unanimous. But free countries don't have to pretend to be unanimous. England is the stronger for facing such matters openly. But what would be the result of an unhampered Gallup survey in Germany or Russia? We shan't know, for neither Government dares to take one, or would dare publish the honest returns.

Clearly, the public-opinion polls have their uses in wartime. In a period of war and national crisis, they help to reveal the impact of regulations upon individuals, and show how people feel about their government and how they react to the conduct of the war itself. No belligerent nation today can afford to ignore the problem of morale and public opinion. No wartime government can continue to survive unless it takes steps to find out what the common people are saying.

★

★

CHAPTER SEVENTEEN

The People and Foreign Policy

ON SEPTEMBER 3, 1939, the headlines of every newspaper and the loud-speakers throughout the nation flashed the news that within a generation after the armistice, Europe had again gone to war. One single thought dominated the minds of millions of people on this side of the Atlantic: what should be the policy of the American government?

In so far as the government of the United States is a representative government, it is the duty of Congress and the President to guide the destiny of the country according to their best judgment. But in so far as this government is also a democratic form of government, its leaders should at all times have full knowledge of what the people, from whom they derive their power, are thinking. In a crisis like war, when not merely the citizen's welfare but his very life may be at stake, the need to hear his voice is imperative. The crisis of 1939, however, did not involve the simple question of a direct attack upon the United States. In such case a man would have little choice but to defend his home and soil. It involved the far more intricate question of what to do about a *foreign* war, and how to maneuver in the field of foreign politics in order to avoid fighting on alien soil, while still preserving the power and dignity of the nation.

At least three courses were open to the country when war broke out. First, it could, as in 1917, take up arms and join the war, join, that is, on the side of the Allies, since there was never any question where the nation's sympathies lay. Second, it could give aid to the Allies in the form of war materials and supplies while not actually participating in the war as a belligerent. Third, it could remain entirely aloof from the conflict, or as aloof as modern conditions would allow.

Which course would the nation support?

Unfortunately, the war had broken out in a year when no national elections were held. Short of a national referendum there was no official way of obtaining a mandate from the people on the policies which lay open. Decisions could not wait upon the next election, more than a year away. Yet to adopt a course of action not popular with the people would run the risk of creating public unrest and dissension, or even repudiation of the administration at the polls, at a time when the gravity of the situation demanded unity on foreign policy. Everything would depend on the ability of the administration to size up public sentiment and adopt a policy which would not create such partisan discord as to leave a great nation hamstrung in its foreign policy through quarrels and bickering between political parties.

All Europe was familiar with the tragic experience of one American statesman, Woodrow Wilson, whose foreign policy of 1919-20, predicated on the League of Nations covenant, did not win the support of the Congress in his own country. Wilson could not speak with the assurance that his country was behind him. Not only were there factional fights in Congress over his foreign policy, but there were no systematic means of discovering from month to month what the rank and file of the people felt during the crucial period between the elections of 1918 and 1920. Contradictory manifestations of sentiment through the press and organized lobby groups gave anything but a clear and satisfying picture. Ironically enough, Wilson was one of the Presidents who cared most about public opinion and felt most keenly the need of its guidance. It was Wilson who wrote: "I would rather hear what men are talking about on trains and in shops and by the firesides than hear anything else because I want guidance and I know I could get it there."

When the shadow of war fell upon Europe in 1939, the situation was vastly different. A reliable instrument was ready to test America's reactions. No longer was it necessary, as' in 1914, to guess about public opinion, or to look to editors and pressure groups in an attempt to discover what the people as a whole were thinking. As a matter of fact, sentiment had been measured and recorded for many months past on the question of America's role in case war did break out. As early as March, 1939, the Institute had begun conducting surveys on the question of sending arms, war supplies, or troops to the Allies. With the actual outbreak of hostilities, both the Institute and the *Fortune* Survey sent out a "war ballot," and at regular intervals thereafter studies of opinion were conducted on the various aspects and problems of the crisis as it affected the United States. Thus, before the war and during the opening weeks of the war, a detailed record of opinion was on hand. The mood of the people, the precise strength of isolationist sentiment, on the one hand, and interventionist sentiment, on the other, were charted. With such information the leaders of the country could know, in advance, what policies the people were likely to accept or reject, and how much "selling" or coaxing was necessary to put any policy across.

The year 1938 had seen a tremendous revival of interest

in European affairs. In contrast to the nineteen twenties, when many Americans were apathetic or indifferent to the problems of foreign countries, voters began to follow with close attention each new move of the dictator nations and the democracies in their grapple for power. In fact, Institute studies found that more voters had an opinion on events in Europe than on many controversial domestic issues such as the T.V.A., the Wagner Act, the Dies Committee, or the C.I.O. Out of this renewed interest in foreign affairs certain public attitudes and convictions began to take shape.

Even before the war the Institute's researches indicated that two dominant aims had developed in the public mind: (1) to keep out of war, and (2) to give England and France every possible aid short of actually going to war.

The first aim—to keep out of war—had been clearly recognizable for some time, for the revulsion against sending American soldiers abroad was widespread and extremely potent. Barely twenty years after the armistice, a decisive majority of voters (70 per cent) were saying that American participation in the last war had been a mistake. Virtually no one favored taking part in a European war a second time—the actual proportion against such participation rising as high as 97 per cent in a survey at the end of 1939. The existence of this sentiment, noted in the Institute studies several years earlier, would have been obvious to virtually anyone who took the trouble to stand on a street corner and talk to a handful of passers-by.

The really significant news of 1938-39 was a marked shift in sentiment toward giving all aid "short of war" to Britain and France. This development was especially interesting because, in some respects, it clashed with the neutrality legislation which had been passed in 1935. In

the hope of keeping the nation off the road to war—a course
heartily approved by the public—the Neutrality Act had
placed an embargo on shipment of arms, airplanes, and
other implements of war. Was the embargo popular? There
seems little doubt that it was in the beginning, for a survey made in 1938 showed a majority opposed to selling war
materials to England and France. It was not long, however,
before this attitude began to change. It changed so rapidly
that within a year sentiment was 2 to 1 in favor of sending
war supplies to the Allied powers.

The Institute's chronological record shows that the shift
in sentiment began with Hitler's seizure of Austria and
was rapidly accelerated by the promises of Munich which
Hitler shattered when he seized the rest of Czechoslovakia
and Memel and stepped up the anti-Jewish campaign. By
that time the relatively cool detachment from European
affairs which had marked American public opinion in the
nineteen twenties and early thirties was gone. While the
voters had taken a relatively neutral view of the Nazi
regime up to 1938, the majority was by 1939 outspokenly
condemning its activities.

The changed attitude toward helping England and
France was clearly defined in three separate surveys between September, 1938, and April, 1939. In September,
when the Czech crisis was brewing, only 34 per cent of
American voters favored selling war materials to England
and France in case of war. By March, 1939, the number had
jumped to 55 per cent, and by April, after Hitler's occupation of Prague and Memel, to 66 per cent. This was a mo-
mentous change, for it meant that the majority of voters
favored doing just what the neutrality laws had for years
sought to prohibit—selling war materials to belligerents.

Why did the change come? From an analysis of the views

expressed by the thousands of persons interviewed, there appeared to be three principal reasons. First, American voters had by the end of 1938 come to regard Nazism and Fascism as serious threats to the security of democratic nations. Second, they feared that if Germany defeated Britain and France in a war, the United States would be next in line as an object of Nazi aggression. Third, a small group of voters, about one person in five, favored selling war materials to England and France for purely economic reasons, arguing that such trade might stimulate clogged business and might reduce unemployment.

Such was the temper of the people when President Roosevelt, in September, 1939, convened Congress for the purpose of reappraising the Neutrality Act. The President proposed to lift the embargo on American arms shipments so that airplanes and military equipment could be sold to the Allies on a cash-and-carry basis. He declared that it would be inconsistent to forbid shipment of war implements while allowing the shipment of other commodities useful in war, such as copper, cotton, wheat, or cloth. Those who wanted an arms embargo would, he felt, by the very logic of their position eventually have to seek an embargo on all foreign trade. To that he was firmly opposed.

A bloc of isolationist Senators, led by Borah and Vandenberg, took up the defense of the arms embargo, maintaining that its repeal would be a step toward war. An historic debate continued for nearly two months. Party lines were almost obliterated, prominent Democrats finding themselves on the same side of the fence as equally prominent Republicans. Taft and Vandenberg, both mentioned as presidential nominees, took opposite sides on the embargo issue.

During the course of the debate not merely Congress,

but the people as well, had an opportunity to vote—the former officially, the latter unofficially, through the sampling referendum. The situation was not unlike the old New England town meeting where the people heard first one side of the issue and then the other, and expressed their sentiments. The Institute conducted a series of studies which revealed the public attitude at the start of the debate and at its close, as well as the trend during the interval. The results show that a rise in repeal sentiment which came after the President proposed his plan was followed by a slight decline as the other side of the case was put forward by the opposition. All through the discussion, however, repeal commanded a majority. The trend:

	For Revising Neutrality Act	Against Revising
Before Roosevelt's speech on Sept. 21	57%	43%
After Roosevelt's speech	62	38
After first week of Senate debate	60	40
After first month of debate	58	42
At close of debate	56	44

An interesting side light was the opinion of persons listed in *Who's Who in America*. This special group of business and professional people was in favor of repeal by a much larger vote (78 per cent) than the general public.

Another interesting revelation was the public's reaction to the argument that repeal would constitute an "unneutral" act. Some of the isolationists had pointed out that if the United States sold war materials on a cash-and-carry basis, England and France alone would reap the chief benefits since they controlled the seas. This argument apparently had little public appeal. Those voters who wanted the embargo lifted advocated that course of action *for the very reason that it would help England and France and not Germany.* In one Institute survey the majority specifically said that if repealing the embargo would help *Germany* and hurt the Allies, they would in that case oppose repeal. The vote on the embargo was thus distinctly not a vote on "true" neutrality. The public's basic aim of giving the Allies every aid short of going to war was asserting itself. That aim having been revealed and described by the Institute many months earlier, it was no surprise that revision of the Neutrality Act was backed by popular support.

Time after time during the period 1939-40, the President's actions relating to foreign affairs closely matched American public sentiment. The Neutrality Act revision was one instance. There were at least eight others which clearly indicated that his policies articulated public sentiment to a remarkable degree. The man who had stirred up so much controversy over domestic issues found his foreign policy supported practically *in toto* by a majority of voters. His actions fitted the known views of the public in much the same way as the vigorous policies of the first hundred days of the New Deal had suited the public temper in that gloomy period of bank failures and despair.

The President's efforts to prevent war in the summer of 1939 were in direct accord with the deep-seated peace sentiment of the country. His known sympathies with the Allied side were also the sympathies of the people, 87 per cent of whom wanted to see the Allies win. His policy of giving every aid to England and France short of going to war had, as we have seen, accurately reflected the majority point of view as measured in Institute studies. When he declared that America must stay out of war, he was reflecting the wishes of 97 per cent of his countrymen. When, early in

1940, he condemned Russia's attack on Finland, he was echoing the sentiment of 9 out of 10 Americans. He suggested that Congress consider a nonmilitary loan to Finland, and the idea was approved by nearly 60 per cent of voters.

The President presented to Congress a program for strengthening the American Army, Navy, and air force; it was approved 9 to 1 by the voters. He opposed Japanese aggression in the Far East and permitted the Japanese trade treaty to lapse. The people were equally opposed to Japanese aggression and approved the denunciation of the trade treaty. In a speech at Kingston, Ontario, in 1938, the President pledged support of the American armed forces to the Dominion if attacked. A subsequent survey found 73 per cent of voters approving military aid to Canada in case of invasion.

The State Department has often expressed its interest in a "sound and lasting peace" at the conclusion of the European war. Many leaders both here and abroad believe this issue overshadows every other modern issue save that of bringing the war to a close.

In one especially interesting survey, the Institute sought to discover how many Americans have given any thought to what should be done to maintain world peace when the fighting is finished. The results showed that about one person in every three (34 per cent) had at least thought about the problem and had some suggestion to offer. About 8 million voters, judging by the survey, were considering some international organization on the League of Nations principle, or some extension of that principle. The main suggestions were a "United States of Europe," "world union," or a "union of democracies," as proposed by Clarence Streit in *Union Now,* and a revived and strengthened League of Nations, which many of these voters said the United States should join. A "United States of Europe" seemed to have the greatest appeal of any single proposal at that time.

Whether or not any of these schemes is feasible lies beyond the scope of this book. Perhaps, too, some other peace idea will come along to attract world attention. The survey results were significant, however, in so far as they showed what ideas for peace were popular at that time.

In this very service the sampling referendum again demonstrates its usefulness. The degree of support which the United States will give to the peace that comes after this war will depend in the long run on how popular that peace is. If there is to be any basic rearrangement of the world setup in which the United States is invited to participate, American public opinion will be a factor of crucial importance. With the sampling referendum, it will be possible to discover in advance what the voters of the country are thinking. If the nation's leaders turn to the people for the kind of guidance Woodrow Wilson wanted, the will of the people will be articulated for them.

PART III

★　　　　　　　　★

EVALUATIONS

★　　　　　　　　★

★

CHAPTER EIGHTEEN

★

The Critics Speak for Themselves

WE ARE now witnessing a paradoxical but unavoidable phenomenon—the polls of public opinion are themselves becoming an issue of public opinion. Actual case studies have already been used to show that the polls perform necessary functions in our democracy since they give a more accurate picture of public opinion. But there are those who see more vice than virtue in this new instrument. During the short space of four years, a considerable body of criticism has been directed at this effort to take the pulse of democracy.

Three main batteries have opened fire on the modern public-opinion poll. The first charge comes from individuals and groups who object to the specific results which a given poll indicates. Politicians and organizations who have already made their own private diagnosis as to the state of public opinion dislike finding that their results are contradicted by a particular survey.

A second type of criticism comes from those who admit the desirability of measuring public opinion, but emphasize defects in the present methods of operation. Some critics point to the possibility of bias due to dishonest sponsorship, and fear that the polls may become "carriers" of propaganda. Others raise such questions as these: Can you really find out people's opinions simply by asking them?

213

Do the polls ignore the intensity with which opinions are held? Without this type of criticism, the modern polls would never have superseded the earlier mass-sampling methods; without continuous analysis, the polls could not hope to improve their standards of performance.

Finally, there is the argument that polls weaken the democratic process, either by destroying interest in elections, or by creating a "band-wagon vote" among the doubtful voters. Polls on issues are said to destroy the foundations of representative government by inducing legislators to bow before the majority opinion which the polls reveal. Still others argue that public opinion itself is not a dependable force on which to base effective government.

In the sections which follow, these various suggestions will be reviewed, and the critics will be permitted to speak for themselves.

At various intervals, Republicans have charged that polls were supporting the Democrats, and Democrats have suggested that polls were in the pay of the Republicans. Socialists have hinted that the polls are in the hands of "reactionaries," while extreme conservatives have accused them of being "too democratic." When the attack comes intermittently from each of the political groups in turn, and when polls are alternately praised and blamed by rival partisans, it would appear that such groups are less interested in the sampling method than in obtaining favorable results for their own causes.

Reform groups, political parties, and all who are trying to mold public opinion sometimes seem to assume that the polls should do their propaganda for them. When a particular result apparently contradicts their claims and slogans, they exhibit annoyance, as the violent reaction of the

Long newspaper, *The American Progress,* to the Institute's Louisiana poll clearly shows. Another illustration may be seen in the Communist-party organ, *The Daily Worker,* which inveighed against the polls in December, 1939, when figures indicated that a slight majority of American voters —some 52 per cent—believed that the policy of the American Communist party was determined after close consultation with Soviet Russia. But who is to blame for the existence of this belief in the American public mind—the public-opinion polls, or the Communist party? Is it not better for any minority political group to know that certain prejudices exist and that they must be modified if the movement is to succeed? The polls showed here that fully 39 per cent of the voting public was undecided or had no opinions on this question—another indication that the propaganda program of the American Communist party has not been carried very far. The real point is that public-opinion polls try to measure the effect of propaganda by charting public reactions. They have no other purpose. Criticism of the polls on the basis of specific results often reveals more about the critics than it does about the polls.

Yet beneath such criticisms lies a problem which must be discussed. Many competent observers have pointed out that the growing prestige of the polls has greatly increased their potentialities. But potency may be for good or evil. Like any other social technique, opinion polls are at once "enormously useful and subtly dangerous." Their usefulness depends on impartial administration. But what can be done to prevent "rigged" polls designed to suit the private interest of the sponsor? What would happen if dishonest persons were to gain control of the polls and abuse their position to create a private view of public opinion? Many people fear that the avowed purpose of the polls—to measure public opinion—may conceal a sinister attempt to influence public opinion. The early straw votes were sometimes accused of attempting to influence opinion in a particular direction, either to suit the sponsor's biases or to make propaganda in favor of certain "interests."

Senator Pat Harrison, Democrat, of Mississippi, for example, saw a plot in the *Digest* poll of 1924, and viewed the *Digest* undertaking as a mammoth plan concocted by the Republican campaign managers to deceive a gullible public into believing that President Coolidge was a "sure winner." Many other observers could not understand why the *Digest* sponsors should periodically spend about $500,-000 in conducting a straw vote unless they had some ulterior political motive, or were being subsidized in secret by some propaganda organization. The Anti-Saloon League journal, *American Issue,* charged that the enormous expenditures for the 1930 *Literary Digest* poll on prohibition were not disinterested. "Evidently," declared the *Issue,* "those who are responsible for *The Literary Digest* poll are against prohibition."

But the fundamental reason why the *Digest* poll conducted its surveys on elections and issues was infinitely more simple. Part of the enormous cost of $500,000 was charged to circulation expenses. William Seaver Woods, the editor of the *Digest,* pointed this out in replying to the charges of Representative Tom Connally, Texas Democrat, on the honesty of the 1924 *Digest* poll:

> The Congressman wants to know who is paying our bill for this straw vote. The answer is that the bill is paid by *The Literary Digest*. It is a business proposition. Attached to each postcard sent for balloting is a subscription blank for the magazine. The returns in subscriptions have been enormous and they have paid the expenses of the polls.

In like manner, newspapers, from the early part of the nineteenth century to the present day, have measured opinion, primarily because their readers are interested in each other. Straw votes on candidates and issues paid dividends in heightened public interest, in increased circulations, and in growing reader confidence.

To the charges of dishonesty brought against the early newspaper and magazine straw votes, Dr. Claude Robinson, a student of the polls with years of practical experience, made this reply: "The general answer to these charges of dishonesty on the part of sponsors of straw votes is that practically without exception straw returns are gathered with honest intent, and that inaccuracies of measurement are due, not to deliberate faking, but almost always to faulty sampling technique. The simple guarantee of this honesty lies in the fact that the cost of such dubious form of support for either candidates or issues is far greater than any newspaper poll sponsor can afford to pay. One of the most jealous possessions of a newspaper is reader confidence. People do not buy publications which they feel they cannot trust. Reader confidence is an essential foundation for circulation; hence the lifeblood of a daily newspaper is to a high degree dependent on the faith the editors keep with the public. It requires long years of patient and costly toil to build up reader confidence, and no editor in his right senses would jeopardize this asset for such a paltry sum as the few votes he might influence by faking the poll returns. The day of reckoning is never far removed in a situation of this kind, for should an editor falsify a poll to help a particular candidate, despite indications pointing to victory for the opposition, he would need to wait only until election day to be exposed. His own readers would notice the discrepancy, and rival editors might also make some observations on the difference between straw and official returns. The offending editor would shortly be accused of dishonesty and double-dealing and reader confidence in his paper would be correspondingly shaken." [1]

The same drives which led single newspapers to try to get better news of public opinion over one hundred years ago still operate. The twin objectives—to interest a wide range of readers and to provide topical information about public opinion simply because to do so is good journalism—continue to motivate the newspapers which support and make possible the Institute's researches. If an editor, for instance, decided not to publish a release which indicated a result contrary to his policy, or if he attempted to modify the returns in some way, some of his readers would soon become aware of such censorship. On one occasion, when an editor, pressed by the demands of space in making up his paper, left out the findings of a particular survey, dozens of protests swiftly followed.

If the modern polls have a bias, it is not likely to come from the subscribing newspapers. Is there, then, a danger that those who administer the Institute's polls will become special pleaders for particular causes? Four main safeguards operate against this source of intentional bias.

The first guarantee that the Institute will not embark on a political crusade rests in the fact that the financial sponsors of its researches are a multipartisan group of over one hundred newspapers. The crudest form of self-interest would suggest that a poll which attempted to favor a particular party or cause would instantly create a demand for "secession" on the part of half its editorial sponsors.

The second check lies in the fact that so long as polls

---

[1] Robinson, Claude, *Straw Votes*, p. 79.

publicly continue to gauge their methods against the acid test of elections, they cannot make propaganda and survive. The poll which attempted to favor a particular side in an election campaign would lose its validity the moment the final returns were announced. Dishonesty offers the surest road to oblivion in this business of testing the nation's opinions, for the dishonest sponsor can be dishonest only once.

One of the most effective guarantees that the modern polls will not be used for propaganda purposes lies in the fact that the widespread discussion of the polls has created an alert and critical attitude toward them. With scores of competent critics eager to pounce upon errors, the surveyor has to meet their objections or go out of business. "A public which reads discussions of the technical accuracy of a *Literary Digest* poll or an American Institute poll," as Professor Harwood Childs has written, "and begins to think in terms of the adequacy of a sample, probable errors, and coefficients of correlation, is certain to become more and more skeptical of statements by individuals or interested minorities that public opinion is thus and so. In time, it may be bold enough to ask: 'What public are you talking about?' 'Did you make a complete enumeration?' 'If not, what method did you employ in sampling your public?' " [1]

Nor will a few specialists monopolize this critical apparatus. The continuous discussion of issues which the modern polls stimulate leads the individual voter to focus attention on specific public problems and thus clarify the issues in his own mind. The growing recognition that such things as propaganda and pressure groups really operate has put the public on the alert against any attempt to organ-

---

[1] Childs, Harwood L., "Rule by Public Opinion," *The Atlantic Monthly*, June, 1936.

ize a dishonest poll. In observing competing polls, the public will be likely to detect bias or fraud.

The fourth check lies in competition—competition between various types of polls and competition between the polls and other guides to public opinion. Free competition has always compelled the polls of public opinion to improve their technique and to check their methods against the rigors of successive elections. Polls which failed to adjust their methods fell by the wayside. Dishonest polls and polls which were well meaning but grossly inaccurate died an early death, as new competitors arose to challenge the old.

Although the record repeatedly shows a high correlation between poll findings and the results of actual elections, some critics have expressed doubt about the accuracy of surveys on issues. How, they ask, can we know whether or not the sampling studies of public opinion on the Supreme Court, the Townsend Plan, or the Neutrality Act represent a true picture of the divisions of public opinion, or merely the picture which the polls want to present?

To those who believe that pre-election polls can be checked more accurately than polls on issues, it must be pointed out that, in one sense, polls on issues are even more likely to hit the bull's-eye. Election forecasts represent at least four separate predictive estimates: The division of sentiment between candidates; the proportion of voters who will actually go to the polls; the effectiveness of the political machine in getting out the vote; the extent of such external factors as political corruption and the weather. A serious miscalculation in any one of these directions may be enough to make a survey inaccurate as compared with the election.

With this point in mind, we may turn to the checks on the reliability of polls on issues:

Polls on issues are based on exactly the same sampling procedures as polls which can be checked against actual elections. They use identical methods of interviewing, tabulation, and checking against information provided by the census and other sources.

Just as polls on candidates are checked by succeeding elections, so polls on issues are often followed by official or semiofficial tests. In the case of the Institute's poll on the question of the Maine sales tax, for example, the official state referendum held soon afterward pointed to the accuracy of the sampling. Again, in July, 1937, nation-wide tests were conducted by the Institute on the question: "In strict confidence and at no cost to you, would you like to be given by your physician a blood test for syphilis?" The same question was also asked of one million Chicago voters in a study conducted about the same time by the Chicago Board of Health. When the Institute's results from Chicago only were compared with the findings of the larger semiofficial study, they were found to tally within 2 per cent.

A final example, based on a study of past behavior rather than opinion, matched the accuracy of the survey technique against another measurement on the same problem. In November, 1937, the government attempted to measure the exact degree of unemployment in the country at large. Special ballot cards went out to 85,000,000 Americans, and persons who were unemployed or only employed part-time were asked to fill in the cards and return them to Washington. Some 7,822,912 cards were returned. Was this the true measure of the country's unemployment? Obviously not, for it did not take account of the unemployed persons who neglected to return the cards. The government then decided

to conduct a smaller census, based on a large sampling of
certain representative areas, in order to find out the proportion of unemployed who had failed to return cards. At
the same time as the government's sampling study was proceeding, the Institute conducted a survey based on its own
small cross section. The government's figure showed that
28 per cent had failed to return cards, while the Institute's
result showed a figure of 26 per cent, a difference well
within the margin of error to be expected in working with
small samples. Although this last example dealt with specific behavior, rather than with opinions, it still checked
the reliability of the sampling technique.

What is the guarantee of reliability in cases where no
immediate objective checks exist? The answer is common
sense. The results of over a thousand surveys of opinion on
issues are available for anyone who wishes to study them.
These results can be examined against the background of
the actual events at the time they were taken and in the
light of subsequent events. Such examination shows that
changes in opinion do not occur in haphazard fashion, but
are obviously related to the march of events. The relationships are not chaotic, but logical.

The precise causes of changes in opinion have not yet
been settled, but we do know that changes seldom take
place unless some event or series of events precedes the
shift. From the various trends which the Institute has
studied, the most complete record of opinion on one issue
is its index of President Roosevelt's popularity. This index,
begun in February, 1934, has been carried on for over
six years, in more than seventy successive surveys. When
the results are charted on a trend line and examined in
relation to events, there are no wild and meaningless gyra-

tions in the trend such as might appear if the surveys were wholly without validity.

When the Roosevelt-popularity studies began, the President had not yet completed his first year in office. The early surveys found him enormously popular throughout the country, with but a slight drop in prestige in 1934 during the controversy over the air-mail contracts. By 1935, however, the situation was quite different. The surveys showed a steady decline in his popularity during the first nine months of that year. Raymond Moley, in his book *After Seven Years*, has pointed to the drop shown by the Institute, and added that the 1935 period was a period of mounting criticism of the President. An extraordinarily long Congressional session lasted almost until September. It was the period of acrimonious debate over Roosevelt's $4,800,-000,000 work-relief bill—one of the largest appropriations ever made available for one President to spend. It was the period of mounting attacks on the N.R.A. before the Supreme Court decision killed the Blue Eagle. It was, finally, the period when the President was ordering "must" legislation and being attacked for attempting to railroad his bills through Congress. During this time, the Institute polls found a steady decline in the President's popularity, the curve sinking from 57 to 50.5. It began to rise again in the fall of 1935 after announcement of the so-called "breathing spell" for business, and continued to rise slowly in 1936. There was a dip when the Republicans nominated Landon, but after the first few weeks of the campaign, the President's popularity started to grow again and continued to the landslide election of November, 1936.

The Supreme Court plan of 1937 had a marked effect and set Roosevelt's popularity back five points. After the

Court issue had been settled, the President began to regain popularity, until the business slump which began early in 1938. The first nine months of 1938 saw a steady decline in Roosevelt's popularity, corresponding with the slump and the unpopular "purge" campaign. Whereas Roosevelt had begun the year with the support of 63 per cent of the voters, he had dropped to 53 per cent by the time the purge campaign ended. Just prior to the 1938 Congressional elections, the Institute index showed Roosevelt at 54 per cent. This figure was objectively confirmed in the election itself, when the Democratic-party strength at the polls was 52 per cent. With the succession of European crises and the final outbreak of war, the President's popularity in 1939 rose considerably above what it had been in 1938.

Such examples will suffice to show that the rise and fall of the Roosevelt-popularity curve bear a logical and demonstrable relation to what is going on in the nation at the time. A similar study of trends on other issues would dispose of the view that public opinion is fickle of changes overnight.

Competition provides the final check on the accuracy of issue polls. So long as there are a large number of competing organizations, plus the future prospect of regular surveys conducted perhaps by governmental departments and other organizations in competition with the existing polls, the public will have the best possible check on the accuracy of the polls on issues. Large divergences in the results of polls taken at the same point of time, and with the same type of question wording on the same issue, will undoubtedly arouse public suspicion and stimulate rechecks in the interest of greater accuracy.

In general, then, the same factors operate in both election polls and issue polls. The nature of present-day sponsorship, the acid test of elections, the growing awareness of sources of error, and the maintenance of free competition provide the essential mechanisms for separating impartial polls from dishonest polls. Such checks help the public to judge for itself.

★

★

CHAPTER NINETEEN

Quantity and Quality

ARE the number of opinions gathered sufficient to represent *public* opinion? Do the opinions thus obtained in direct interviews express basic convictions, or are they mere "snap judgments"? The problems of the adequacy and character of the opinions obtained by the polls appear frequently on the agenda of the critics.

For the most part, analysis of the statistical phases of procedure has yielded to a discussion of the nature of the opinions collected, and the dangers of faulty question wording. Occasionally, however, some people are puzzled by the sampling principles on which the polls are based. Frequently the question is raised: "But why haven't *I* been interviewed?" General Hugh S. Johnson has expressed skepticism concerning public-opinion polls because he claims that he has seldom met anyone who has been interviewed by one of the modern polls:

> Polls of public opinion of wide publication should be required to state, by areas and groups, the number of persons polled and a detail of the methods used each time. Last Thursday I talked to a convention of 1650 "Little Fellows" in business representing every part of the country. The subject of such polls came up in the closing forum. A question recently asked in the most widely publicized of them was asked of me. The opinion of that group was clearly not the opinion reported by the poll as being held by 88 per cent of

the people polled. So I asked all in that very *representative group* [italics ours] who had been polled in any enquiry to raise his hand. One hand went up.[1]

To those engaged in sampling public opinion, intense surprise could have been occasioned only if *more than one* "Little Fellow" had put up his hand. In a population of some 60,000,000 eligible voters, an opinion poll would not cover as many as 500,000 voters in a year, and it would take about 120 years to get around to the entire population. For this reason, by the very nature of representative sampling, the chance of striking a particular individual is remote. The protest: "I have never been interviewed!" is rather like the plaintive cry: "I have never won the Irish sweepstakes." In both cases, the odds are against it. But every poll will include individuals of every possible type. There will be farmers, Democrats, city folk, Republicans, people of every economic group and age level, and from every section of the country. In the sense that people with similar characteristics are included in the poll, every citizen of voting age is represented in the final returns.

But there is still another point to be considered. While General Johnson and the opinion surveyor agree on the need for a "sample" of some kind, they apparently disagree on the best methods of obtaining it. General Johnson implies that 1650 "Little Fellows" from all over the nation would constitute a "very representative group." The basis on which the polls proceed is that while such a group might be thoroughly representative of "Little Fellows," the proportion of "Little Fellows" must be set in its true context, among Big Fellows, Poor Fellows, Old Fellows, Young Fellows, and even Odd Fellows, not to mention a

---

[1] Hugh S. Johnson, "The Duty of Congress," column in *New York World-Telegram*, October 3, 1939.

fair proportion of Little Women, Big Women, and their various counterparts in the different economic, age, political, and geographical groups throughout the nation. Only in this fashion can a truly representative cross section of the American people be secured.

Emil Hurja describes a discussion he once had about polling techniques with William Allen White. Hurja had been enlarging on the various devices he used to build up his cross section of the voting public.

"That's all right," said Mr. White, "you spend a lot of time and a lot of money getting a national sample of public opinion. All I have to do is to get into my car and drive out to Clay Township and talk to the folks."

Between Mr. White's method and the method of the public-opinion poll, there is no essential contradiction. What the polls try to do is to project Clay Township on a nation-wide canvas. They select similar "typical" areas throughout the country and see people of all types and classes within these areas. The opinion surveyor's job is to get a faithful picture of sentiment, by "talking to the folks," always taking care to talk to the "right" folks in their "right" proportions. Larger averages and careful sampling assure the necessary measure of security.

The opinion surveyor is often asked: "How can you be sure that you are *really* getting at the convictions of the voters you interview? Doesn't a brief conversation with voters of all kinds raise many insuperable barriers that make it impossible to discover what people think? Must not their behavior and habits receive much more careful study than you are able to give in your short interviews? Isn't it true that people may answer 'yes' or 'no' only because they think they should answer, or because they would like to get rid of the interviewer?"

Such questions rest on the distinction between the "public" opinion which an individual expresses and the "private" opinion which he keeps to himself. Gordon W. Allport has emphasized this distinction in his discussion of attitudes and their measurement: "Many people," he wrote, "reserve for themselves the right to say one thing and to think another. Caught off his guard, an individual may disclose his innermost attitude, but the direct frontal attack which many psychological enquiries make provokes him to give merely a conventional answer. For this reason the task of investigating attitudes is difficult and hazardous." [1]

It is clear, at the outset, that in dealing with the responses of large numbers of people, the opinion surveyor must make certain assumptions. He lacks the time and the clinical facilities to conduct private psychological studies of each individual case, and like all other students of opinion who use question-and-answer techniques, his raw material must be the individual's own statement of his attitude. But while it is true that the individual's expressed opinions merely *indicate* his basic attitudes, and while he may have related underlying convictions which his opinions do not completely reveal, it is equally true that any other method of assessing public opinion must also measure overt indications. In an election, for example, the vote which an individual casts for a particular candidate is also

---

[1] Allport, G. W., "Attitudes," in Murchison, Carl, *A Handbook of Social Psychology*. Public-opinion surveys face similar problems to those which emerge in the psychological studies of attitude such as those conducted by Bogardus, Thurstone, Allport, and Hartman, and other students.

an *index* of his underlying attitude, and not the entire complex of attitudes which make up his whole personality.

Voting is only one way of revealing attitudes; writing an ear-splitting radio speech is another. So are political demonstrations, picket lines, campaign contributions. The opinion surveyor proceeds on the theory that a friendly interview in which the individual tells the way he feels about specific issues is perhaps the best method of finding out what his convictions really are. Clearly, then, it is never a question of "Do opinions represent basic convictions?" Such a question is unanswerable. The only valuable question is "Under what conditions do opinions *most nearly represent* basic convictions?" The final reply to this second question can only be given by abandoning speculation and referring to the field experience of the surveys themselves.

Ward canvassers for political parties engaged in a pre-election checkup know how hard it can be to get prospective voters to co-operate. Many of them will point out heatedly that how they are going to vote is their own damned business and then slam the door in the canvasser's face. Apart from being shown the door, the weary canvasser will encounter many other forms of resistance. He knows how easily the suspicions of people can be aroused, how they bluff or lie in an effort to conceal their true convictions. In the frigid manner of the housewife who answers the doorbell after dinner, the political canvasser can detect a lingering suspicion. What is this annoying person so inquisitive about? What business is it of his how a person votes? Isn't the information going to be used to stop Uncle Jake getting his job with the W.P.A.?

But it is just this kind of example that reveals the strong position of the public-opinion surveys once people become familiar with their objectives. They are nonpartisan. They represent no political party, no special "cause." They are interested not in molding, but in measuring, opinion. Investigators do not obtain the names of those selected for interviews. They use no coercion to obtain answers. Since the work that the surveys do is quasi-public, people who have seldom had a chance to express their views are given the opportunity of making their voices heard.

This point is underlined in the letters which come from field interviewers throughout the country. An interviewer in Indiana writes:

> The field interviewer's first problem in approaching a prospective respondent is to break down the natural barrier which is usually facing the stranger seeking information. The general rule I have found is that if the respondent has heard of the Institute's surveys, the rest is simple. All interview resistance vanishes. I have never known anyone who, when he knew the significance of the polls, didn't evidence a keen delight in answering the questions even when they concerned his religious and political faiths.

Another, in New York City, makes the same point:

> No matter what a person's first reaction is, but especially if it is adverse, it is inspired by ignorance of the work of the surveys and the very human suspicion in the great city of a stranger. It has become more than a theory to me that if the survey is properly explained, the first reaction of a respondent changes immediately to one that is both helpful and considerate.

An investigator in upstate New York strikes the same note:

> The greatest aid in starting the interview off on the right foot is when the respondent has heard of the polls of public opinion. Then the natural reaction is one of eagerness to take part in the surveys. When the poll is thoroughly understood, common obstacles, such as suspicion of motives, fear of saying the wrong thing, fear of sales follow-up, are re-

moved. It seems to me that as the work of the polls becomes more widely known and understood, the work of the interviewer will be more pleasant and accurate.

Thus the anonymity of the surveys, their fact-finding objectives, and the natural though often shy curiosity which most people feel in their own and in their neighbor's opinions—all these factors dispose the public to co-operate with the surveys. The resistance which arose frequently in the early days has tended to disappear as the polls have become more widely known. Once the interviewer has introduced himself, it is not uncommon for an individual to summon his whole family to see "the man who's come to get our opinion." In these cases it is the interviewer's task to single out the person he requires to fill the assignment, disregarding the side comments of the other members of the group. Sometimes, on the other hand, opinions will not be forthcoming while anyone else is listening. In nearly every instance, the interviewer will seize the first opportunity to assure the voter, "I don't want your name—just your opinion. You don't have to sign anything. I don't want to sell you anything."

The first question usually dissipates any suspicion that may exist. Especially in the poorer districts a man may believe that he is being asked to take an intelligence test, and that he will be graded on the "rightness" or "wrongness" of his replies. The first question usually reassures the hesitant individual; he is pleased to find that he can answer the question, that it is not too difficult for him. He takes more and more command of the situation, and his answers come more readily, often with his own spontaneous comments for personal flavoring. Interest generally increases as the interview proceeds, and at the end most people show genuine satisfaction and ask: "How do my opinions stack up with the other people's answers?"

For every individual who refuses to take the surveys seriously, there are fifty who earnestly try to give their own answers to the front-page issues of American life. However crudely people may speak, they generally make a sincere and honest effort to express their personal convictions. Interrupt the average American when he has a few minutes to spare, win his confidence, make him understand that his opinions really do count, and he will take up the questions slowly and carefully, like a man pondering the next move in a game of checkers. Concrete evidence that people do not merely "say one thing and think another" is to be found in the successful predictions of voting behavior. Interviewers' experiences with many thousands of voters —in offices, in homes, or on farms throughout the country —show that most people respond with honesty and directness to the survey questions.

What about "snap" replies? Are there not many people who simply have no opinion on a subject, or whose minds are so confused that their opinions are of little value?

No surveyor would deny that superficial replies frequently occur in the course of investigation. All the people interviewed do not have an opinion on every issue. An interviewer, in Texas, once divided the people she had met in four years of interviewing into the "positive class," the "pondering class," and the "parasite class." The first group, she wrote, were people who "usually answer the questions almost before I have finished reading them," and who may "want to add more of their own views on the back of the ballot." These are the "party men," the one hundred per centers. The pondering class "includes the great mass of people who preface their answers with 'Well, now let me think a few minutes.' " It is the third group, or "parasite class," which concerns us most here:

> The parasite class is composed of those to whom a genuine opinion is unknown. The nearest they come to conviction is "Well, yes, I guess so." Their usual answer is "Well, I just don't know. I can't say as to that." Most of them are in the lowest economic levels, but if there is someone else conveniently near they try to tap his opinion. If it is a woman (and unfortunately, the bulk of this class is made up of women), she will look for her husband and say with an explanatory air, "Ask him. I always think just like he does." Many of these people are foreigners, some of whom cannot read the papers and consequently have little interest in the questions on the ballot. Many of these "I don't knows" are women well up in the economic level who "just don't believe women have any place in politics." They don't want to be bothered with answering a lot of questions. "What difference does it make what I think anyway?" How will they vote on election day? Just exactly as they were told the night before.

Undoubtedly, the epithet "parasite class" is too hard. There are pockets in our democracy where the daily task is too time consuming and monotonous to provide an opportunity for thinking about public affairs. Undoubtedly, there are also stupid people in every walk of life, from the highest economic rung to the lowest. But a false stereotype of the composite public opinion would be created by forgetting the other side of the picture—the thousands of people who try to explain their attitudes and their reasons for holding them, in the hope that their voices will be heard.

One reason why people give ignorant and careless answers is that the issues have not been brought directly before them. People cannot hold opinions until they have heard about the issues. They must have had the chance of "listening in" on a full debate between the interested partisans. One investigator quoted a machine worker as saying at the end of the interview, "And if I'd had more time to study up on these questions, I might have done a whole lot better. You kinda took me by surprise."

This kind of situation reveals a problem which the polls can high-light, but which they cannot solve. The ultimate solution lies with the press, the radio forums, and the political parties, which must interest ordinary citizens in the central issues of the day. Survey results point to the deficiencies and shortcomings in public thinking and to the educational needs which can be met only by wide action on many fronts.

Frequently, the polls paint a graphic picture of the inconsistencies and contradictions in the public mind. Voters may favor lower taxes and general economic retrenchment and at the same time support greater expenditures for relief or more funds for guns and battleships. Some people may want a foreign policy in which the United States will take resolute action against aggressor nations, and continue to favor a policy of absolute neutrality. They may say, as a transport worker is reported to have said, that the "Reds should all be shut up by the government," and in the next breath assert that the government should support all the needy "even if it means the end of the capitalistic system." The answers may be inconsistent and confused. They may reflect the stereotypes of propaganda rather than the results of cool reflection. But surely it is wise to know that such inconsistencies exist, to try to chart the areas in which they are most prevalent, as the first step to knowing how far democratic education has gone and how far it has yet to go in order to complete its work.

It has been argued that people have certain basic attitudes, covered with a heavy "protective coating," which are too personal for the polls to reach. And must not the polls scrupulously respect certain "taboos"?

Some subjects may be embedded in so much emotional content that an impersonal questionnaire would reveal little, but surely we should test the approach itself before reaching any dogmatic conclusions. It is remarkable how freely people speak their minds to strangers. "It's not at all unusual for people to confide their troubles," one interviewer has pointed out; "after all, I'm a complete stranger—and it's someone to talk to."

Many of the taboos that arouse so much discussion have been found to be nonexistent so far as the mass of the people are concerned. When, for example, the Institute ignored the moralists and went directly to the people on the issue of preventing the spread of venereal diseases, it found that voters wanted to see all secrecy removed from the subject, and were anxious to support a nation-wide prevention drive. The taboo supposedly surrounding this subject did not exist in the minds of the people, but in the preconceptions of those who believed they knew what the people thought. And there are other questions on which most people have quite definite convictions and which they are surprisingly willing to discuss. "When *Life* published its picture of the 'Birth of a Baby,'" James Wechsler has written in *The Nation*, "all the decency legionnaires cried out in protest. It sounded as if America were unanimous in its repudiation of the facts of life. The Gallup Institute reported that a large majority of the persons it interviewed approved of the publication. This was important and useful news, and it is not a unique example; the polls have encouraged the suspicion that Americans have minds. Undoubtedly, there are 'blanks,' but one 'blank' is no proof that the 'masses is asses.'"

The truth of this contention emerges time and again in the course of meeting the public. Since 1936, for example, the Institute has conducted various surveys on the question of birth control, and the results show that people throughout the country have been perfectly willing to express their views on this topic. Even before the courts made it possible to send birth-control information through the mails, the Institute asked in one of its surveys:

"Should the distribution of information on birth control be made legal?"
Seventy per cent of those questioned voted "yes." Later, in July, 1936, voters were asked:
"Do you favor the birth-control movement?"
Seventy-one per cent voted in its favor. On later questions:
"Would you like to see a government agency furnish birth-control information to married people who want it?" and:
"Would you approve or disapprove of having government health clinics furnish birth-control information to married people who want it?" majorities of the same size registered. One voter expressed the attitude of those who favored these policies by saying that "people might as well get information instead of quackery." A final example may be taken from the experience of the French Institute of Public Opinion. A few weeks before the outbreak of war in September, 1939, one of its surveys dealt with the decline of the birth rate and the reasons for childlessness. The French public co-operated willingly in the experiment, giving reasons for the conditions as they saw them and suggesting possible remedies. In such cases, experience has shown that ordinary people eagerly spoke out on questions which might seem too intimate for the method of the opinion surveys.

Various other studies dealing with such "private" topics as living standards, size of the family, money income, and morals have also been conducted by the Institute and the *Fortune* Survey, and, in nearly every case, the people themselves have co-operated. The inference is clear. To the people who say, "You can't ask that!" the surveyor must point out that the proof of the pudding is in the eating.

Is there a danger that the polls oversimplify the picture of opinion by reducing the variety of points of view to a "yes" and "no" kind of response? Are not many questions too complex for such a formula?

The point has been raised from time to time and deserves close attention. "Publicized polls," it has been suggested,[1] "accentuate stereotyped thinking on political and economic questions. The use of a dichotomized technique instead of a graded scale makes for an oversimplification of issues. One must be either For or Against; one must answer Yes or No. For example, in *The Literary Digest* poll on the New Deal in 1935, people were asked 'Do you approve on the whole of the acts and policies of the Roosevelt Administration?' This all-or-none type of question discourages discriminating analysis and forfeits a host of individual attitudes by forcing people into two opposite camps."

This criticism does not rest on the claim that the polls are wholly responsible for the habit of dividing things into black-and-white categories. That is an age-old human trick. But some feel that the polls encourage this habit on occasions when it would not usually exist and when people would often prefer to qualify their attitudes. In the case of the *Digest* poll in 1935, many people wrote letters stating that they favored certain parts of the New Deal, but dis-

---

[1] Katz, D., and Cantril H., "Public Opinion Polls," *Sociometry*, p. 172.

liked others, and that they would probably have preferred
to check intermediate possibilities.

The modern polls have taken various steps to break
down the for-and-against responses into more than two
mutually exclusive categories. In the first place, increasing
attention has been paid to those voters who express a
"no-opinion" or "undecided" vote. In this way the sphere
of choice has been widened. This "no-opinion" vote may
frequently be of great importance and even modify the
proportions considerably. While the shouting and battle
cries usually come from those who have already chosen
their side—the crusaders and propagandists for rival causes
—this "no-opinion" or "undecided" group is sometimes
crucial.

"This third group," writes Elmo Roper, "is composed
in part of those who do not know what they think, and in
part by those who regard the proposal under consideration
as having some merit, but object to certain parts of it or to
the methods of achieving it. This is the group which looks
on, sometimes with amused tolerance, sometimes with dis-
may, sometimes with disgust, at the heat and disorder gen-
erated by the two warring camps. From this group come
the converts. From this group also frequently comes the
compromise proposal which the two other groups accept,
reluctantly or with relief. It is in some respects a balance
wheel group." [1]

At the present time, considerable attention is being paid
to this "no-opinion" vote, to find out under what conditions, on what sorts of issues, and in what social groups, it
is highest or lowest. In general, studies indicate that regular voters generally register a lower "no-opinion" vote

---

[1] Roper, Elmo, "Neutral Opinion and the Court Proposal," *Public
Opinion Quarterly*, July, 1937.

than nonvoters. The size of the "no-opinion" vote also tends
to increase as people in the lower economic groups, or as
the proportion of women, is increased. Again, the nature of
the issue may also modify the size of the undecided vote.
Hypothetical or remote issues increase the ratio of indecision. Questions such as: "If President Roosevelt runs next
year will you support him?" or: "Do you think Japan will
attack the U.S. in the next twenty years?" invite a high "no
opinion." Lowest "no-opinion" votes are secured on questions referring to immediate past behavior: "Did you hear
the President's last radio speech?" or personal and concrete questions like: "Would you be prepared to pay higher
taxes for rearmaments?" or questions on which opinion is
overwhelmingly one way: "Do you think the United States
should send our Army to fight Germany?" Undoubtedly,
the size and character of this "no-opinion" vote are inti-
mately related to the point of time at which the survey is
taken. If the questions are posed before the people have had
the chance to relate them to their personal values and experiences, a high degree of indecision can be expected.
Wider discussion and protracted conflict crystallize opinion about the rival banners of parties and programs, and
reduce the proportion of "I guess so" and "I haven't made
my mind up yet" opinions.

To measure public opinion is to imply that general
trends and common tendencies can be pigeonholed. But
surveyors are continually trying to register the shades of
difference between expressed opinions. The *Fortune* Survey regularly uses a graded scale of questions or a check
list of many alternatives. In this way, even in the presidential election of 1936, the *Fortune* Survey relied on
the old Shakespearian adage: "By indirection seek direction out." The *Fortune* ballot, in 1936, did not ask voters

directly whether they were going to vote for Roosevelt, but instead asked four *indirect* questions:

With which of the following statements do you agree?
a. Roosevelt's re-election is essential for the good of the country.
b. Roosevelt may have made mistakes, but there is no one else who can do much good.
c. Roosevelt did many things that needed doing, but most of his usefulness is over.
d. About the worst thing that could happen to this country is another Roosevelt administration.

These questions were graded to bring out the qualitative differences in public attitudes.

The Institute has developed another kind of approach by collecting the people's own comments as recorded by interviewers. The analysis of these comments sheds further light on the background of the opinions and on the reasons which people give for their choices. Such methods, coupled with the ordinary breakdowns by age, sex, political party, and other variables, give new life to the proportions and percentages. They yield a more accurate statement of what people are thinking and a more comprehensive analysis of what determines public opinion.

It has frequently been pointed out that while a minority may vote "no" on a question about the dissemination of birth-control information, this minority may be so well organized, cohesive, and powerful that it will outweigh, politically, an organized group in a numerical majority. But scientific polls are constructed to provide a simple numerical statement of the replies of a sample of individual voters. Within the limits of the quotas which set the proportion from each class, the Benthamite conception holds: "Everybody to count as one, nobody for more than one." How can the polls take account of qualitative factors such as the intensity with which opinions are held?

Quantitative measurement, or any device based on a counting of heads, runs the risk of ignoring certain qualities and characteristics in the materials it studies. Constructive research is also needed in the direction of "intensity" measurements. Numerous checks are beginning to be employed, both objective and subjective. A voter is asked his opinion for example, on the Wagner Labor Relations Act, and is then asked: "How convinced are you of that?" The replies to the second question provide a means of singling out the undecided individual or the person with little interest in the issue. It may well be, however, that the most effective way of measuring the intensity of an opinion will continue to be the study of majority and minority trends over regularly spaced intervals. A proposition that gains the support of an increasing number of voters, whether intensely approved by all of them or not, challenges our legislatures and forums.

Undeniably, the intensity of opinion is an important factor. It operates equally in elections, in political demonstrations, in pressure-group activities, and in all other ways that public opinion is expressed. But periodically a final estimate must be made, a vote must be taken, or a resolution passed. Elections, too, call for "yes" and "no" answers, and even dare to ignore the "no-opinion" vote completely. At some point, the members of the public are forced to choose between competing alternatives. Thus, opinion intensity can be seen in true perspective only in relation to time.

An issue arises, let us say, and instantly small interest groups form in defensive and attacking positions. Key

groups put forward propaganda to maintain the support
of their component members, to counteract the propaganda of the rival public, and to win adherents from the
ranks of the neutral and the uninterested. As the partisans
emerge more clearly, and the propaganda "for" and
"against" increases in intensity, the ranks of the opposed
publics close and the members gird themselves for battle
at the polls. Professor Lasswell's discussion of political action brings out the same sequence of events. Political
action, he writes, "begins in unrest. People act upon one
another excitedly, but their diagnoses of what the matter
is, and their prescriptions about what ought to be done, are
notably vague. Then public opinion develops. General symbols are invented into which restless individuals read their
private meanings. As discussion and agitation develop,
these symbols are gradually arranged in the form of a 'this
or that,' 'yes' or 'no' situation. The community is enabled
to pass *over* from controversy into action." [1]

Thus, whether the dispute is over a new taxation proposal, a change in the membership of the Supreme Court,
or the question of declaring war, public opinion moves
in successive stages. James Bryce saw this sequence clearly;
he was careful to distinguish between the amorphous profusion of individual impressions and points of view on public questions, the organized opinions which develop as the
result of social influences and controls, and the predom-
inant opinion which is known and accepted when the
members of the community have had a chance to express
their views. The development of a "typical" public-opinion
situation was seen in four stages: the *stage of spontaneous
impression*—the first response of the individual to the prob-

[1] Lasswell, Harold, "Types of Political Personalities," in Burgess, E.,
Personality and the Social Group, pp. 161-71.

lem at issue—was followed by the *stage of crystallization,* in which the press, local discussions, and public meetings helped to integrate individuals into opposed groups; crystallization led to the *stage of controversy,* which operated to drive the partisans still farther apart, and finally the *stage of resolution,* when public opinion is asked to choose between conflicting alternatives.

During the development of this crisis of public opinion, some people are affected intensely by the issues at stake, while interest and excitement tend to disappear as the circumference of the public is reached. But if the polls conduct their studies *continuously* through the successive changes from stage to stage, they will reflect the effects of the propaganda of those who hold their views intensely on the other groups who are lukewarm. When democracy is "standing at ease," the polls show indecision; when, at the final stages of the conflict, democracy "stands to attention," they show the crystallized opinions of the mass of people.

For making decisions is the essence of politics. These decisions may at times have to be made even before *all* the facts are in, for the simple reason that in real life *all* the facts *never* come in. Democratic government rests on the premise that people finally make up their minds and push their weight in one direction rather than another. The task of the polls of public opinion is to mirror these divisions while they are taking place and after opinion has been formed. When the polls interview people before the opinion-forming process has begun, they may find much confusion in the public mind. But even here, the poll technique will probably show a high "no-opinion" vote—as a warning beacon that the public has not yet had time to make up its mind. When issues are chosen and interviews timed to reach the public after full opportunity has been given for discussion of the issue, the polls will do their work well.

There can be little doubt that continuous polling has thrown much light on the nature of public opinion itself. Older conceptions of public opinion as the "social conscience," as some "superindividual force" which controls and molds men's minds, rather than as the interaction of individual points of view, are out of harmony with the facts. The idea that public opinion is compounded of the opinions of individuals in all walks of life outmodes older conceptions, and places the modern emphasis squarely on the rational and irrational factors in individual thought. Is it not possible that continuous tests of public opinion will force people out of the older dichotomies and exclusive stereotypes, in which they have at times sought refuge, and will stimulate them to think for themselves along nontraditional lines? By helping to focus attention on the fact that public affairs are, for good or ill, bound up with private affairs, the polls can perhaps play a part in the continuous educative process that is at the heart of effective popular government. The discovery of ignorance or confusion, as well as the discovery that people are often wiser than many critics of democracy think, is of equal significance for the successful working of democracy. The grave danger to democracy arises when the ordinary citizen begins to say: "It doesn't matter what I think—they'll run things their own way anyway."

CHAPTER TWENTY

Is There a Band-Wagon Vote?

PRACTICAL politicians occasionally criticize the public-opin-ion polls, because they believe that measuring the pulse of democracy will do serious harm to the patient. It has fre-quently been asserted that public-opinion polls are "dan-gerous," that they place the voting process in jeopardy by announcing the result before the electorate has ex-pressed its will on Election Day, and reduce popular inter-est in the election itself. Many political observers express the fear that the polls create a "band-wagon" rush to what-ever is presented as the popular side. Politicians appear to have devoted so much time and effort to swinging voters to their support by prophesying and publicizing ultimate victory that they have convinced themselves that this band-wagon technique is effective at all times and in all places.

The first charge is that polls tend to destroy the demo-cratic process by reducing the number of people who vote. "Winning" voters, urged Congressman Walter Pierce of Oregon, would feel that they were unnecessary for victory, while voters on the "losing" side would remain away from the polls because they thought it useless to go, since their candidate appeared doomed to hopeless defeat.

Congressman Pierce has also argued that election polls tend to handicap the losing side because, in his opinion, the publication of pre-election standings tends to swing voters to the band wagon, and influences doubtful voters to cast their votes for the winning candidate. The polls, it was urged, prejudice the presentation of the minority case, by making fickle or undecided voters swing in behind the majority.

To these contradictory arguments, certain facts must be opposed. In the first place, careful examination of the evidence reveals no sign that the polls operate to decrease the popular vote. In the period from 1920 to 1932, when the findings of *The Literary Digest* poll were widely followed, the popular vote in successive presidential elections rose from over 26,705,000 to more than 39,817,000 votes. The year 1936, when polling interest reached its peak, saw the introduction of improved sampling methods; more than 45,646,000 Americans cast their votes—an increase of 6,000,-000 votes over 1932, and the highest popular vote in the history of the nation. If it is plausible to argue that the polls decrease the popular vote, it might equally well be pointed out that the polls may have partially contributed to the increase in participation, by stimulating a more widespread interest in political questions. But all we really know is that a steady rise has taken place and that it has been caused by a combination of many factors.

More serious is the charge that "one person out of every five is a band-wagon voter" and will always come down on the "winning" side. But before going on to test the truth of this hypothesis, it must be observed that polls have no monopoly in the field of election forecasting. Predictions by newspaper correspondents, party leaders, and candidates have been an accepted part of every political campaign in the United States for generations. In the 1936 presidential election, the most accurate state-by-state forecast was not made by a poll, but by the Democratic Party

Chairman, James Farley. The Republican House Leader, Joseph Martin of Massachusetts, was extremely accurate in his prediction of the probable division of seats in the Congressional elections of 1938. If, in 1940, the polls are to be scrutinized on the grounds that they discourage voting or induce a band-wagon vote, undoubtedly some attention should also be paid to the pronouncements of the professional politicians. How many Republicans will turn around and vote for the Democratic candidate in November, 1940, if Mr. Farley again declares that the Democrats will carry every state but Maine and Vermont?

The real truth of the matter is that political partisans get news of the probable success or failure of their cause every day an election campaign is in progress. To hear that a farmer's organization has thrown its support to the Democratic candidate does not cause a Republican-party worker to wash his hands of the election. The news that the Republican candidate was booed at a local outdoor meeting does not ordinarily deter the Republican voter from going to the polls. Indeed, it might well be argued that party organizations would welcome some more objective technique for testing the division of sentiment and the effect of their campaign propaganda. The minority candidate and his agents at party headquarters would then know where the candidate's chances were weakest, and where further intensive work was needed. It is of more than passing interest to note that the Democratic National Committee employed a poll expert, Emil Hurja, to help chart the movements of political sentiment in 1932 and 1936.

A careful examination of the record reveals little evidence for the band-wagon theory. If Congressman Pierce's argument is correct, if one voter in five eagerly watches the poll returns to see which candidate is leading, and then suddenly decides to vote the "winning" side, it would always be true that between the first pre-election poll forecasts and the actual vote on Election Day, a substantial rise in the popularity of the winning candidate could be logically expected. Actually, however, scores of past-election checkups show that in most cases there is no such rise—the curve of sentiment indicating the support for each candidate is usually flat and, in fact, usually goes down toward the end of a campaign. In most cases, research indicates that the shift is actually in the opposite direction to that required by the band-wagon theory. In Ohio, in 1932, for example, the first preliminary poll taken by the *Columbus Dispatch* indicated that Roosevelt would receive 65 per cent of the total votes cast in the state. If surveys "make" as well as "measure" public sentiment, the band-wagon factor should have operated here. The *Dispatch* polls were well known. For thirty-odd years, that newspaper had conducted polls in Ohio, and its measurements had been widely acclaimed on the score of accuracy. Yet, when the *Dispatch* took its second pre-election poll, Roosevelt's strength had dropped in Ohio to 51 per cent—the approximate figure he received in the election. The trend of the *Dispatch* poll in Ohio in 1932 provides no basis for the view that voters hastened to climb on the band wagon.

In 1936, *The Literary Digest* conducted its poll on presidential candidates. Earlier successes had given the *Digest* poll tremendous prestige. There is little doubt that, of all the polls conducted in 1936, the *Digest* was easily the most widely known. But even with the backing of three successful predictions in previous presidential campaigns, with its returns widely publicized in the press of the entire country and over a nation-wide radio network, the fact remains that the *Digest*'s indication of a sweeping Landon victory ap-

250   THE PULSE OF DEMOCRACY

parently did not result in attracting voters to Landon. In
the election more than 27,000,000 voters cast their ballots
for the *Digest* "loser," while less than 17,000,000 voted for
the *Digest* "winner." Moreover, in states where all other
polls had little publicity, but where the *Digest* results were
given wide circulation through newspapers and radio,
Roosevelt's majority was just as large as in states where the
Institute's polls showing a Democratic victory were widely
publicized.

In 1938, the American Institute conducted a series of
surveys among Kentucky voters on the Barkley-Chandler
campaign for the Democratic nomination for Senator. These
surveys took place over a period of four months. The following table shows the trend of sentiment toward the two
candidates, as revealed by the successive surveys:

American Institute of Public Opinion Surveys

	Barkley	Chandler
	%	%
April 10	67	33
May 15	65	35
July 8	64	36
July 24	61	39
August 5	59	41
Election Result		
August 6	57	43

The Institute's surveys were published in the Louisville
Courier-Journal, the leading paper in Kentucky, and were
given wide publicity throughout the state. According to the
band-wagon theory, Senator Barkley should have continued
to gain strength from the time of the first survey, when he
had the support of about two thirds of the Democratic voters.
Instead, however, as time went on and Governor Chandler
carried his aggressive campaign to the rural voters among

Kentucky's unmapped back roads, Senator Barkley's share of the popular vote steadily declined.

In connection with its measurement of public opinion in this campaign, the Institute asked, in addition to the regular questions, which candidate the voters interviewed expected would win. Among Barkley supporters, 82 per cent expected Barkley to win, 16 per cent did not know which candidate would win, and 2 per cent expected Governor Chandler to win. Among Chandler supporters, only 52 per cent expected Chandler to win, 36 per cent did not know which candidate would win, and 12 per cent actually expected that Senator Barkley would win. A comparison of the survey results with those of the election indicates that, in this election at least, the band-wagon factor was not present. Instead, it appears that in Kentucky, in 1938, the voters moved toward the candidate of their choice, and that a substantial block of votes shifted from the side of the majority candidate to the side of the minority candidate as the campaign progressed.

Shortly after the Kentucky Democratic senatorial primary, the American Institute conducted a survey in another election, in which the band-wagon influence again seemed to be absent. This was the Georgia Democratic senatorial primary, held on September 14, 1938. The candidates were: (1) Senator George, candidate for renomination; (2) ex-Governor Eugene Talmadge; (3) Lawrence E. Camp, New Deal attorney, and (4) W. G. McRae, Townsendite. President Roosevelt had singled out Senator George as an opponent of the New Deal, and backed the candidacy of Mr. Camp.

During the election, Senator George referred to the Institute's early findings in his campaign literature and in several public speeches. The poll was widely publicized by the *Atlanta Constitution,* and its various reports showing the standing of the different candidates reached a considerable section of the voting public. The following table shows the trend of sentiment during the campaign as revealed by the Institute's published surveys:

	Camp %	George %	McRae %	Talmadge %
Distribution of Popular Vote [1]				
American Institute of Public Opinion Surveys				
Sept. 4	28	52	1 [2]	20
Sept. 9	24	52	1 [2]	24
Sept. 13	25	46	1	28
Election Results				
Sept. 14	24	44	—	32

According to the band-wagon theory, the strength of Senator George should have increased from September 4 on, at the expense of Mr. Camp and Mr. Talmadge. But just the reverse happened, and this in spite of the widespread publicity which the Institute's results received.

If the band-wagon psychology prevailed among the mass of voters, one might expect it to be especially apparent in the months before a party nominating convention. In testing the attitudes of voters to possible presidential candidates about six months preceding the 1940 party conventions, the Institute asked the following supplemental questions:

Do you happen to know which Democratic candidate is leading today in the polls on presidential candidates?

Do you happen to know which Republican candidate is leading in these polls today?

[1] The Democratic senatorial nomination is based on a county-unit-vote basis, but whenever a candidate has a large margin in popular vote, he usually also wins the convention vote. This was the case in the 1938 Georgia election.

[2] The small vote for McRae, who withdrew before the election, was not included in compiling the figures for the other three candidates.

By obtaining answers to these questions, the Institute was able to separate into two groups, the Republicans, for example, who said they followed the polls on candidates and those who said they did not. The members of each group were then asked which candidate they preferred for 1940.

Those who were reading the polls favored Dewey, Vandenberg, and Taft, in that order—which corresponded with the estimate of opinion polls at that time. But Republican voters *who had no opportunity to see the surveys* and did not know what they were showing voted *in exactly the same way*—for Dewey, Vandenberg, and Taft—and the percentage vote for each candidate was virtually the same as among those who knew the poll results.

The discovery that people continue to support their own chosen candidates, in spite of early estimates made by the polls of public opinion, should come as no surprise to contemporary observers of politics. Everyone is aware that the Socialists in this country keep polling a few hundred thousand votes in every campaign, yet most of these voters know that their candidate has little chance of being victorious. In 1936, the Institute found that 81 per cent of the Lemke voters thought Lemke would be defeated, but were voting for him anyway.

Thus, previous studies of the trends of opinion during past elections, and investigations of the relationship between the voter's actual behavior and his expectation of being on the winning side, fail to reveal any real evidence for the belief that polls create a band-wagon vote among the mass of voters. Undoubtedly, politicians and various partisan groups *act as though* such a theory had a real basis in fact. All of them picture their own side sweeping on to victory, but there are occasions when the actions of politicians are based on political mythology rather than on political science.

The view that the band-wagon vote operates on issues has even less validity. The Institute's research staff has carefully investigated past trends on issues to obtain proof or disproof of the view that people are mob-minded. Hundreds of questions on which at least two sets of figures at successive time intervals had been published were tabulated under various headings: (1) questions where the trend of majority sentiment was upward in accordance with the band-wagon theory; (2) questions where the trend of majority sentiment was downward contrary to the theory, and (3) questions where the trend was either nonexistent or inconclusive. In two out of every three issues studied the *trend was downward, and the vote for the "popular side" declined.* All cases which showed an upward trend were then carefully examined. The broad conclusion which emerged was that events rather than a knowledge of majority opinion were the fundamental determinants of movements of opinion. When, for example, the question was asked: "Which labor leader do you like better—Green of the A.F. of L. or Lewis of the C.I.O.?"

In July, 1937,   Green got 67%
In October, 1938,   Green got 78%
In June, 1939,   Green got 80%

The shift in favor of Green, which some might possibly take to indicate the presence of a band-wagon vote, is far more likely to be due to the hostile public reaction to the wave of sit-down strikes in which members of the C.I.O. were engaged during 1936-37.

Similarly on the question: "How far should we go to help

England and France?" the proportion of voters favoring selling food supplies rose from 57 per cent in September, 1938, to 76 per cent in March, 1939, and finally to 82 per cent in April, 1939. But, obviously, the significant factor here was the public's reaction to the real movement of events in Europe between the Munich Agreement and the German annexation of Bohemia and Moravia, rather than a simple-minded desire to imitate the majority.

The Institute's experience, both in elections and in issues, would seem to point conclusively to the fact that events and actions are infinitely more potent factors in influencing the formation of opinion than a mere desire to imitate one's fellow citizens. Polls of public opinion, claims of victory which come from competing candidates in a close-fought political campaign, the prognostications of political commentators—none of these factors *measurably affects* the voting conduct of the mass of the people.

The urge to follow the majority, which the psychologists call the "impression of universality," must be interpreted to mean not opinion of the nation as a whole, but rather the small intimate group who make up the individual voter's circumscribed universe. Thus, he may listen with some respect to the opinions of his friends, his associates, and the workaday groups with whom he is in daily contact, and the majority opinion of this group may at times be an important element in the formation of his attitudes. But there is no evidence to support the belief that public-opinion polls, making estimates on the basis of a national cross section of voters, have this effect on the individual voter. The case studies to date which describe the movements of opinions on the issues of the day reveal absolutely no tendency for voters to herd together in order to be on the winning side.

Final proof, or disproof, of this band-wagon theory must

await future research. It is possible that the use of a "panel" technique will make possible more precise knowledge of the fundamental causes behind shifts in sentiment. One thing is clear at the present time: of all the devices in the politician's bag of tricks, the technique of appealing to band-wagon voters is most out of harmony with the available facts. *It is the impact of events, and the everyday conditions and experiences of the mass of the people, which supply the motive force of political action.*

★

CHAPTER TWENTY-ONE

★

Will the Polls Destroy Representative Democracy?

ANOTHER accusation leveled at the modern polls is based on the assumption that they intensify the "band-wagon" instinct in legislators and undermine the American system of representative government. "Ours is a representative democracy," a newspaper editorial suggested soon after the polls had become prominent in 1936, "in which it is properly assumed that those who are chosen to be representatives will think for themselves, use their best judgment individually, and take the unpopular side of an argument whenever they are sincerely convinced that the unpopular side is in the long run in the best interests of the country."

The point has been made more recently by a student of public opinion. "If our representatives were told," it has been written, "that 62% of the people favored payment of the soldier's bonus or 65% favored killing the World Court Treaty, the desire of many of them to be re-elected would lead them to respond to such statistics by voting for or against a measure not because they considered it wise or stupid but because they wanted to be in accord with what was pictured to them as the will of the electorate." [1]

Beyond such criticisms, and at the root of many objections to the polls of public opinion, lies a fundamental conflict be-

---

[1] Smith, C. W., *Public Opinion in a Democracy*, New York, 1939, p. 411.

257

tween two opposed views of the democratic process and what
it means. This conflict is not new—it is older than American
political theory itself. It concerns the relationship between
representative government and direct democracy, between
the judgments of small exclusive groups and the opinions
of the great mass of the people. Many theorists who criticize
the polls do so because they fear that giving too much power
to the people will reduce the representative to the role of
rubber stamp. A modern restatement of this attitude may
be found in an article written by Colonel O. R. Maguire in
the November, 1939, issue of the *United States Law Review*.[1]

Colonel Maguire quotes James Madison: ". . . pure democracies . . . have ever been spectacles of turbulence and
contention; have ever been found incompatible with personal security or the rights of property; and have in general been as short in their lives as they have been violent in
their deaths."

To support these statements made by an eighteenth-
century conservative who feared the dangers of "too much
democracy," Maguire insists that the ordinary man is incapable of being a responsible citizen, and leans heavily on
the antidemocratic psychological generalizations of Ross,
Tarde, and Le Bon. He follows James Madison and the
English Conservative, Edmund Burke, in upholding the
conception of representative government under which a
body of carefully chosen, disinterested public representatives
"whose wisdom may best discern the true interest of their
country, and whose patriotism and love of justice will be
least likely to sacrifice it to temporary or partial considerations," interpret the real will of the people. Under such

[1] Maguire, O. R., "The Republican Form of Government and the Straw
Poll—an Examination," *U.S. Law Review*, November, 1939.

conditions, it is argued, "it may well happen that the public voice, pronounced by the representatives of the people, will be more consonant to the public good than if pronounced by the people themselves, convened for that purpose." The polls are condemned because, in his view, they invite judgments on which the people are ignorant and ill-informed, on which discussion must be left to representatives and specialists. Finally, a grim picture is drawn of the excesses that will follow the growth of "direct democracy": ". . . the straw ballot will undermine and discourage the influence of able and conscientious public men and elevate to power the demagogue who will go to the greatest extremes in taking from those who have and giving to those who have not, until there has been realized the prophecy of Thomas Babington Macaulay that America will be as fearfully plundered from within by her own people in the twentieth century as Rome was plundered from without by the Gauls and Vandals."

This case against government by public opinion reveals suspicion not only of the public-opinion surveys, but also of the mass of the people. By and large, the thesis that the people are unfit to rule, and that they must be led by their natural superiors—the legislators and the experts—differs only in degree, and not in essence, from the view urged by Mussolini and Hitler that the people are mere "ballot cattle," whose votes are useful not because they represent a valuable guide to policy, but merely because they provide "proof" of the mass support on which the superior regime is based. It must not be forgotten that the dictators, too, urge that the common people, because of their numbers, their lack of training, their stupidity and gullibility, must be kept as far away as possible from the elite whose task it is to formulate laws for the mass blindly to obey.

Many previous statements and charges of just this kind can be found throughout history. Every despot has claimed that the people were incapable of ruling themselves, and by implication decided that only certain privileged leaders were fit for the legislative task. They have argued that "the best" should rule—but at different times and in different places the judgments as to who constituted "the best" have been completely contradictory. In Burke's England or Madison's America, it was the peerage or the stable wealthier classes —"the good, the wise, and the rich." In Soviet Russia, the representatives of the proletariat constitute "the best."

But the history of autocracy has paid eloquent testimony to the truth of Lord Acton's conclusion that "Power corrupts —absolute power corrupts absolutely." The possible danger of what has been called "the never-ending audacity of elected persons" emphasizes the need for modifying executive power by the contribution of the needs and aspirations of the common people. This is the essence of the democratic conception: political societies are most secure when deeply rooted in the political activity and interest of the mass of the people and least secure when social judgment is the prerogative of the chosen few.

The American tradition of political thought has tried to reconcile these two points of view. Since the beginning of the country's history, political theorists have disagreed on the extent to which the people and their opinions could play a part in the political decision.

"Men by their constitutions," wrote Jefferson, "are naturally divided into two parties: 1.—Those who fear and distrust the people and wish to draw all powers from them into the hands of the higher classes; 2.—Those who identify themselves with the people, have confidence in them, cherish and consider them as the most wise depository of the public interests." [1] Jefferson himself believed that the people were less likely to misgovern themselves than any small exclusive group, and for this reason urged that public opinion should be the decisive and ultimate force in American politics.

His opponents have followed Alexander Hamilton, whose antidemocratic ideas provide an armory for present-day conservatives. "All communities divide themselves into the few and the many," Hamilton declared. "The first are the rich and well-born, the others are the mass of the people. The voice of the people has been said to be the Voice of God; and however generally this maxim has been quoted and believed, it is not true in fact. The people seldom judge or determine right." Those who have followed the Federalist philosophy have largely been concerned with the liberties and property of the minority and have continually urged the necessity of building checks against the people's power.

Those who favor rule of "the best," through the gifted representative, and those who desire to give the common people more power are frequently at loggerheads because their arguments do not meet each other. The need exists to find the right balance between the kind of mass judgments and comments obtained by the public-opinion polls and the opinions of legislators. Both extreme views contain a kernel of truth. No one would deny that we need the best and the wisest in the key positions of our political life. But the democrat is right in demanding that these leaders be subject to check by the opinions of the mass of the people. He is right in refusing to let these persons rule irresponsibly. For in its most extreme form, the criticism that opposes any effort, like the modern polls, to make the people more articu-

---

[1] Agar, Herbert, *Pursuit of Happiness*, p. 42.

late, that inveighs against the perils of a "direct democracy," leads directly to antidemocratic government. If it is argued that legislators understand better than the people what the people want, it is but a short step to give legislators the power to decree what the people *ought* to want. Few tendencies could be more dangerous. When a special group is entrusted with the task of determining the values for a whole community, we have gone a long way from democracy, representative or any other kind.

The debate hinges to some extent on which particular theory of the representatives' role is accepted. There is the view which the English Conservative, Edmund Burke, advanced in the eighteenth century to the electors of Bristol: "His unbiased opinion, his mature judgment, his enlightened conscience, he ought not to sacrifice to you; to any man, or to any set of men living. These he does not derive from your pleasure. They are a trust from Providence, for the abuse of which he is deeply answerable. Your representative owes you, not his industry only, but his judgment; and he betrays instead of serving you, if he sacrifices it to your opinion." This view has been restated more sharply in the words of the Southern Senator who is reported to have told a state delegation: "Not for hell and a brown mule will I bind myself to your wishes." But, on the other hand, it must be remembered that the electors of Bristol rejected Burke after his address, and that there are many in our own day who take the view that one of the legislator's chief tasks in a democracy must be to "represent."

Unless he is to be the easy prey of special interests and antisocial pressure, he must have access to the expression of a truly "public" opinion, containing the views of all the groups in our complex society. For free expression of public opinion is not merely a right which the masses are fortunate to possess—it is as vital for the leaders as for the people. In no other way can the legislators know what the people they represent want, what kinds of legislation are possible, what the people think about existing laws, or how serious the opposition may be to a particular political proposal. A rigid dictatorship, or any organization of political society which forbids the people to express their own attitudes, is dangerous not only to the people, but also to the leaders themselves, since they never know whether they are sitting in an easy chair or on top of a volcano. *People who live differently think differently.* In order that their experience be incorporated into political rules under which they are to live, their thinking must be included in the main body of ideas involved in the process of final decisions. That is why the surveys take care to include those on relief as well as those who draw their income from investments, young as well as old, men and women of all sorts from every section of the country, in the sample public.

Another form which the case against the people takes is the argument that we are living today in a society so complex and so technical that its problems cannot be trusted to the people or their representatives, but must be turned over to experts. It has been urged that only those who know *how* to legislate should have the power of decreeing what type of legislation *ought* to exist. The Technocracy movement put this view squarely before the American public. If it is true, it means that the kind of mass value judgments secured by the polls and surveys is quite useless in political life. It means that the people and their representatives must abdicate before the trained economist, the social worker, the expert in public finance, in tariffs, in rural problems, in foreign affairs. These learned persons, the argument runs, are the only ones who know and understand the facts and, therefore, they alone are competent to decide on matters of policy.

There is something tempting about the view that the people should be led by an aristocracy of specialists. But Americans have learned something from the experience of the past decade. They have learned, in the first place, that experts do not always agree about the solutions for the ills of our times. "Ask six economists their opinion on unemployment," an English wag has suggested, "and you will get seven different answers—two from Mr. John Maynard Keynes."

The point is obviously exaggerated. Certainly today a vast body of useful, applicable knowledge has been built up by economists and other specialists—knowledge which is sorely needed to remedy the ills of our time. But all that experts can do, even assuming we can get them to agree about what need be done, is to tell *how* we can act.

The objectives, the ends, the basic values of policy must still be decided. The economist can suggest what action is to be taken if a certain goal is to be reached. He, speaking purely as an economist, cannot say what final goal *should* be reached. The lawyer can administer and interpret the country's laws. He cannot say what those laws should be. The social worker can suggest ways of aiding the aged. He cannot say that aiding aged persons is desirable. The expert's function is invaluable, but its value lies in judging the means—not the ends—of public policy.

Thus the expert and his techniques are sorely needed. Perhaps Great Britain has gone even further than the United States in relating expert opinion to democratic government. The technique of the Royal Commission, and the other methods of organizing special knowledge, are extremely valuable ways of focusing the attention of the general public on specific evils and on solutions of them. In these Commissions, expert opinion is brought to bear, and opportunities for collective deliberation are created for those with special knowledge of political and economic questions. But even these Royal Commissions must remain ineffective until the general public has passed judgment on whether or not their recommendations should be implemented into legislation.

As a corollary of this view that expert opinion can bear only on specific questions of means, on the technical methods by which solutions are to be achieved, we must agree that most people do not and, in the nature of things, cannot have the necessary knowledge to judge the intimate details of policy. Repeated testing by means of the poll technique reveals that they cannot be expected to have opinions or intelligent judgments about details of monetary policy, of treaty making, or on other questions involving highly specialized knowledge. There are things which cannot be done by public opinion, just as there are things which can only be done by public opinion. "The people who are the power entitled to say what they want," Bryce wrote, "are less qualified to say how, and in what form, they are to obtain it; or in other words, public opinion can determine ends, but is less fit to examine and select means to those ends." [1]

All this may be granted to the critics. But having urged the need for representatives and experts, we still need to keep these legislators and experts in touch with the public and its opinions. We still have need of declarations of attitudes from those who live under the laws and regulations administered by the experts. For only the man on relief can tell the administrator how it feels to be on relief. Only the

---

[1] Bryce, James, *The American Commonwealth*, p. 347.

small businessman can express his attitude on the economic
questions which complicate his existence. Only women
voters can explain their views on marriage and divorce.
Only all these groups, taken together, can formulate the
general objectives and tendencies which their experience
makes them feel would be best for the common welfare. For
the ultimate values of politics and economics, the judgments
on which public policy is based, do not come from special
knowledge or from intelligence alone. *They are compounded from the day-to-day experience of the men and
women who together make up the society we live in.*

That is why public-opinion polls are important today.
Instead of being attempts to sabotage representative government, kidnap the members of Congress, and substitute the
taxi driver for the expert in politics, as some critics insist,
public-opinion research is a necessary and valuable aid to
truly representative government. The continuous studies
of public opinion will merely *supplement,* not destroy, the
work of representatives. What is evident here is that representatives will be better able to represent if they have an
accurate measure of the wishes, aspirations, and needs of
different groups within the general public, rather than the
kind of distorted picture sent them by telegram enthusiasts
and overzealous pressure groups who claim to speak for all
the people, but actually speak only for themselves. Public-
opinion surveys will provide legislators with a new instrument for estimating trends of opinion, and minimize the
chances of their being fooled by clamoring minorities. For
the alternative to these surveys, it must be remembered, is
not a perfect and still silence in which the Ideal Legislator
and the Perfect Expert can commune on desirable policies.

It is the real world of competing pressures, vociferous demonstrations, and the stale cries of party politics.

Does this mean that constant soundings of public opinion will inevitably substitute demagogery for statesmanship? The contrary is more likely. The demagogue is no unfamiliar object. He was not created by the modern opinion surveys. He thrives, not when the people have power, facts, information, but when the people are insecure, gullible, see and hear only one side of the case. The demagogue, like any propagandist of untruths, finds his natural habitat where there is no method of checking on the truth or falsity of his case. To distinguish demagogues from democratic leaders, the people must know the facts, and must act upon them.

Is this element secured by having no measurement of public opinion, or by having frequent, accurate measurement? When local Caesars rise to claim a large popular support for their plans and schemes, is it not better to be able to refer to some more tangible index of their true status than their own claims and speeches? The poll measurements have, more than once, served in the past to expose the claims of false prophets.

As the polls develop in accuracy, and as their returns become more widely accepted, public officials and the people themselves will probably become more critical in distinguishing between the currents of opinion which command the genuine support of a large section of the public and the spurious claims of the pressure groups. The new methods of estimating public opinion are not revolutionary —they merely supplement the various intuitive and haphazard indices available to the legislator with a direct, systematic description of public opinion. Politicians who introduced the technique of political canvassing and door-to-door surveys on the eve of elections, to discover the voting intentions and opinions of the public in their own districts, can hardly fail to acknowledge the value of canvassing the people to hear their opinions, not only on candidates, but on issues as well. It is simply a question of substituting more precise methods for methods based on impressions. Certainly people knew it was cold long before the invention of the thermometer, but the thermometer has helped them to know exactly how cold it is, and how the temperature varies at different points of time. In the same way, politicians and legislators employed methods for measuring the attitudes of the public in the past, but the introduction of the sampling referendum allows their estimates to be made against the background of tested knowledge.

Will the polls of the future become so accurate that legislators will automatically follow their dictates? If this happened would it mean rule by a kind of "mobocracy"? To the first point, it may be suggested that although great accuracy can be achieved through careful polling, no poll can be completely accurate in every single instance over a long period of time. In every sampling result there is a small margin of error which must never be overlooked in interpreting the results. The answer to the second question depends essentially on the nature of the judgments which people make, and on the competence of the majority to act as a directive force in politics.

There has always been a fear of the majority at the back of the minds of many intelligent critics of the polls. Ever since the time of Alexis de Tocqueville, the phrase, "tyranny of the majority," has been used widely by critics of democratic procedure, fearful lest the sheer weight of numbers should crush intelligent minorities and suppress the criticism that comes from small associations which refuse to conform to the majority view. It has been asserted that the same tendencies to a wanton use of power which exist in a despotism may also exist in a society where the will of the majority is the supreme sovereign power.

What protection exists against this abuse of power by a majority scornful of its weaker critics and intolerant of dissenting opinions? The sages of 1787 were fully aware of the danger, and accordingly created in the Bill of Rights provisions whereby specific guarantees—free speech, free association, and open debate—were laid down to ensure the protection of the rights of dissident minorities.

Obviously, such legal provisions cannot guarantee that a self-governing community will never make mistakes, or that the majority will always urge right policies. No democratic state can ever be *certain* of these things. Our own history provides abundant evidence pointing to the conclusion that the majority can commit blunders, and can become intolerant of intelligent minority points of view. But popular government has never rested on the belief that such things *cannot* happen. On the contrary, it rests on the sure knowledge that they *can* and *do* happen, and further, that they can and do happen in autocracies—with infinitely more disastrous consequences. The democratic idea implies awareness that the people *can* be wrong—but it attempts to build conditions within which error may be discovered and through which truth may become more widely available. It recognizes that people can make crucial mistakes when they do not have access to the facts, when the facts to which they have access are so distorted through the spread of propaganda and half-truths as to be useless, or when their lives are so insecure as to provide a breeding ground for violence and extremes.

It is important to remember that while the seismograph does not create earthquakes, this instrument may one day help to alleviate such catastrophes by charting the place of their occurrence, their strength, and so enabling those interested in controlling the effects of such disasters to obtain more knowledge of their causes. Similarly, the polls do not create the sources of irrationalism and potential chaos in our society. What they can do is to give the people and the legislators a picture of existing tendencies, knowledge of which may save democracy from rushing over the edge of the precipice.

The antidote for "mobocracy" is not the suppression of public opinion, but the maintenance of a free tribunal of public opinion to which rival protagonists can make their appeals. Only in this atmosphere of give-and-take of rival points of view can democratic methods produce intelligent results. "The clash and conflict of argument bring out the strength and weakness of every case," it has been truly said, "and that which is sound tends to prevail. Let the cynic say what he will. Man is not an irrational animal. Truth usually wins in the long run, though the obsessions of self-interest or prejudice or ignorance may long delay its victory."

There is a powerful incentive to expose the forces which prevent the victory of truth, for there is real value in the social judgments that are reached through widespread discussion and debate. Although democratic solutions may not be the "ideally best," yet they have the fundamental merit of being solutions which the people and their representatives have worked out in co-operation. There is value in the method of trial and error, for the only way people will ever learn to govern themselves is by governing themselves.

Thus the faith to which the democrat holds is not found so much in the inherent wisdom of majorities as in the value of rule by the majority principle. The democrat need not depend upon a mystic "general will" continually operating to direct society toward the "good life." He merely has to agree that the best way of settling conflicts in political life is by some settled rule of action, and that, empirically, this lies in the majority principle. For when the majority is finally convinced, the laws are immeasurably more stable than they would be were they carried out in flagrant opposition to its wishes. In the long run, only laws which are backed by public opinion can command obedience.

"The risk of the majority principle," it has been said, "is the least dangerous, and the stakes the highest, of all forms of political organization. It is the risk least separable from the process of government itself. When you have made the commonwealth reasonably safe against raids by oligarchies or depredations by individual megalomaniacs; when you have provided the best mechanisms you can contrive for the succession to power, and have hedged both majorities and minorities about with constitutional safeguards of their own devising, then you have done all that the art of politics can ever do. For the rest, insurance against majority tyranny will depend on the health of your economic institutions, the wisdom of your educational process, the whole ethos and vitality of your culture." [1] In short, the democrat does not have to believe that man is infinitely perfectible, or that he is infinitely a fool. He merely has to realize that under some conditions men judge wisely and act decently, while under other conditions they act blindly and cruelly. His job is to see that the second set of conditions never develops, and to maximize the conditions which enable men to govern themselves peacefully and wisely.

The "tyranny of the majority" has never been America's

---

[1] Lerner, Max. *It Is Later Than You Think,* 1938, p. 111.

biggest problem. It is as great a danger to contemplate the "tyranny of the minority," who operate under cover of the Bill of Rights to secure ends in the interests of a small group. The real tyranny in America will not come from a better knowledge of how majorities feel about the questions of the day which press for solution. Tyranny comes from ignorance of the power and wants of the opposition. Tyranny arises when the media of information are closed, not when they are open for all to use.

The best guarantee for the maintenance of a vigorous democratic life lies not in concealing what people think, but in trying to find out what their ultimate purposes are, and in seeking to incorporate these purposes in legislation. It demands exposing the weakness of democracy as well as its values. Above all, it is posited on the belief that political institutions are not perfect, that they must be modified to meet changing conditions, and that a new age demands new political techniques.

★

★

CHAPTER TWENTY-TWO

A Guide to the Public

How can the polls best be administered in the years immediately ahead? What role will they play in the future? Apart from the abortive suggestion that there should be no polls at all, and that all polls—good, bad, and indifferent—should be prohibited, various constructive proposals have been advanced from time to time dealing with the question of alternative types of sponsorship. Some individuals take the view that the power to conduct opinion surveys should be centered exclusively in the hands of the government; others think that tomorrow's surveys should be supported by some permanent endowment or trust fund. Most students of public opinion believe that supplementary government polls would be valuable, but maintain that the expanding frontiers in this new field of public-opinion research can be most thoroughly mapped by competing polls, tempered with some form of regular audit in the interests of both polls and public.

Few people urge that the polls are so dangerous they must be completely prohibited by law. In principle, any legislative ban on the right to conduct studies of public opinion would represent a gross violation of the Bill of Rights. In actual practice, the absurdity of trying to distinguish between the systematic study and publication of descriptions of public opinion and the informal study of opinion,

273

which is the daily occupation of every editor, politician, and observer of politics in the country, makes such a proposal as unworkable as it would be fantastic.

Would the polls be more honestly and more accurately conducted if they were run as a government monopoly? Those who have occasionally suggested that the government itself should take over all the present polls and establish a single bureau for periodically sounding public opinion have not always realized the implications of their views. In a political crisis a government which had the sole power to measure public opinion might be tempted to ask only those questions on which a clear majority for its own objectives could be secured, and to frame questions in such a way as to prove that the legislation is itself desired by public opinion. To grant a government the exclusive power to assess public reactions toward its own legislation would be a source of danger to the health of any community. The power of making laws and the right to judge the effects of those laws must, in a democracy, be separate and distinct functions. Only in a dictatorship are these powers of action and judgment unified in the same hands. When modern autocrats can be heard to shout: "I am Public Opinion," the critic is skeptical of the validity of his instrument and the reliability of his results. The guarantee of freedom rests in ensuring that the means of announcing what public opinion thinks do not rest solely in the hands of the government.

This does not mean that the agencies of national, state, and local government should not use this new instrument to find out more about the mass of the public and its needs. The last decade has witnessed an enormous growth in the number and power of government agencies which are responsible for the administration of legislation dealing with agriculture, business, and labor, with old-age pensions and unemployment, with housing, the security markets, and the problem of relief, with communication and transport, with natural resources, and trade practices. There has been a steady growth in the importance of the administrative branches of government in the continuous effort to cope with the technical and social problems of a changing society. One of the chief political tasks of our age lies in devising ways for maintaining democratic controls over these essential agencies, and in relating the special skills and knowledge of the expert and the administrator to the needs and opinions of the general public whom they serve. The suggestion made by Elmo Roper of the *Fortune* Survey that ". . . all governing units should seriously weigh the possibilities inherent in allowing the public to express its wants and its fears, its likes and dislikes," and should adapt sampling techniques to their special needs, is one that must command attention.[1]

There are indications that these needs are being increasingly met by reliance on accurate methods of measuring public opinion. To the indices provided by letters, newspaper comment, and other methods of keeping the administrative ear more closely to the ground, contemporary agencies are adding the results, and occasionally the methods of sampling studies of opinion. "The administrative publicity official," writes James McCamy, the author of a well-documented study of government publicity, "wants to know what the public thinks of his agency so he can plan his program to remove misconceptions. He wants to know too, whether the objectives set for his agency are approved by the public at large." [2]

---

[1] In "Democracy Must Think": Round Table Discussion of Public Opinion, 44th Annual Conference of National Municipal League.

[2] McCamy, James, *Government Publicity*, 1939, Ch. V.

Both the Institute and the *Fortune* Survey have asked a large number of questions which are highly pertinent to the aims and methods of the existing administrative agencies. Studies of opinion toward the social-security program, the public-health program, the administration of relief, and agricultural assistance, to name only a few, have provided the experts who deal with these problems with a better knowledge of public opinion than was previously obtainable. Perhaps the most interesting development for the future is the fact that the need to get frequent measures of public opinion is being met by the government agencies themselves. The recent creation of a public-opinion-survey branch of the Department of Agriculture in Washington, which conducts its own sampling tests of information and sentiment among the country's farm population, is an example. Such government efforts are a step in the right direction of building closer relations between the people and the agencies through which public policy is finally expressed.

Although the use of sampling techniques by government agencies would undoubtedly mark an advance, there can be little doubt that any government's exclusive control over these surveys, as over any agency through which public opinion is expressed, would not result in improved and more accurate methods. Rather would it be a long, and perhaps disastrous, step backward.

Could the polls operate more effectively if they were permanently subsidized by some trust fund or foundation? Such an endowment might sponsor some future poll. It would, however, work under a great disadvantage—the results would not reach a large public with the speed of daily newspaper publication. The prime condition for the successful working of public opinion is widespread publicity. Polls, therefore, can function well only if their results are disseminated to every part of the country, thus stimulating nation-wide discussion of common issues and problems. To maintain the results of public-opinion research in the archives of a library would give a few scholars and specialists valuable source material, but such data would do little to stimulate an interchange of ideas in a far-flung society.

To those who express the fear that private influences will inevitably operate to distort the picture presented by the polls, it must be plain that the accurate measurement of public opinion is in itself a necessary and important undertaking. Getting an honest account of public opinion is a direct interest of a growing number of groups in present-day society. In 1922, Walter Lippmann could write that "American political writers . . . have wished either to tame opinion or to obey it." In 1940, there is a growing perception—even on the part of American political writers —that it is equally necessary to study and chart its movements. The need to know the facts about public opinion as it is, and not as some particular group would like it to be, continues to be the driving force behind present-day opinion research. The objective of the surveyor is neither to tame nor to obey public opinion, but rather to describe its operation.

It is certain that the future will see the application of polling techniques to many phases of political, economic, and social problems. But in spite of the occasional and dryly humorous charges that the polls have now superseded elections and that with increasing accuracy the need for complete canvasses of the public can be met by frequent sampling surveys, there is no basis for alarm on this point.

As elections are at present decided, one single vote can provide the margin between victory and defeat. No poll, no matter how impartial its sponsorship, or how accurate its methods, can ever expect to reach a measure of accuracy sufficient to match this hair-line degree of precision.

Secondly, elections in which most of the people participate are essentially training schools in civics, which no public-opinion poll can possibly hope to rival. Where millions of citizens can listen to speeches, take their stand on the issues, and cast their vote, there is a real experience of what the rights of suffrage and free citizenship actually mean. The polls are not intended to supplant elections, although with intelligent use they can help to supplement them.

Projecting present-day tendencies, the development of hundreds of uses and organizations employing the sampling method can be safely prophesied. For in our own day, sampling techniques are not secret or mysterious rites to be practiced only by the initiated. They are widely used in the field of industrial and commercial research to solve a hundred and one problems which deal with statistical data, and to provide a basis of fact on which more intelligent decisions may be made. These decisions are not only concerned with consumers' attitudes, but with the whole range of business and labor problems within the general field of public relations.

"As the science of measuring public opinion is further developed," writes Robert Updegraff in his study of the polls, "one can predict a very bright future for it. Though it grew out of commercial researches carried on by advertising agencies and private research organizations, its possibilities in the field of commerce and industry have by no means reached their limit. In the future, there will be few questions that merchants or manufacturers will guess about, as applied to their products or services, their policies, or their relations with the public or their workers. They will employ the science of opinion testing and know for certain. Furthermore, this public opinion auditing will be carried on as matter-of-factly as the auditing of their books of account."

Polling is a valuable technique wherever the interests or opinions or activities of large groups of people need to be consulted. Recent years have seen universities and colleges running their own polls to obtain information about the interests and attitudes of college students. Practical politicians and newspaper editors have occasionally organized polls and surveys. The future alone will dictate the uses and limitations of the sampling method.

For the protection of those earnestly engaged in polling public opinion, as well as for the general public which uses the surveys as an index of trends and probabilities, it will be necessary to establish some form of public audit to check the various phases of polling procedure. The public is entitled to know all the facts about the polls of public opinion. The people should be informed of the nature of the sponsorship of various polls, and should know where the money for the polls comes from. They are entitled to know the methods used, the number of people in the sample, the method of collecting the ballots, and the margins of error within which the published figures are to be interpreted. Just as the daily newspapers and the general public are protected by the Audit Bureau of Circulations which makes it necessary to reveal the size of circulations and the methods by which circulation is obtained, the polls of public opinion should also be protected by a similar form of audit. The mechanics of such a system would not be difficult to evolve.

An advisory council composed of statisticians, psychologists, and representative members of various political groups could check the methods and accuracy of polling organizations at regular intervals. This kind of audit would be useful both to the public and to those engaged in opinion research.

This much is clear. The real difficulties confronting those engaged in polling public opinion would also exist under any system of sponsorship. Whether the poll of the future is conducted by competing organizations, by the government, or by a group of individuals as morally impeccable as Plato's guardians, the major problems will not arise from the pressure of "powerful interests." They will emerge in the day-to-day effort to refine the polling procedures and to eliminate the detectable sources of bias.

There can be little doubt that 1940 and succeeding years will bring forward a spate of polls. Some will be good, others bad. The methods built up in the past four years by the existing surveys will no doubt be modified as better ways of testing opinion are demonstrated. In the bewildering profusion of polls of all sorts, the people must have a guide against which to check the competing estimates. Measuring public opinion is only one aspect of the whole problem—the other important aspect lies in the use of critical principles of interpretation on the part of the members of the public.

The critical individual who follows public-opinion polls and wants a set of rough criteria by which to judge between competing estimates may find the following list of interpretative principles a useful guide to understanding:

1. Who is conducting the poll? How is the poll financed?
2. How were the ballots collected? By ballot-in-the-paper methods? By spot canvassing? By mail interviews? By the

use of personal interviews? If the ballot-in-the-paper method or the mail poll has been used, what proof is there that the groups who respond are representative of the whole?

3. What controls have been used to ensure that the sample shall be as representative as possible of the total voting population?

4. Are the returns given according to how the various groups voted in the previous election? Is this vote according to past affiliation proportionate to the actual division of the previous vote in various sections?

5. Are the returns presented by different income groups, age groups, sex, geographical area? Is there evidence that any of these groups was underestimated in the total sample?

6. If the poll is conducted by mail or by a ballot-in-the-paper technique, is there any evidence of "stuffing the ballot box" on the part of pressure groups, or of a failure to co-operate in the poll on the part of large sections of the public?

7. What kind of a cross section was used? A social cross section, or a cross section based on eligible voters? Is there reason to believe that individuals or groups were included in the poll who might be excluded by voting requirements in certain areas?

8. How large was the sample? Was it large enough to meet the requirements of scientific sampling?

9. When was the survey taken? Is the result an early figure, or were the opinions collected near enough to the actual election to avoid error due to changing sentiment over time? Were successive and comparable samples used to provide a measure of the changing trend, or were the results cumulated throughout the campaign?

Such general principles are equally important in polls on issues, as well as certain other points which are especially relevant here:

1. Is it the kind of issue on which a considerable section of the public can reasonably be expected to have an opinion? If not, has the "no-opinion" vote been reported?

2. Is the question worded fairly to permit the expression of competing points of view? Does it use emotional words and "stereotypes," or is it worded neutrally?

3. Has the result been interpreted in the light of the actual wording of the question?

4. When was the poll taken? Is there any evidence that opinion has shifted since the poll was taken?

Such a brief guide can perhaps act as a yardstick against which competing polls may be placed, and may provide general directives for the public in interpreting future estimates of opinion.

Of all the safeguards which may be devised to regulate and check either the antisocial or inaccurate use of this instrument, no legal formula or mathematical tables of precision can take the place of an interested and enlightened public opinion. When all possible precautions have been taken, when every source of error has been thoroughly accounted for, the future role and limitations of the polls, and their relation to other modes of public expression, will ultimately be determined by the people themselves.

What is becoming clearer with each passing day is that techniques like the press, the radio, or the polls of public opinion are instruments which may be used either to make democracy work better or to enchain it in its own fetters. Undoubtedly, they are "instruments of power," but, in the last analysis, it is not those who administer them, but the public itself, which sets the limit within which they can operate. The limitations and shortcomings of the polls are the limitations and shortcomings of public opinion itself.

★

CHAPTER TWENTY-THREE

★

The Average Opinion of Mankind

ON THE afternoon of November 15, 1939, President Roosevelt formally dedicated the Thomas Jefferson Memorial on the rim of the Tidal Basin, in Washington. To the large audience of government officials, foreign diplomats, and citizens gathered on the Basin shore below, he recalled Jefferson's contribution to the political philosophy of America.

"Jefferson lived as we live," declared the President, "in the midst of a struggle between rule by the self-chosen individual or the self-appointed few on the one hand, and rule by the franchise and approval of the many on the other. He believed as we do that the average opinion of mankind is in the long run superior to the dictates of the self-chosen."

Thomas Jefferson's faith in government by public opinion was a source of strength in the political struggle against his Federalist opponents. John Adams and Alexander Hamilton distrusted and feared the common man. They condemned democracy as "rule of the worst," and compared its advance to the slow but certain approach of death. They defended a monopoly of public thought and action by an exclusive, propertied minority. They regarded an elite of wealthy and educated citizens as the only safe depository of the public interest.

Our own faith in democracy has to meet the combined

challenge of the dogmas of dictatorship, and the more
subtle but also more dangerous doctrines promulgated by
those in our midst who speak in the name of democracy
only to achieve antidemocratic purposes. The current
denunciations differ little from those of a century ago.
There is the same insistence that the opinions of the
common man are founded on quicksand, the same charges
that public opinion is too stupid and unreliable to form
the basis of sound public policy, the same praise of government by a dominant elite.

Throughout the historical debate, the case against the
common man has frequently proceeded on the basis of the
flimsiest circumstantial evidence. He has been led meekly
to the bar of justice and pronounced guilty. He has not
been granted a fair chance to call his key witnesses and make
his own defense. Whether the final sentence has been that
the People is a Great Beast, or that the Masses are Unfit to
Rule, the critics of democracy frequently issue their verdict
on the basis of fear rather than fact.

Those who followed Thomas Jefferson in combating the
arguments of the Federalists based their case on a profound
belief in the fundamental wisdom of the people. In attacking entrenched privilege, the protagonists of the emergent
democratic creed declared that the voice of the people was
the voice of God. But even Jefferson's own conception of
"the people" was restricted in its political application. He
envisaged an ideal democratic society based largely on independent farmers and small landowners. "Those who labor
in the earth," he wrote, "are the chosen people of God,
if ever He had a chosen people, whose breasts He has made
His peculiar deposit for substantial and genuine virtue."
Yet the task of building a continent was too tremendous

THE AVERAGE OPINION OF MANKIND 285

to be bound by the narrow political qualifications suited to the needs of a local, agricultural economy.

Jacksonian democracy and the drive for manhood suffrage were the inevitable consequences of the growing equality of frontier economic and social conditions. An expanding industrialism sustained the march of political democracy. Each successive step in the rise of the common man produced a new resurgence of faith. "Throughout the nineteenth century," Walter Lippmann writes, "the people were flattered and mystified to hear that deep within a fixed percentage of them there lay the same divine inspiration and the same gifts of revelation which men had attributed previously to the established authorities." It was inevitable that the fight against dogmatism made faith in democracy itself dogmatic.

This fight against dogmatism is on again. The wheel of history has turned full circle, and once more the idea of rule by public opinion is challenged by those who favor rule by the self-chosen. But we cannot meet today's attack with yesterday's slogans. Each generation must fight its own democratic struggle, on its own terms and with its own weapons. Our epoch is re-examining the mysticism that encrusts so many political habits in an attempt to discover fundamental truths. Americans today are no less devout in their attitude toward democracy than the pioneers of a century ago. If they are tired of lip service, they are also more eager to grapple with the underlying realities. They still answer their critics of democracy, but they make reply in the light of actual experience. The modern answer will continue to rest on faith, but it will be a faith based on reason and evidence.

In providing an objective and continuous record of

public opinion at work, the polls of public opinion supply an indispensable part of this evidence. For the first time in democratic history, these continuous surveys of what America thinks are enabling us to collect the facts about public opinion. Public-opinion research provides an objective week-to-week description of the values to which the people hold, and the prejudices and attitudes which they have formed out of their own experiences. Their judgments on hundreds of recent social, political, and economic issues are on file for all to examine and to evaluate.

Those who review the accumulated evidence and observe the trends of public opinion on the dominant issues of the last few years—foreign policy, unemployment, relief, labor problems, business recovery, domestic politics, and social questions—will gain a refreshing insight into the private worlds of the people who seldom make the front pages, but who, in the last analysis, make democratic history.

In scanning the record, it is not difficult to find individual cases of ignorance, stupidity, and apathy. The polls have discovered some people who do not know the difference between the Supreme Court and the local police court. They have discovered others who would willingly follow any golden voice which promised forty acres and a mule in return for their political support. They have talked with individuals who admit that they have never cast a vote. But when many of these instances of ignorance, stupidity, and apathy are studied closely, it becomes apparent that somewhere the machinery of our democratic institutions has gone wrong. The public contains many people who have never been fitted by education for the task of citizenship. Others have found their economic life so insecure that they readily fall victim to false panaceas. They are so engrossed in the daily struggle to make ends meet that they have neither the time nor the opportunity to think coherently about the nation's problems.

But there are two fundamental reasons for optimism about the quality of public opinion in our democracy. In the first place, the evidence shows that some people judge badly and that a few people have no equipment at all for forming intelligent opinions. This will stimulate all who have the future of our democracy at heart to ask two questions: "Why is this so?" and "What are we going to do about it?" To relate these "pathological" conditions of opinion to the social and psychological background in which they arise is the first step. It eliminates the use of such emotional epithets as the "swinish multitude," and brings into focus the social conditions under which public opinion can work most effectively. If the central problem of public opinion is really, as Jeremy Bentham once said, "to maximize the rectitude of the decisions by it," the solution of that problem will depend on analytical study of public opinion as it is.

In the second place, it is important to realize that ignorance, stupidity, and apathy are the exception, not the rule. The serious observer of public opinion on scores of issues cannot fail to come away with a feeling of intense admiration for the honesty and common sense with which an enormous number of ordinary people in all walks of life and at all levels of the economic scale have continued to meet their responsibilities as citizens. He will be profoundly impressed with the grasp of broad principles which voters of all types possess, and with their capacity to adjust themselves to the ever-changing movement of events.

By helping the people speak for themselves, the polls

have rediscovered the vital truth which the philosopher Aristotle saw so clearly, when he wrote: "A man may not be able to make a poem, but he can tell when a poem pleases him. He may not be able to make a house, but he can tell when the roof leaks. He may not be able to cook, but he can tell whether he likes what is prepared for him." The analysis of public-opinion trends indicates that a man may not be able to decipher a Congressional appropriation bill, but he can tell whether or not he approves of the objects for which it is to be passed; a man may not be able to understand the technological causes of his unemployment, but he knows what it means to be out of work, and his experience will contribute to the solution of the general problem; and a man may not grasp the subtle details of diplomacy, but he can tell whether or not the main principles of his country's foreign policy conform to his standards of judgment.

The conduct of government does not merely involve specialized knowledge. It deals primarily with human needs and human values. It knows no fixed and timeless standard of right, no revealed formula for the avoidance of error. The attempt to create an absolute standard by setting up a supreme ruling group to pass judgment for the whole community has always debased a nation's political ideals. Whenever a small clique has seized power and proceeded to dictate not only where the nation's political destination lies, but also what each individual citizen must do, the interests of the excluded majority have invariably been sacrificed to the ambitions of the dominant minority. The moral abdication of the individual in favor of the twentieth-century leviathan has led to oppression, conquest, and war.

The democratic way of life rests firmly on the premise that the surest touchstone of political action is the actual experience of the mass of its citizens. It rests on the realization that because there are no rigid standards of absolute value, it is all the more vital to measure the standards which the people set for themselves. There can be no sure guarantee of agreement with the majority's decision in every single case. Ethical values and standards of "rightness" in politics cannot be measured so easily as the size of a majority, and, since the assumption of omniscience on the part of any single group—even the majority—is dangerous, it is essential at all times to have a measure of the opinions of the opposition. But the democratic process is not inflexible. It operates so that goals of common effort gradually evolve, and the value of these goals depends on how accurately they reflect the values in which the individuals who compose the general public believe.

As a democratic nation, we have chosen to take the road of majority rule. Our leaders are chosen by the mass of the people, and the main lines of governmental and social policy are continuously referred back to the people for their approval. There is a wealth of available evidence proving that the common people can see through the shams of political life and can hold fast to what they value. Conclusive evidence supports the late Theodore Roosevelt who wrote: "The majority of the plain people of the United States will, day in and day out, make fewer mistakes in governing themselves than any smaller group will make in governing them."

Some of this evidence has already been presented in these pages. The people themselves are continuously supplying new facts which justify an intelligent rational faith in the future of our democracy. On the basis of the "early returns" from the common people, the prediction may be made—with little probability of error—that government responsive to the average opinion of mankind will continue to survive long after dictatorial systems have become mere bogey stories to frighten our great-grandchildren.

★

APPENDIX ONE

★

COMPLETE compilations of the actual questions and results of past surveys conducted by the American Institute of Public Opinion are published in the *Public Opinion Quarterly*, School of Public Affairs, Princeton University. The following pages contain a brief selection of some of the major issues on which public opinion has been measured in the last few years. Each of these results must be interpreted in the light of the specific question asked, and, above all, against the background of the actual date of the survey. Political issues of the immediate present have been omitted, because in continuous surveys opinion on candidates and parties changes from week to week.

Domestic Issues

PARTY STRENGTH

Which party would you like to see win the presidential election in 1940?

	Dem.	Rep.
Apr., 1939	49%	51%
Oct., 1939	57	43
Nov., 1939	54	46
Jan., 1940	54	46
Mar., 1940	55	45

REPUBLICAN PARTY POLICY

Would you like to see the Republican party be more liberal or more conservative than it was in the presidential campaign of 1940?

	Feb., 1940	July, 1939	Oct., 1938	Dec., 1937
More liberal	59%	55%	56%	47%
More conservative	17 ·	17	15	12
About the same	24	28	29	41

Do you think the Republican party has a better chance or a worse chance of winning this year's election if it nominates a liberal candidate and adopts a liberal program? (Feb., 1940)

Better	77%
Worse	10
No diff.	13

293

CONSERVATIVE-LIBERAL CANDIDATES

How do you consider each of the following political leaders—
as a conservative, a liberal, or a radical? (July, 1939)

	Conservative	Liberal	Radical
Hopkins	4%	55%	41%
Roosevelt	1	62	37
LaGuardia	8	64	28
Farley	13	63	24
Dewey	45	47	8
Hull	51	46	3
Garner	64	32	4
Vandenberg	67	29	4
Taft	86	13	1
Hoover	92	5	3

SIX-YEAR TERM

Would you favor changing the term of office of the President
of the United States to one six-year term with no re-election?

June, 1936		Jan., 1939	
Yes	26%	Yes	24%
No	74	No	76

THIRD TERM

Would you favor a constitutional amendment prohibiting any
President of the United States from serving a third term?

Aug., 1937		Sept., 1938	
Yes	49%	Yes	48%
No	51	No	52

Would you like to see the Senate go on record against a third
term for President Roosevelt? (Feb., 1939)

Yes	49%
No	51

LIBERAL-CONSERVATIVE TRENDS

During the next two years would you like to see the Roosevelt Administration continue along its present lines or become more conservative? (Aug., 1938)

> More conservative   66%
> Continue on present lines   34

NEW DEAL OPPOSITION

If you had been a member of Congress during the past two years, would you have supported every bill recommended by President Roosevelt? (Aug., 1938)

National Vote		Democratic Vote	
Yes	23%	Yes	38%
No	77	No	62

POLITICS IN RELIEF

Should employees of the Federal government be prohibited from contributing money to political campaigns? (Jan., 1939)

> Yes   62%
> No   38

TYPE OF RELIEF

Which way do you think relief should be given—in the form of work relief (such as a W.P.A. job), or as direct cash relief? (May, 1939)

> Work relief   89%
> Cash relief   11

INDEPENDENT VOTERS

In politics do you consider yourself a Democrat, Independent, Socialist, or Republican? (Jan., 1940)

> Democrat   42%
> Republican   38
> Independent   19
> Other   1

HATCH ACT

Do you think it is all right for people to solicit money for political campaigns from government employees or do you think this should be prevented by law? (Feb., 1940)

All right to solicit	23%
Should be prevented	77
	100

No opinion   12%

CIVIL SERVICE

Should government positions, except those which have to do with important matters of policy, be given to (1) those who help put their political party in office, or (2) those who receive the highest marks in Civil Service examinations? (Mar., 1936)

Civil Service	88%
Put political party in	12

Should all Washington employees of the special emergency agencies created by the New Deal be placed under Civil Service? (Mar., 1936)

Yes	69%
No	31

OLD-AGE PENSIONS

Do you believe in government old-age pensions?

	Sept., 1938	Feb., 1939	Nov., 1939
Yes	91%	94%	90%
No	9	6	10
	100	100	100
No opinion	3%	2%	3%

Would you be willing to pay a sales tax or an income tax to provide for these pensions? (Feb., 1939)

Yes	87%
No	13
	100

No opinion   7%

Do you think pensions should be given to all people, or only to old people who are in need?

	Sept., 1938	Nov., 1939
Needy only	79%	77%
All old people	21	23
	100	100
No opinion	4%	6%

How much per month should be paid to a single person?

	Sept., 1938	Feb., 1939
(median)	$40	$40

How much per month to a husband and wife?

	Sept., 1938	Feb., 1939
(median)	$70	$60

"PURGE" OF COURT-PLAN OPPOSITION

Do you think the Roosevelt Administration should try to defeat in the primary elections Democratic Senators who opposed the President's plan to enlarge the Supreme Court? (Democratic voters only, July, 1938)

No	69%
Yes	31
	100
No opinion	23%

Do you approve or disapprove of President Roosevelt's campaign to defeat Democrats who oppose his views? (Sept., 1938)

	Disapprove	Approve	No Opinion
All Democrats	61%	39%	20%
Southern Democrats	66	34	18

A.A.A.

Are you in favor of the A.A.A.? (Poll reported day before Court decision, Jan., 1936)

No	59%
Yes	41

Would you like to see the A.A.A. revived? (Aug., 1937)

No	59%
Yes	41
	100

No opinion 23%

FARM TENANCY

Would you favor government loans, on a long-time and easy basis, to enable farm tenants to buy the land they now rent? (Dec., 1936)

Yes	83%
No	17
	100

No opinion 17%

SURVEY OF FARMERS

Do you think Henry Wallace has done a good job or a poor job as Secretary of Agriculture?

	Dec., 1937	Mar., 1940
Good job	69%	73%
Poor job	31	27
	100	100

No opinion 32% 32%

Would you be interested in buying a farm if the government loaned you the money at 3% interest and gave you thirty years to repay the loan?

Yes	74%
No	26
	100

No opinion 12%

C.C.C.

Are you in favor of continuing the C.C.C. camps? (July, 1936)

Yes	82%
No	18

Do you think the C.C.C. should be made permanent? (Apr.,
1938)

Yes	78%
No	22
	100

No opinion   7%

Should military training be part of the duties of those who
attend?

	July, 1936	Aug., 1938
Yes	77%	75%
No	23	25
	100	100

No opinion   7%

N.R.A.

Do you think Congress and the President should try to enact
a second N.R.A.? (Mar., 1937)

Yes	53%
No	47
	100

No opinion   8%

WAGES AND HOURS

Should Congress set a limit on the hours employees should
work in each business and industry? (June, 1937)

Yes	58%
No	42
	100

No opinion   10%

Do you think the Federal government ought to set the lowest
wages employees should receive in each business and industry?
(June, 1937)

Yes	61%
No	39
	100

No opinion   10%

Should Congress pass a law regulating wages and hours before ending this session? (May, 1938)

Yes	59%
No	41
	100

No opinion   16%

WAGNER ACT

Do you think the Wagner Labor Relations Act should be revised, repealed, or left unchanged?

	Revised	Repealed	Left Un-changed	Unfamiliar with the Act or No Opinion
May, 1938	43%	19%	38%	56%
Nov., 1938	52	18	30	—
Mar., 1939	48	18	34	54
Nov., 1939	37	18	45	57
Jan., 1940	53	18	29	58

SOCIAL SECURITY

Do you approve of the Social Security tax on wages? (Jan., 1938)

Yes	73%
No	27
	100

No opinion   5%

The present old-age pension and unemployment-insurance act does not cover household help, sailors, farm hands, and employees in small shops. Do you think this law should be extended to include these workers? (Jan., 1938)

Yes	74%
No	26
	100

No opinion   11%

Do you think the Social Security Law should be changed to make the employer pay the whole amount of the Security tax? (Jan., 1938)

No	85%
Yes	15
	100
No opinion	13%

RELIEF

Do you think it is the government's responsibility to pay the living expenses of needy persons who are out of work? (Jan., 1938)

Yes	69%
No	31
	100
No opinion	8%

Do you think that people on relief in your community are getting as much as they should? (Apr., 1938)

Yes	71%
No	29
	100
No opinion	19%

Do you think the United States will have to continue relief appropriations permanently? (Apr., 1938)

Yes	67%
No	33
	100
No opinion	10%

Would you favor a law making it a crime for a relief official to attempt to influence the vote of persons on relief? (May, 1938)

Yes	86%
No	14
	100
No opinion	6%

In general, how much money do you think W.P.A. workers
should be paid? (Aug., 1939)

Less than workers in private industry	73%
About the same as workers in industry	26
More than workers in private industry	1
	100

No opinion   3%

RELIEFER'S POINT OF VIEW

Do you think relief assistance would be harder or easier to get
if we had a Republican President? (Reliefers only, July, 1938)

Harder	89%
Easier	11
	100

No opinion   46%

Do you think you would be better off or worse off if there were
a Republican administration in the White House? (Reliefers
only, June, 1939)

Better	24%
Worse	44
No difference	32
	100

No opinion   16%

If you had a job and then lost it, do you think it would be
hard to get relief assistance again? (Reliefers only, July, 1938)

Yes	61%
No	39
	100

No opinion   23%

If you were given a chance to go on a farm where you could
have a house and make enough to pay living expenses, would
you take it? (Reliefers only, Aug., 1938)

Yes	52%
No	48

What do you blame for the present unemployment in this country? (Reliefers only, June, 1939)

Increased use of machinery	23%
Shortsighted attitude of business	13
Capital not being invested	10
Policies of Roosevelt Administration	8
All other causes	46
	100

Do you think jobs in private industry are harder to get now than ten years ago? (June, 1939)

Yes	94%
No	6
	100
No answer	1%

Do you expect you or your husband will be able to get a job in private industry in the next two years? (June, 1939)

Yes	52%
No	48
	100
No opinion	22%

SUPREME COURT

Would you favor curbing the power of the Supreme Court to declare acts of Congress unconstitutional? (Dec., 1936)

No	59%
Yes	41
	100
No opinion	19%

Should Congress pass the President's Supreme Court plan? (June., 1937)

No	59%
Yes	41
	100
No opinion	21%

Would you favor a compromise on the Court plan which would permit the President to appoint two new judges instead of six? (May, 1937)

No	62%
Yes	38
	100

No opinion   21%

Would you favor a constitutional amendment requiring Supreme Court justices to retire at some age between 70 and 75? (Apr., 1937)

Yes	64%
No	36
	100

No opinion   10%

Would you like to have President Roosevelt continue his fight to enlarge the Supreme Court? (Sept., 1937)

No	68%
Yes	32
	100

No opinion   19%

Do you believe the Roosevelt administration should try to defeat the re-election of Democratic congressmen who opposed the Supreme Court plan? (Sept., 1937)

Democrats Only		National Total	
No	73%	No	80%
Yes	27	Yes	20
	100		100
No opinion	26%	No opinion	25%

Do you think Felix Frankfurter will make a good United States Supreme Court judge (Jan., 1939)

Yes	82%
No	18
	100

No opinion   48%

In general, do you think that judges in the Federal courts of the
country are honest? (June, 1939)

Yes	86%
No	14
	100

Refused to say and don't know   19%

In general, do you think judges in the state courts are honest?
(June, 1939)

Yes	76%
No	24
	100

Don't know   18%

In general, do you think judges in the municipal or local courts
are honest? (June, 1939)

Yes	72%
No	28
	100

Refused to say and don't know   18%

LABOR DISPUTES

In the current General Motors strike, are your sympathies with
the strikers or with the company? (Feb., 1937)

Company	56%
Strikers	44

Should sit-down strikes be made illegal?

	Yes	No	No Opinion
Mar., 1937	67%	33%	
Mar.,1939	75	25	12%

Should state and local authorities use force in removing sit-
down strikers? (Apr., 1937)

Yes	65%
No	35
	100

No opinion   10%

Should employers and employees be compelled by law to try to
settle their differences before strikes can be called? (July, 1937)

Yes	89%
No	11
	100
No opinion	8%

Would you favor laws regulating the conduct of strikes? (July,
1937)

Yes	84%
No	16
	100
No opinion	8%

Do you approve of citizen groups, called vigilantes, which have
sprung up recently in strike areas? (Aug., 1937)

No	76%
Yes	24
	100
No opinion	10%

LABOR UNIONS

Do you think labor unions should be regulated by the government? (May, 1937)

Yes	69%
No	31
	100
No opinion	14%

Should labor unions be required to incorporate? (May, 1937)

Yes	86%
No	14
	100
No opinion	20%

Are you in favor of labor unions?

	Yes	No	No Opinion
July, 1937	76%	24%	9%
June, 1939	70	30	11

Which labor leader do you like better: Green of the A.F. of L. or Lewis of the C.I.O.?

	Green	Lewis	No Opinion
July, 1937	67%	33%	43%
Oct., 1938	78	22	43%

Should government employees join labor unions? (Aug., 1937)

No	74%
Yes	26
	100
No opinion	14%

Do you think the attitude of the Roosevelt Administration toward union labor is too friendly or not friendly enough? (Sept., 1937)

Too friendly	45%
Not friendly enough	14
About right	41
	100
No opinion	17%

Would you like to see the C.I.O. and A.F. of L. labor unions settle their differences and work as one labor organization? (Oct., 1937)

Yes	79%
No	21
	100
No opinion	24%

★ II ★

Social Issues

MOST VITAL ISSUE

What do you regard as the most vital issue before the American people today?

Dec., 1936
1. Unemployment
2. Economy
3. Neutrality

Jan., 1937
1. Unemployment
2. Neutrality
3. Social security

May and Dec., 1939
1. Keeping out of war
2. Solving unemployment
3. Business recovery

PROHIBITION

If the question of national prohibition should come up again, would you vote for it?

	Dec., 1936	Feb., 1938	Dec., 1938	Jan., 1940
Yes	33%	34%	36%	34%
No	67	66	64	66
	100	100	100	100
No opinion	7%	4%	5%	5%

308

Do you think drunkenness is increasing or decreasing in this community? (Dec., 1938)

Increasing	40%
Decreasing	24
About the same	36
	100
No opinion	10%

Do you think liquor regulations here are too strict, not strict enough, or about right?

	Dec., 1938	Jan., 1940
Too strict	4%	7%
Not strict enough	53	51
About right	43	42
	100	100
No opinion	8%	9%

SOCIAL CLASS

To what social class in this country do you feel you belong? Middle class, upper class, or lower class? (April, 1939)

Upper	6%
Middle	88
Lower	6
	100

MARRIED WOMEN IN JOBS

Do you approve of a married woman earning money in industry or business if she has a husband capable of supporting her? (Nov., 1936)

No	82%
Yes	18
	100
No opinion	4%

DIVORCE

Should divorce be easier to obtain in your state? (Dec., 1936)

No	77%
Yes	23
	100
No opinion	19%

SCHOOLS

Should schools teach the facts about Socialism, Communism, and Fascism? (May, 1936)

Yes	62%
No	38

Should college teachers be free to express their views on all subjects, including politics and religion? (May, 1936)

Yes	59%
No	41

VENEREAL-DISEASE CONTROL

Would you favor a government bureau that would distribute information concerning venereal diseases? (Dec., 1936)

Yes	90%
No	10
	100
No opinion	16%

Should this bureau set up clinics for the treatment of venereal diseases?

Yes	88%
No	12
	100
No opinion	19%

In strict confidence and at no expense to you, would you like to be given by your physician a blood test for syphilis? (Aug., 1937)

Yes	87%
No	13
	100
No answer	8%

Would you favor a law requiring doctors to give every expectant mother a blood test for syphilis? (Jan., 1938)

Yes	88%
No	12
	100

| No opinion | 14% |

Do you think Congress should appropriate money to aid states in fighting venereal diseases? (May, 1938)

Yes	86%
No	14
	100

| No opinion | 9% |

Would you be willing to pay higher taxes for this purpose?

Yes	69%
No	31
	100

| No opinion | 12% |

BIRTH CONTROL

Do you favor the birth-control movement? (July, 1937)

Yes	71%
No	29
	100

| No opinion | 14% |

Would you like to see a government agency furnish birth-control information to married people who want it? (Oct., 1938)

Yes	72%
No	28
	100

| No opinion | 14% |

Would you approve or disapprove of having government health clinics furnish birth-control information to married people who want it? (Jan., 1940)

Approve	77%
Disapprove	23
	100
No opinion	11%

MATERNITY CARE

Should the Federal government aid state and local governments in providing medical care for mothers at childbirth? (Nov., 1937)

Yes	81%
No	19
	100
No opinion	10%

HEALTH INSURANCE

Have you ever put off going to the doctor because of the cost? (June, 1938)

Yes	42%
No	58
	100
No opinion	3%

Do you think the government should be responsible for providing medical care for people who are unable to pay for it?

Yes	81%
No	19
	100
No opinion	4%

Would you be willing to pay higher taxes for this purpose?

Yes	59%
No	41
	100
No opinion	9%

POLL OF PHYSICIANS ONLY

Do you approve of the principle of voluntary health insurance, where an individual insures for himself medical or hospital care by making regular payments to a health fund? (June, 1938)

Yes	73%
No	27
	100

No opinion	6%

Do you think the movement for voluntary health insurance will grow in this country during the next ten years?

Yes	82%
No	18
	100

No opinion	14%

If voluntary health insurance is widely adopted, do you think it will increase or decrease the income of the medical profession?

Increase	51%
Decrease	49
	100

No opinion	27%

Do you think the standards of medical practice are raised when physicians practice in groups, as in clinics?

Yes	53%
No	47
	100

No opinion	9%

Do you believe many persons in your community go without adequate medical care because they are unable to pay doctors' fees?

No	63%
Yes	37
	100

No opinion	3%

★ III ★

Foreign Issues

GERMAN POLICY

Hitler says he has no more territorial ambitions in Europe. Do you believe him? (Nov., 1938)

No	92%
Yes	8
	100
No opinion	9%

Do you believe that England and France did the best thing in giving in to Germany instead of going to war? (Oct., 1938)

Yes	59%
No	41
	100
No opinion	9%

Do you think that Germany's demand for the annexation of the Sudeten German areas in Czechoslovakia was justified? (Oct., 1939)

No	77%
Yes	23
	100
No opinion	13%

Do you think that this settlement (Munich Agreement) will result in peace for a number of years or in a greater possibility of war? (Oct., 1938)

Greater possibility of war	60%
Peace	40
	100
No opinion	28%

Do you approve or disapprove of the Nazis' treatment of the Jews in Germany? (Dec., 1938)

Disapprove	94%
Approve	6
	100
No opinion	7%

Do you approve or disapprove of the Nazis' treatment of the Catholics in Germany? (Dec., 1938)

Disapprove	97%
Approve	3
	100
No opinion	13%

Do you think the United States will have to fight Germany again in your lifetime?

	Apr., 1938	Oct., 1939
Yes	46%	48%
No	54	52
	100	100
No opinion	13%	15%

WAR REFERENDUM

In order to declare war should Congress be required to obtain the approval of the people by means of a national vote?

	Oct., 1937	Oct., 1938	Mar., 1939
Yes	73%	68%	58%
No	27	32	42
	100	100	100
No opinion	7%	7%	9%

Should the Constitution be amended to require a national vote
before the country could draft men to fight overseas?

	Mar., 1939	Sept., 1939	Jan., 1940
Yes	61%	51%	60%
No	39	49	40
	100	100	100
No opinion	10%	8%	5%

SPANISH CIVIL WAR

Which side do you sympathize with in the Spanish Civil War—
the Loyalists or Franco?

	Feb., 1937	Feb., 1938	Dec., 1938
Loyalists	65%	75%	76%
Franco	35	25	24
	100	100	100
No opinion	26%	52%	35%

FAVORITE EUROPEAN COUNTRY

Which European country do you like best? (July, 1939)

England	43%	Sweden	4%
France	11	Ireland	3
Finland	4	Germany	3
Switzerland	4	Others and no answer	28

Our present neutrality law prevents this country from selling
war materials to any countries fighting in a declared war. Do
you think the law should be changed so that we could sell war
materials to England and France in case of war? (Apr., 1939)

Yes	57%
No	43
	100
No opinion	13%

AMERICA AND JAPAN

In the present fight between Japan and China, are your sympathies with either side?

	Sept., 1937	June, 1939
Japan	2%	2%
China	43	74
Neither	55	24

Would you join a movement in this country to stop buying goods made in Japan?

	Oct., 1937	June, 1939
Favor boycott	37%	66%
Oppose boycott	63	34
	100	100
No opinion	6%	

Do you approve of Secretary Hull's action in serving notice on Japan that the United States may end its trade treaty with Japan in six months? (July, 1939)

Approve	81%
Disapprove	19
	100

Don't know about action	16%
No opinion	12%

Do you think the United States should forbid shipment of arms or ammunition from this country to China? (June, 1939)

Yes	40%
No	60%
	100

No opinion	9%

Do you think our government should forbid the sale of arms, airplanes, gasoline, and other war materials to Japan? (Feb., 1940)

Yes	75%
No	25
	100

No opinion	6%

THE WAR IN EUROPE

Do you think it was a mistake for the United States to have entered the World War?

	Apr., 1937	Nov., 1939
Yes	70%	68%
No	30	32
	100	100
No opinion	8%	13%

Why do you think we entered the last war? (Dec., 1939)

America was the victim of propaganda and selfish interests	34%
America had a just and unselfish cause	26
America entered the war for her own safety	18
Other reasons	8
No opinion	14

Do you have confidence in the news from Germany at the present time? (Sept., 1939)

Complete confidence	1%
Some confidence	33
No confidence	66
	100
No opinion	5%

Do you have confidence in the news from England and France at the present time? (Sept., 1939)

Complete confidence	8%
Some confidence	62
No confidence	30
	100
No opinion	5%

About how long do you think the present war will last? (Sept., 1939)

1 year or less	49%
More than 1 year	51
	100
No opinion	28%

Which side do you think will win? (Sept., 1939)

Allies	82%
Germany	7
No opinion	11
	100

Do you think the United States will go into the war in Europe or do you think we will stay out of the war?

	Oct., 1939	Feb., 1940
Go in	46%	32%
Stay out	54	68
	100	100
No opinion	13%	13%

Which side do you want to see win the war, England and France, or Germany?

	Oct., 1939	Mar., 1940
Allies	84%	84%
Germany	2	1
No opinion	14	15

Do you feel more sympathetic or less sympathetic toward that side today than you did when the war began? (Mar., 1940)

	Those who say "England and France"
More	28%
Less	17
Same	55

In the present crisis are your sympathies with Finland or Russia? (Dec., 1939)

Finland	88%
Russia	1
Neutral or no opinion	11

Do you think all able-bodied young men twenty years old should be made to serve in the Army or Navy for one year?

	Dec., 1938	Oct., 1939
Yes	37%	39%
No	63	61
	100	100
No opinion	6%	5%

Would you be willing to pay more money in taxes to support a
larger Army? Navy? Air force? (Nov., 1939)

Army	64%
Navy	67
Air force	70
No opinion	7

Do you think the United States should do everything possible
to help England and France win the war—short of going to war
ourselves? (Oct., 1939)

Yes	62%
No	38
	100
No opinion	5%

Should we declare war and send our Army and Navy abroad to
fight against Germany?

	Sept., 1939	Oct., 1939	Dec., 1939	Apr., 1940
Yes	16%	5%	3.5%	3.7%
No	84	95	96.5	96.3
	100	100	100	100
No opinion 6%		4%		

If Canada is actually invaded by a European power, do you
think the United States should use its Army and Navy to aid
Canada? (Oct., 1938)

Yes	73%
No	27
	100
No opinion	7%

Do you think the United States should do everything possible
to help England and France win the war, even at the risk of
getting into the war ourselves? (Oct., 1939)

Yes	34%
No	66
	100
No opinion	6%

If it appears that Germany is defeating England and France, should the United States declare war on Germany and send our Army and Navy to Europe to fight?

	Sept., 1939	Oct., 1939	Feb., 1940
Yes	44%	29%	23%
No	56	71	77
	100	100	100
No opinion	10%	8%	5%

Would you favor a conference of the leading nations of the world to end the present war and settle Europe's problems? (Oct., 1939)

Yes	69%
No	31
	100
No opinion	10%

If such a conference is called, should the United States take part in it? (Oct., 1939)

Yes	50%
No	50
	100
No opinion	10%

Would you like to see the United States join in a movement to establish an international police force to maintain world peace? (Sept., 1939)

Yes	53%
No	47
	100
No opinion	14%

Do you think now is the right time for the leading countries of the world to have a conference to try to settle Europe's problems and end the war between Germany and England and France? (Mar., 1940)

Yes	58%
No	42
	100
No opinion	13%

If such a conference is held, should the United States take part
in it? (Mar., 1940)

Yes	55%
No	45
	100
No opinion	9%

NEWSPAPERS PUBLISHING FINDINGS OF THE AMERICAN INSTITUTE OF PUBLIC OPINION (as of MAY, 1940)

(The political classifications are those made by the newspapers themselves)

DEMOCRATIC
Atlanta Constitution
Clarksburg Exponent
El Paso Times
Fairmont Times
Fort Smith Southwest
  American
Fort Wayne Journal Gazette
Great Falls Tribune
Rock Springs Rocket
Sheboygan Press
Lynchburg News
Charlotte News

INDEPENDENT DEMOCRATIC
Amarillo Globe-News
Baltimore Sun
Birmingham News
Cleveland Plain-Dealer
Dallas News
Dayton Daily News
Harrisburg Patriot

Hartford Times
Jacksonville Journal
Memphis Commercial Appeal
New Orleans Item-Tribune
New York Times
Norfolk Virginian Pilot
Richmond Times Dispatch
Roanoke Times
St. Petersburg Times
Wheeling News-Register
Wichita Falls Times
Winston-Salem Journal &
  Sentinel
Miami Herald
Durham Herald

INDEPENDENT
Aberdeen News
Anderson (Ind.) Tribune
Appleton Post-Crescent
Bloomington (Ill.) Daily
  Pantagraph

323

INDEPENDENT (*Cont.*)
Boise Capital News
Boston Globe
Burlington Daily News
Chattanooga News-Free Press
Cincinnati Enquirer
Chicago Daily News
Decatur Herald & Review
Colorado Springs Gazette-
   Telegraph
Columbus Citizen
Detroit News
Denver R. M. News
Des Moines Register &
   Tribune
Duluth Herald
Erie Dispatch-Herald
Elkhart Truth
Fall River Herald-News
Gary Post-Tribune
Grand Rapids Press
Green Bay Press-Gazette
Greensboro News
Houston Post
Huron Huronite
Indianapolis Times
Knoxville News Sentinel
LaCrosse Tribune
Lewistown Sentinel
Lincoln Journal Star
Louisville Courier-Journal
Madison State Journal
Minneapolis Star
Mitchell Daily Republican

Nashville Banner
Newark Evening News
Peoria Journal-Transcript
Pittsburgh Press
Portland (Ore.) Journal
Providence Journal
Pueblo Star-Journal
Quincy Herald-Whig
Rock Island Argus
St. Joseph News-Press Gazette
St. Louis Globe-Democrat
St. Paul Dispatch
Salt Lake City Tribune
San Antonio Express
San Francisco News
Seattle Star
Sioux City Tribune
Sioux Falls Argus-Leader
South Bend Tribune
Springfield (Mass.)
   Republican
Tacoma Times
Tucson Citizen
Tulsa Tribune
Washington Post
Spokane Spokesman Review-
   Chronicle
Wisconsin Rapids Tribune

REPUBLICAN
Anderson (S.C.) Herald
Bloomington (Ind.)
   Telephone

REPUBLICAN *(Cont.)*
Bradford Newspapers
Cheyenne Wyoming State
Tribune
Galesburg Register-Mail
Hibbing Tribune
Johnstown Tribune
Los Angeles Times
Oil City Derrick
Parkersburg News
Racine Journal Times
Rochester Democrat and
Chronicle
San Diego Union and
Tribune
San Jose Mercury Herald

Springfield (Ill.) State
Journal
Topeka Capital

INDEPENDENT
REPUBLICAN
Bellingham Herald
Buffalo Evening News
Davenport Times
Honolulu Star-Bulletin
Jamestown Journal
Kewanee Star-Courier
Philadelphia Bulletin
Portland (Me.) Sunday
Telegram
Toledo Times and Blade

★

BIBLIOGRAPHY

★

THE following list of books and articles are representative of the literature which bears on public-opinion polls.

ALLPORT, F. H. "Towards a Science of Public Opinion," *Public Opinion Quarterly,* Vol. 1, No. 1, Jan., 1937.

ALLPORT, G. W. "Attitudes," in Murchison C. (ed.), *A Handbook of Social Psychology.* Worcester: Clark Univ. Press, 1935.

ALBIG, W. *Public Opinion.* New York: McGraw-Hill, 1939.

AMERICAN INSTITUTE OF PUBLIC OPINION. *See* surveys in *Public Opinion Quarterly.*

AMERICAN INSTITUTE OF PUBLIC OPINION pamphlets: *The New Science of Public Opinion Measurement.* Princeton, N.J.

BOWLEY, A. L. "Application of Sampling to Economic and Social Problems," *Journal of American Statistical Association,* Vol. xxvi, Sept., 1936.

BRITISH INSTITUTE OF PUBLIC OPINION. *What Britain Thinks.* London, 1938.

BRYCE, JAMES. *Modern Democracies.* London, 1920.

BRYCE, JAMES. *The American Commonwealth,* 2 vols. New York, 1888.

CHILDS, H. L. "Rule by Public Opinion," *The Atlantic,* June, 1936.

CROSSLEY, A. M. "Straw Polls in 1936," *Public Opinion Quarterly,* Vol. 1, No. 1, Jan., 1937.

CRUM, W. L. *Straw Polls.* Harvard University Press, 1928.

DROBA, D. "Methods of Measuring Public Opinion," *American Journal of Sociology,* Vol. xxxvii, No. 3, Nov., 1931.

326

Fortune Surveys. Published monthly in *Fortune* magazine, and summarized in the *Public Opinion Quarterly*.

GALLUP, G. H. "Government and the Sampling Referendum," *Journal of American Statistical Association,* March, 1938.

GALLUP, G. H. "Public Opinion in a Democracy," *Stafford Little Lectures.* Princeton, N. J.

GALLUP, G. H. (with Pollock, J., and Wirth, L.) "Testing Public Opinion," *University of Chicago Round Table,* Nov. 5, 1939.

GALLUP, G. H. "Testing Public Opinion," *Public Opinion Quarterly* (suppl.), Jan., 1938.

GOSNELL, H. "How Accurate Were the Polls?" *Public Opinion Quarterly,* Vol. 1, 1937.

HERRING, P. "How Does the Voter Make up His Mind?" *Public Opinion Quarterly,* Vol. 2, No. 1, Jan., 1938.

HOUSE, F. N. "Measurement in Sociology," *American Journal of Sociology,* Vol. xl, No. 1, July, 1934.

HURJA, EMIL. "The Importance of Straw Votes," Washington Letter, August 25, 1939.

KATZ, D., and CANTRIL, H. "Public Opinion Polls," *Sociometry,* Vol. 1, No. 1, July, 1937.

LIVINGSTONE, DAME A. *The Peace Ballot.* London, 1935.

LUNDBERG, G. "Public Opinion From a Behavioristic Viewpoint," *American Journal of Sociology,* Vol. xxxvi, No. 3, 1930.

MENEFEE, S. C. "Stereotyped Phrases and Public Opinion," *American Journal of Sociology,* Vol. xliii, No. 4, February, 1938.

MERRIAM, C. E., and GOSNELL, H. *Non-Voting: Causes and Methods of Control.* Chicago, 1924.

PEARSON, E. S. "Sampling Problems in Industry," *Supplement to Royal Statistical Society,* Vol. vi, No. 2, 1934.

RAE, S. F. *The Concept of Public Opinion and its Measurement.* University of London, 1938.

RAE, S. F. "The Oxford By-election," *Political Quarterly,* London, Vol. x, No. 2, June, 1939.

RHODES, E. C. "Voting at Municipal Elections," *Political Science Quarterly,* London, Vol. ix, No. 1.

RICE, S. *Statistics in Social Studies*. University of Pennsylvania, 1930.

RICE, S. *Quantitative Methods in Politics*. New York, 1924.

ROBINSON, C. E. *Straw Votes*. Columbia University Press, 1932.

ROBINSON, C. E. "Recent Developments in the Straw-Poll Field," *Public Opinion Quarterly*, Vol. 1, No. 3, July, 1936.

ROBINSON, C. E. "The Straw Poll," *Encyclopedia of the Social Sciences*, Vol. xiv.

ROGERS, L. "Dr. Gallup's Statistics," *The New Republic*, Nov. 1, 1939.

ROPER, E. "Democracy Must Think." Columbia University Press. (Round Table on Public Opinion, National Municipal League's 44th Annual Conference.)

SCHOENBERG, E. H., and PARTEN, M. "Methods and Problems of Sampling Presented by the Urban Study of Consumer Purchases," *Journal of American Statistical Association*, July, 1937.

SMITH, C. W. Chapter 18, "Straw Votes and the Measurement of Opinion," in *Public Opinion in a Democracy*, 1939.

SPINGARN, J. "These Public Opinion Polls," *Harper's*, No. 1063, Dec., 1938.

STEPHAN, F. F. "Practical Problems of Sampling Procedure," *American Sociological Review*, Vol. 1, No. 4, August, 1936.

TINGSTEN, H. *Political Behaviour*. London, 1937.

UPDEGRAFF, R. R. "Democracy's New Mirror," *The Forum*. Jan., 1940.

WARNER, L. "The Reliability of Public Opinion Polls," *Public Opinion Quarterly*.

WECHSLER, JAMES. "Polling America," *The Nation*, Jan. 20, 1940.

WILCOX, W. F. "An Attempt to Measure Public Opinion About Repealing the Eighteenth Amendment," *Journal of American Statistical Association*, Vol. xxvi, Sept., 1931.